HOW TO DO BIOGRAPHY

HOW TO DO

Biography

A Primer

NIGEL HAMILTON

Harvard University Press

CAMBRIDGE, MASSACHUSETTS · LONDON, ENGLAND

First Harvard University Press paperback edition, 2012

LIBRARY OF CONGRESS CATALOGING-IN-PUBLICATION DATA

Hamilton, Nigel.
How to do biography : a primer / Nigel Hamilton.
p.   cm.
Includes bibliographical references and index.
ISBN 978-0-674-02796-1 (hardcover : alk. paper)
ISBN 978-0-674-06615-1 (pbk.)
1. Biography as a literary form.   2. Biography—Research—
Methodology.   3. Autobiography—Authorship.   I. Title.

CT22.H36 2008
808'.06692—dc22   2007047583

For Oskari Gray Hamilton

né June 9, 2007

and

Joyce Seltzer

Contents

HOW TO DO BIOGRAPHY

Introduction

We live—at least in the Western world—in a golden age for biography. The depiction of real lives in every medium from print to film, from radio to television and the Internet, is more popular than ever. More people are undertaking biographies (and autobiographical works, such as blogs and memoirs) than ever before. Yet there is still, to my knowledge, no book or primer to guide the would-be biographer in tackling the record and interpretation of a human individual, past or present.

Given the contribution that biography makes to knowledge and understanding in the modern democratic world, this is, to say the least, disappointing. A society in which no biographies could be produced is almost unthinkable—yet we do not teach the study and composition of biography, in all its aspects, in higher education. Its ethics, like the history and theory behind it, thus go largely unaddressed, while at a practical level there are still relatively few courses offered to those who wish to write a biography, whether big or small. Would-be biographers are thus left largely to their own devices, scrabbling for advice and examples in every direction.

Having spent a lifetime in the business of biography—as a writer, teacher, bookseller, publisher, and filmmaker—I therefore wondered whether it would be useful to write a short book of advice on how to do biography, a manual that would follow *Biography: A Brief History,* my survey of biography's long and storied past up to the present day.

The project proved more challenging than I anticipated. For instance, I had hoped, initially, to cover the many different media in which life-depiction can be tackled in our time. This was beyond me; the manuscript filled with subjunctives, subsidiary clauses, subsidiary cases, multiple choices. It lacked clarity—which is essential in tackling a life. I therefore began again, confining myself to print biography. Perhaps one day this can be extended to the visual and aural media of film, radio, television, the fine arts, and the Internet, where the biographical impetus is now such a burgeoning force. Meanwhile I hope that *How To Do Biography* will provide a building block, and a start.

I have structured the book in sixteen chapters, to cover the main elements of the biographical undertaking, from conception to composition and publishing—but although they reflect the stages in which you accomplish the work, I must emphasize that the real process of biography is like juggling: you must learn to manage several aspects simultaneously. The business of research, for example, constantly affects your agenda, your design, and your composition—as does a concern with your audience's needs and expectations.

Because interest in memoir has been increasing exponentially of late, I have included several chapters on autobiography as well. I hope they, too, will be useful.

In the course of this work, I've chosen a number of brief extracts from well-known biographies: examples of good practice that illustrate the sheer range of approaches you can adopt, from great beginnings to memorable death scenes.

My intention was to write a primer that would be readable, informative, instructive—and, to a degree, entertaining. Biography has been my passion for more than forty years—and I hope it will be yours, too, for it offers a raft of pleasures and fulfillments, if you get it right—as well as interesting life-experience if you don't!

Enjoy!

I

GETTING STARTED

ONE

The Task of Biography

No species of writing seems more worthy of cultivation than biography, since none can be more delightful or more useful, none can more certainly enchain the heart by irresistible interest, or more widely diffuse instruction to every diversity of condition.

—SAMUEL JOHNSON,
The Rambler, 60 (October 13, 1750)

You wish to write or produce a "life," but wisely pause to think about the task. I have no wish to hold you up; but no would-be biographer, in my view, should embark on the depiction of a real life without bothering to know something about how—and why—previous biographers have addressed the lives of real individuals in the

past—and with what results. From canonizations, peer-
ages, and professorships to trials, punishments, and even
beheadings, it is a fascinating story.

When did the biographical urge arise in humans? How
was it first manifested? How did the invention of writing—
in cuneiform and, later, in ink on papyrus—affect the course
of life-depiction? Was the purpose to commemorate the
dead—or to judge them? Was it individuals' achievements
that were important to record, or their characters—and
why? Did readers want to learn *of* the dead—or *from* the
dead? And where did art—the art of storytelling and composition—come in?

These are important questions for us, because they've
remained more or less constant throughout Western history, and are still valid today. Dr. Johnson, who had undertaken to write the lives of the eminent English poets, put
the matter very well. "Most accounts of particular persons
are barren and useless," he commented—English biographies of his time (circa 1750) having been "allotted to writers who seem little acquainted with the nature of their
task."[1]

What the *task* of biography is, then, must be your first
concern, if you wish to avoid Dr. Johnson's penitentiary!
How did your predecessors see their task, how did they
carry it out—and with what results? Even though biogra-

phy is seldom, if ever, taught at the university level, it *is* a discipline, and awareness of its history and rationale can only enrich your view of what you're undertaking as a life-chronicler in today's society. It may also help you avoid some of the pitfalls—or, if not avoid them, may help you take consolation in the pitfalls already encountered by biographers past. After all, Xenophon, Plutarch, Julius Caesar, Suetonius, Tacitus, Matthew, Mark, Luke, and John, the Gnostic gospelers, Saint Augustine, Holinshed, Sir Walter Raleigh, Shakespeare, Vasari, Bellini, Dr. Johnson, Boswell, Rousseau, Casanova, de Quincy, Lockhart, Carlyle, Froude, Morley, Leslie Stephen, Gosse, Freud, Strachey, Woolf, Nicolson, and others who brought biography into the modern age, as well as innovators like Flaherty, Gance, Riefenstahl, Welles, Brecht, Capote, Holroyd, Plath, Hughes—their hard-won experience in depicting real lives has shaped our biographical conventions, and we would be daft to ignore them as we start out.

Briefly put, Dr. Johnson is really the father of modern biography in the Western world—most famous for the book that James Boswell wrote about him, *The Life of Samuel Johnson, LL.D.* However, it was Johnson's own essays on biography, in his twice-weekly journal *The Rambler,* that truly redefined the aims and practice of written biography. Regarding the quality of contemporary biographical works, in the mid 1700s, he was caustic. Their authors "rarely afford any other account than might be collected from public papers"—whereas it was vital, if a true and honest portrait was to be attempted, to look behind the public mask of an individual: in other words, to explore the individual's private life.

Dr. Johnson's interest was not prurient. What he wanted to see, in biography, was the recording and evaluating of people's moral character, the way Plutarch and Suetonius had practiced this art in classical times: how, in facing the vicissitudes of life, an individual did or didn't cope, was or was not tempted into sin, felt or did not feel remorse. Though Johnson could see the value in historical accounts of the past, such as the rise and fall of kings and emperors, he was more interested, within such chronicles, in those episodes and stories that resonated with the reader, and whose lessons could be applied to his or her own life—in other words, the practical usefulness of biography. "I esteem biography," Johnson told Boswell on their tour of the Hebrides, "as giving us what comes near to ourselves, what we can put to use." Like Plutarch, Johnson distrusted history—or the history being written in his time; for although historians claimed to give the facts of people's actions, they did not give credible motives. "We cannot trust to the characters we find in history," he objected, memorably.[2] They were straw men, unreal: "whole ranks of characters adorned with uniform panegyrick," as he put it.[3] Stuffed with pointless, commemorative information, most English biographies were, he claimed, fatuous. Between "falsehood and useless truth there is little difference," he remarked—adding: "As gold which he cannot spend will make no man rich, so knowledge which he cannot apply will make no man wise."[4]

Applicable knowledge, then, was Johnson's goal for biography—and here he distinguished himself from the "ancients," as he referred to them. Biography was the record of real lives; but if its great benefit to society was its ability to provide insights into human nature that could be useful to the reader in his own life, then there was no intrinsic reason biographers should chronicle only the lives of the famous. It was not improper to "gain attention" by writing about celebrities, Johnson assured readers, but the intrinsic aim of biography remained the same for all biographical subjects: to penetrate to the moral core of a life, to interpret it—and thereby not only learn facts and information, but acquire insight and lessons that could be serviceable in one's own life, either as warnings or inspiration. "I have often thought that there has rarely passed a life of which a judicious and faithful narrative would not be useful," he wrote—and he did not mean faithful in the fawning sense![5]

The real "business of the biographer" was to "pass slightly over those performances and incidents, which produce vulgar greatness, to lead the thoughts into domestick privacies, and display the minute details of daily life, where exterior appendages are cast aside" so as to reveal the moral center of an individual's life.[6] What Johnson called "the mischievous consequences of vice and folly, of irregular desires and predominant passions,"[7] were most readily apparent in private life. This belief prompted him to one of his most famous remarks—namely, that "more knowledge may be gained of a man's real character, by a short conversation with one of his servants, than from a formal and studied narrative, begun with his pedigree, and ended with his funeral."[8]

This perception was crucial to the development of modern biography—at least in its justification of the need for a biographer to enter the private life of his subject, and not rest content with the public image. It is in his own home that a man, after all, "shrinks to his natural dimensions, and throws aside the ornaments or disguises, which he feels in privacy to be useless incumbrances"; it is "at home that every man must be known by those who would make a just estimate either of his virtue or felicity; for smiles and embroidery are alike occasional, and the mind is often dressed for show in painted honour, and fictitious benevolence." Nor was it so difficult for the resourceful biographer to find out the true story of the man—or woman—behind the mask. There were "very few faults to be committed in solitude," he pointed out, "or without some agents, partners, confederates, or witnesses"—evidence it was the business of the biographer to collect, collate, and present in depicting the moral character of a real individual.[9]

I quote these comments of Johnson on biography at such length because they are often forgotten, yet are timeless. Johnson's younger companion, James Boswell—whose own morals were deeply suspect—certainly took the Doctor's prescription to heart: penning in 1791 *The Life of Samuel Johnson, LL.D.,* one of the greatest biographies in the English language. Since then, an army of practitioners and critics have discussed and debated the objectives, merits, ethics, and failings of biography—and autobiography. Although there are no ultimate answers, you can take heart from the fact that many before you have struggled with the issues, just as you will. Knowing, in advance, a little of the history of biography in the Western world, and the nature of the debates it has engendered over time, will not only help inure you to the poisoned arrows of detractors on the day your work is published, but perhaps help you predict many of those attacks in advance, so that you can structure and formulate your work to meet them. Forewarned is forearmed! Real-life depiction has *always* been controversial, in a manner that long predated Johnson's time—and this is something you need to understand. How could it be otherwise when the biographer is not only tackling the record of a person's life, but his or her reputation?

Think, if you question this, about the life of Jesus of Nazareth—and how, once the Christian church decided to adopt the four Gospels of Matthew, Mark, Luke, and John as *the* "official biography" or authorized version of his life, all alternative biographies—such as the gospels of Thomas, Judas, and Mary Magdalene—were damned as heretical and ordered to be destroyed. "Hagiography" was the name given to the biography of saints during the Christian era—but the matrix of hagiography was the policing and censoring of life stories viewed as subversive by the church.

Biography, then, has always negotiated the line between what is socially acceptable in recounting real lives, and what is unacceptable. As the power of the church waned at the end of the Middle Ages, this concern spilled over into secular biography—with similar controversies (and censorship). Sir Walter Raleigh, thinking on the perils of biographical candor—especially when it concerned reigning princes—warned potential practitioners not to tackle lives too close in time to their own, since "whosoever in writing a modern history shall follow truth too near the heels, it may haply strike out his teeth."[10] Unhappily, in the case of Raleigh, it did: he was beheaded in 1618. How could the outcome have been any different? Biography deals, after all, with reputations—and as Shakespeare's Othello puts it, "He that filches from me my good name, robs me of that which not enriches him, but makes me poor indeed." Small wonder that men and women—as well as their families, friends, and loyal supporters—have always fought fiercely to defend their good names, by invoking the laws of libel, challenging slanderers to a duel, imposing censorship, vilifying their critics, or threatening other sorts of retaliation.

Knowing something of the biographical evolution that has taken place between Dr. Johnson's time and ours will help ground your approach and your work. Boswell's warts'n'all life of Johnson was rapturously received in 1791—but within a generation the mood in Victorian Europe and America had changed, and, along with it, standards for what was permissible in biography. As studiously as the best Victorian biographers attempted to put the great Doctor's precepts into practice in life-stories and autobiography, they were defeated by the new social, political, judicial, and sexual mores of their time—shifting imperatives that affected women even more than men. In her comic novel *Orlando: A Biography* (1928), Virginia Woolf lamented the fact that, after Queen Victoria's accession, "love, birth, and death were all swaddled in a variety of fine phrases," while "the sexes drew further and further apart. No open conversation was tolerated. Evasions and concealments were sedulously practised on both sides."[11] The patriarchal "spirit of the nineteenth century" was "antipathetic to" Orlando in the extreme; "it took her and broke her, and she was aware of her defeat at its hands as she had never been before."[12] Woolf had cause to know— her father was the founding editor of the *Dictionary of National Biography,* in which only a handful of women were allowed to be included in its twenty-eight volumes.

Even within the lives that could be written in Victorian times, censorship and evasion held sway. Peering into a biographee's private life—so crucial to Johnson's vision of biography—was nearly impossible in those days; the achievements, and the struggle to achieve, were the only subjects a biographer was licensed to address. Johnson's "mischievous consequences of vice and folly" could be seen everywhere in Victorian society—in homes for foundlings, in widescale prostitution, and in hospitals where syphilis and gonorrhea abounded—but were unmentionable in

Victorian biography, which Lytton Strachey, in 1918, likened to the *"cortège* of the undertaker," wearing "the same air of slow, funereal barbarism."

Victorian biography, then, exuded panegyric—spun out at vast length, devoted to public lives, and restricted to males. As the *Oxford English Dictionary* defined the term in 1888, "biography" was simply "the history of men's lives," and a sub-branch of English literature.

All this changed, however, in the twentieth century. Not overnight, but year by year, decade by decade, the century witnessed a veritable cultural revolution in life-writing and real-life depiction, in media ranging from painted portraits to print and new technologies such as film. Moreover, the very frontier between biography (nonfiction) and the novel (fiction) became blurry—was attacked, crossed, moved, and then recrossed. Seeing biographers so enchained by the rules of convention, social acceptability, and sheer hypocrisy, the best Victorian writers had moved into the fictional arena of the novel and short story—a domain where they couldn't be sued for libel, or challenged to a duel for defamation, or ostracized from polite society for daring to explore the private life of famous individuals behind the ubiquitous virtuous masks. As a result, the Victorian novel abounded in fictional biographies: *David Copperfield, Oliver Twist, Eugénie Grandet, Jane Eyre, Henry Esmond, Silas*

*Marner, The Warden, Madame Bovary, The Idiot, Anna Kare-
nina, Tess of the D'Urbervilles, Thérèse Raquin, Nana, Lord
Jim* . . . These are among the pearls of modern literature,
and maintain their timelessness in part because of their
quasi-biographical form—their authors having recognized
the very opportunities and challenges to which Johnson
had alluded, but which had been legally and socially off
limits to real-life biographers.

   The world of biography changed in the early decades of
the twentieth century, as did, eventually, the laws safe-
guarding people's reputations and the social mores restrict-
ing biographers' access to private lives. There are two key
texts that you might with profit read as the biographical
"shots heard 'round the world." The first is *Father and Son*
(1907), Edmund Gosse's childhood memoir which posthumously exposed his father, the distinguished British natu-
ralist Philip Henry Gosse, as a religious (Plymouth
Brethren) tyrant. The second is *Leonardo da Vinci* (1910),
Sigmund Freud's outing of the great Renaissance poly-
math as a homosexual. These two works marked the beginning of the modern age in biography—the one daring
to tell the sort of intimate, private-life truths that would ultimately lead to the dizzying rise of memoir in the late
twentieth-century, the other opening the gates of biography to the kind of psychological and sociological interpretation that characterizes almost all biography today.

It was, however, the struggle between democracy and totalitarianism in World War II, followed by the Cold War, that really spurred biography as the study of the individual in Western society—and fulfilled Johnson's dictum regarding ordinary people's lives, as well as extraordinary ones. From GIs, generals, aircraft technicians, air raid wardens, to secretaries, Rosie the Riveter, and housewives, millions of people participated in the war for the individual's rights against those of a tyrannical leader and state, validating and ennobling the cause of human rights—which was then taken up domestically in the postwar world, in movements to promote civil rights, gender rights, and sexual rights. From Richard Wright's *Black Boy* to the accounts of gulag prisoners in the Soviet Union, the voices of the marginalized and oppressed were finally heard, alongside those of the successful and self-satisfied.

Inexorably, the public altered its expectations of biography, as biographers and memoir writers broke down the barriers holding back innovation—in every medium, from television to museums. The personal truly became the political, an adage epitomized when the U.S. Supreme Court in 1964 struck down the law of libel as biography's biggest barrier to the criticism and depiction of living public figures—enshrined in the lawsuit of a bigoted Alabama police commissioner named L. B. Sullivan, who had sued the *New York Times* for defamation in an editorial advertisement.

New York Times v. *Sullivan* changed the practice and possibilities of biography. Not only did written and graphic life-depictions (which had begun in 15,000 B.C. as matchstick men on cave walls) proliferate, but biography exploded in *all* the new technologies of the twentieth century: in celluloid, on the airwaves, on TV, and ultimately on the Internet—where blogging became the autobiographical rage.

Learning more about that evolution will not inhibit you in becoming a biographer. Rather, a historical overview will deepen your understanding of biography's rich and conflicted past, its 250-year struggle to fulfill Dr. Johnson's vision of its importance, and will enable you to appreciate the legal, religious, social, and other barriers with which biography has had to contend, from laws governing defamation, obscenity, copyright, and plagiarism, to academic prejudice and the minefield of poststructuralism. The cross-pollination between media, between genres, and between nonfiction and fiction has been immense—generating intense debate over the ethics of biography and issues of trivialization, intrusiveness, copyright, access rights, even nomenclature. Was Thomas Keneally's book *Schindler's List* a novel (for which it was awarded the Whitbread Prize for Fiction) or a biography? Should James Frey's *A Million Little Pieces* have been published as fiction instead of memoir—as Frey first intended? Is Steven Shainberg's 2007 film *Fur: An Imaginary Portrait of Diane Arbus,* starring Nicole Kidman and Robert Downey Jr., a fictive drama seeking to exploit what Virginia Woolf called the "granite" of biography as the narrative of a real person? Or is it simply a postmodern biopic for sophisticated audiences who appreciate erotica?

Biography, today, remains, as it has always been, the record and interpretation of real lives—the lives of others and of ourselves. But the *way* we record and interpret those lives has varied enormously from age to age. Knowing more of biography's past, you'll be wiser, more alert to what you can attempt without ruffling feathers, and more prepared to be challenged by vested interests (a likely event, if we can judge from past experience).

With the past in mind, then, let's move on to the future—*your* future, as a biographer—beginning with your agenda.

TWO

What Is Your Agenda?

He that writes the life of another is either his friend or his
enemy, and wishes either to exalt his praise or aggravate
his infamy.

　　—DR. JOHNSON, *The Idler*, 84 (November 24, 1759)

What life do you wish to tell—and why?

When I first drafted this chapter I tried to boil down my
advice to a sequence of bullet points, a sort of questionnaire you might ponder and mentally fill out. It covered
what I saw as the primary factors that make for success
or failure in tackling an individual's life-story: your aims,
your motivation, your suitability, your stamina. On paper,
though, the questionnaire looked . . . phony. No biographer ticks off a list before starting, however logical and

helpful such a procedure might be. So I scrapped the bullet points; I'm not going to ask you anything. What I will do, though, is run through the "bare necessities" you should consider when deciding whether to tackle a life, and I'll provide some examples.

The Proposal

At some point—sooner rather than later—you will, if you are serious about writing a life, have to produce what's called the "proposal," in order to get funding for what will take several years of research and writing. In other words, you'll need to convince *someone else* that the biography is a good idea: that there's an audience and thus a market for it, and that you are the right person to undertake it. Clarifying, for others, your conception of the biography you'd like to write is the first hurdle you'll have to overcome. As we'll see, it's not something you can do without some preliminary research, but recognizing that this is Goal Number One is the initial step in "doing" a biography.

The proposal must set forth your agenda with clarity and purpose: whose life you wish to record; why; and how.

Although the proposal will be a real document and, if accepted, the basis of an agreement or contract between you and a publisher or funding body, it is of course a figment of your imagination—not unlike Christopher Columbus' assurance to Ferdinand and Isabella in 1492, when he was seeking Spanish support and investment, that he would find a western sea route to India. Its real value, however, is as a spur to self-discipline, and as a test of your persuasiveness. It's a document which compels you to think through, in advance, the aims and objectives of your undertaking, then sets them out in such a way that the publisher or sponsoring institution has full confidence in you, as biographer-to-be. In other words, it's a rehearsal—not so much of the eventual or eventuating book, but of your abilities at the outset, both in conceptualization and in presentation. It must articulately convey, in writing, your sense of purpose and your mastery of what will be of interest and importance to others.

A publisher, reading the proposal, will be calculating whether there is a market for such a subject—and specifically for the sort of book you have in mind. The proposal must therefore convey not only the importance of a fresh route to the Indies, but your reliability: why and how you think *you* can successfully find and navigate the passage. It must display complete confidence in your idea, your motivation, and the application of that motivation—strong enough to withstand the inevitable storms!

Before attempting the proposal (which usually takes some research and many iterations before you're satisfied), it will be worth your time to think through your agenda: why you really want to write this life, whether it is possible, and whether you are the right person to do it.

Motivation

Tackling the mystery of a life is no mean enterprise. It'll involve research—often years of it. It'll require writing ability. It'll also test your skills of human understanding, insight, and appreciation—and then some—as you face the trials of true, rather than invented, portraiture. Motivation is therefore a key requirement.

Why do you wish to write this particular life? What interests you about it? Are you merely responding to a commission—that is, are you being paid to carry out someone else's idea—or are you responding to your own curiosity about the individual? Is there some deeper reason than money or curiosity? What, really, is the impulse—*your* impulse—in tackling the project?

These are not things you can necessarily know for certain, since they will be embedded in your psyche as much as your intellect. Moreover they will not necessarily be mentioned in your proposal—yet they will and must fuel that document, if it is to get you a sponsor. I remember when I was first asked if I would be willing to tackle a biography of Field Marshal Montgomery, after he died in

1976. I'd been very close to him in my youth, in fact I had loved him like a second father, and he had—or claimed to have—regarded me as a "second son." "Of course, you'll write about me when I'm gone," he would say—and I would protest that I had no interest in military matters, and no wish to write about someone so vain. He would laugh, and we'd leave it there.

In my fondness for "Monty," I did not like to think of him as dead—and when he finally passed away, I was, in any case, already in mourning, as my wife had recently died. Writing about his life, for publication, did not come into question in my mind. Others felt differently, however, and in due course I was asked if I would write an authorized biography of Monty, based on his private papers.

Again, I demurred. I had loved him—therefore I would be too prejudiced from the start. Moreover, I had by then moved abroad, to Finland, and had remarried, in an effort to fashion a new life as a self-made exile. Taking the job would mean returning to England, and would lead to upsetting memories. But when I was asked who I would therefore recommend among historians or biographers of my generation (I was thirty-two), I was troubled. I had spent my vacations with Monty; his home had been my second home. We'd had many an argument and spat, but over the years I felt I'd gotten to understand him—his eccentricities, strengths, and weaknesses. Suppose someone was appointed who got him wrong? Most American historians did, and many British ones too. Wouldn't I feel that I had let him down?

And so I agreed to at least look through Monty's unpublished papers and make a determination, either for myself or with an eye toward recommending someone else. Once I did that, of course, I was hooked—for there, in hundreds of letters to his mother, his father, his siblings, and others, was the quasi-father I'd never known: in his childhood, his early years, his first battles on the Western Front in World War I . . . Moreover, at a moment when Monty's reputation had been savaged, thanks to his boastfulness and exaggerations (asked who he thought were the three greatest commanders in English history, he named himself and two others), I saw an opportunity to rehabilitate that tainted public image. I therefore accepted the task and became his official biographer.

My point is that your motivation for tackling a life may be unclear, conflicted, contradictory, naïve, even stupid, but motivation there must be: motivation strong enough to start you off, even if at some point you abandon ship—or, conversely, assemble a fleet. (My proposed single volume became two volumes and then three, plus a BBC television documentary and subsidiary works relating to the field marshal. Sir Martin Gilbert, undertaking Churchill's biography on the death of Churchill's son, Randolph, had a similar experience.)

En bref, biographers need years to research, to write, and to publish a life. Unless you are powerfully motivated, don't even think of it.

Aims, Feasibility, Credentials

Assuming, then, that you are motivated at a deep enough level to undertake the years of work necessary for a biography, you will have to convince others, in your proposal, that such a book is worthwhile, doable, and of sufficient interest to generate an audience. For this, you must set out your aims and objectives—which may, as I've shown, be distinct from your motivation.

I've always been impressed by Robert Caro's approach to the biography of President Lyndon Johnson. Caro had spent seven years researching and writing *The Power Broker,* a study of Robert Moses, the "master builder" and urban planner who helped to shape New York City in the twentieth century. *The Power Broker* had enabled Caro to educate himself, and eventually others, about the nature of nonelected power in running a great city like New York. The insight he had gained led him to consider a new study. "I knew if I ever somehow could, I'd like to do the same thing for national power as I had done in *The Power Broker* with urban power," he later explained. "And I knew I wanted to do it with Lyndon Johnson, because I felt he understood national power better than any other president in our time."[1]

Caro's aim, in other words, was not so much to reveal the character and persona of Lyndon Johnson—which, as he acknowledged, had already been done by at least fifteen others, including Doris Kearns Goodwin in her wonderful book *Lyndon Johnson and the American Dream*. Rather, it was to explore, as he had done with Robert Moses, the trail Johnson had followed—or had established—in achieving and wielding power in America.

The important thing is to be clear, and remain clear, about your avowed aims in tackling a biography; for you will be challenged on these, not only in your proposal, but all the way through the research, writing, publication, and reception of your book. For example, each time you ask for an interview or for access to papers, you'll be asked to state your aim in writing such a biography. If it seems disingenuous to attempt this when your internal agenda and motivation are so hard to know, get over it. In the real world, other people need a simple, clear articulation of your intent. Give it to them. Think Columbus!

Now, let's assume you have clarified for a publisher your

initial aims and objectives: your search for a western passage to the Indies. No one, you argue, has tackled the subject before, or in the way you propose. The publisher's
next question about the project will be: Is it doable?

I remember vividly the most exciting proposal I ever
saw. I was working for a publishing house, where I'd gotten a job right after earning my university degree. The proposal came inside a smart blue folder and was about seven
pages long. It laid out a plan to undertake the life-story of
Sir Stewart Menzies, the legendary director of the British secret service (MI6) during World War II, who had
been the counterpart of Admiral Canaris, the head of the
equivalent German agency, the Abwehr. Marked "Strictly
Confidential," the beguiling proposal opened with a haunting description of a visit by the would-be biographer to Sir
Stewart's rural home in England's Cotswold district, and a
dinner at which there was an unoccupied seat and table
setting. When the author asked for whom the place had
been set, Menzies ("M" in Ian Fleming's *James Bond* novels)
replied, with an air of mystery: "It is in memory of my opposite number, Admiral Wilhelm Canaris"—who was arrested by Hitler after the July Plot in 1944, and executed
less than a month before Hitler's own suicide and the end
of the war. For the first time ever, Sir Stewart would, the
proposal promised, cooperate with a biographer and reveal all.

The publisher, accordingly, gave the author an immediate cash advance. This proved a blunder, as we soon found out! I mentioned the proposal in confidence to my father, a newspaper editor who had made his reputation for buying serialization rights to biographies and memoirs, many of them concerning World War II. He shook his head. "There's no way Menzies can cooperate!" he snorted— "He signed the Official Secrets Act—he'd be arrested!" And went back to reading his paper.

Crestfallen, I told my boss, the publisher. It was true. In 1932 the famous British novelist Compton Mackenzie had been fined £100, and all copies of his autobiography *Greek Memories* had been withdrawn and pulped, merely because he mentioned (as a former employee) the *existence* of MI6! Did the would-be biographer know this? Gingerly, my boss began calling the directors of other houses—and found that the aspiring author had already sold the proposal to a number of other gullible publishers!

Unless you're a fraud, then, you must convince a publisher that your project can be lawfully undertaken and that it's feasible. Being the authorized biographer—that is, authorized by those who hold copyright to the documents you will want to quote—is a tremendous advantage. Even in this case, however, you'll need to be careful. Do you have signed consent that you may write the book *and publish it without interference?* Have the individual, the family, the designated legal representatives signed off, in advance, on your right to publish copyrighted documents?

Perhaps the best-known case, in this respect, is the biography of Eric Blair (alias George Orwell) which Bernard Crick undertook, having first obtained written consent from Orwell's widow, Sonia. "She agreed to my firm condition that as well as complete access to the papers, I should have an absolute and prior waiver of copyright so that I could quote what I liked and write what I liked," Crick later explained. "These were hard terms, even if the only terms on which, I think, a scholar should and can take on contemporary [authorized] biography."[2]

It was just as well. Once Sonia saw the typescript, she was appalled, and attempted to annul the arrangement by taking Crick to court. She failed; her consent could not be legally revoked.

If you have not been specifically authorized to undertake a life by family members or representatives who have copyright control of essential documents, you will need to show the publisher how you propose to undertake the research; what sort of materials you hope to assemble; how available they are; what interviews you propose to conduct; and how likely you are to obtain access and copyright permissions.

This is by no means as straightforward as people generally imagine. Bernard Crick was tough enough not to be halted or intimidated by Mrs. Blair, and he produced a very fine biography of Orwell.[3] But when Ian Hamilton (no relation to me), tackled the unauthorized life of J. D. Salinger in the 1980s, he was not so lucky.

Hamilton had published a highly regarded and commercially successful life of Robert Lowell, and so had been given a very generous advance by Random House in anticipation of similar sales and reception for the Salinger biography. Yet not only did Salinger refuse to cooperate or give copyright permission for his writings to be quoted; he made it legally impossible for any of his relatives, friends, or colleagues to be interviewed—and then, in 1986, he sued to halt publication of Hamilton's completed manuscript!

The moral, then, is simple. Your aims and objectives must not only be well stated in your proposal, but must be achievable. And this leads to the question of whether you are the right person to undertake the biography: in other words, to the question of your credentials.

Sadly, there is still, to the best of my knowledge, no university that offers a degree in biography or biographical studies. Your suitability for the task of writing a proposed biography is therefore difficult for the publisher to assess, other than on past evidence. Would-be authors often have wonderful notions for a biography, as well as excellent-sounding specific credentials—such as access to crucial people or documents, and good research skills. But that doesn't necessarily translate into a credible proposal or biography. A biographer has to be, or become, a good *writer;* and your proposal will be, among other things, a test of your writing skill, as you rehearse, in advance and for an advance, your aim, your approach, your prospects for success in obtaining the necessary access and copyright permissions, and your own suitability for the project.

Robert Caro was given a paltry $2,500 advance royalty for his Moses book. When, after five years' work on a project which he had said would take only nine months, he dared to ask for another advance, he got short shrift—perhaps understandably. The "uncut manuscript of *The Power Broker* ran to 1.1 million words," Nicholas Von Hoffman later reported in *Vanity Fair.* "Flat broke and five years into the project, he submitted the first 400,000 or 500,000 words in hopes of getting a second $2,500 payment, due on completion. His editor took him out to a cheap Chinese restaurant at the corner of 107th and Broadway, and told him that while the people at the [*Newsday*] office [where Caro worked as a journalist] thought he was writing 'one of the most important works of nonfiction in the twentieth century' they were 'not prepared to go beyond the terms of the contract.'"[4]

Caro's publishers saw no prospect of commercial success—but the Pulitzer Prize committee didn't worry about that, and after *The Power Broker* won the Pulitzer it went on to become a classic. It also provided Caro with a stepping stone to his great biography of Lyndon Baines Johnson.

"Suitability" in biography, then, is an impossible quality to predict, even to define. What is important, however, is that *you* should believe you are a suitable candidate. Only you can know whether you have the sustained interest and the commitment to successfully record the life of your chosen subject. And somehow you must be able to convey that confidence through your proposal.

Quitting While You're Ahead

Conversely, it behooves you, if possible, to assess your *unsuitability*—however tempting the project, however strong the pressure to tackle it. A publisher, or the relative of a possible subject, may suggest a subject to you. Think hard before you accept such a commission, however well credentialed the publisher may think you. Reflect, for example, on Virginia Woolf's life of her close friend Roger Fry, the early twentieth-century artist and art critic. Virginia's father, Leslie Stephen, had been knighted for his biographical work, and Virginia had already written her best-selling spoof biography, *Orlando*, as well as some of her generation's finest essays on biography. Roger Fry's long-time lover, Helen Anrep, and Fry's sister Margery both begged her to write Fry's life. Since the staff of the Hogarth Press—the publishing company Virginia had established with her husband, Leonard—was keen to publish such a work, she accepted the commission.

The result was Virginia Woolf's worst manuscript—one which even her loyal husband thought a failure and which Woolf herself regretted, once she'd started it. Friendship had impelled her to accede to Helen and Margery's request. Once she realized she'd have to leave out at least half of Fry's private life (such as his affair with Virginia's own sister, the painter Vanessa Bell, and his many other adulterous relationships), Virginia became increasingly frustrated. She was simply not equipped (or interested enough) to record Fry's development as a painter, nor was she free to depict his private life. The book was a commercial and critical failure, and did not endure.[5]

Anne Stevenson's biography of Sylvia Plath, *Bitter Fame*, fared similarly. Dr. Stevenson, an American poet living in England, had seemed the ideal person to tackle a life of Plath—but the project proved a nightmare. Having been appointed the authorized biographer by Plath's widower, Ted Hughes, Stevenson found her path crossed at every turn by Hughes's sister Olwyn, who acted zealously to protect *his* reputation and estate. "Ms. Hughes has contributed so liberally to the text that this is in effect a work of joint authorship," Stevenson finally wrote despairingly in her original acknowledgments. Ms. Hughes made her remove even that comment.

As Janet Malcolm would write in her seminal account of the problem of writing Plath's biography (indeed, all biography), what emerged was "a piece of worthless native propaganda" by Dr. Stevenson on Ted Hughes's behalf. Stevenson was, as Janet Malcolm made clear, the last person able to stand up to Hughes's sister, or even the mysterious Hughes himself. "You never saw him alone?" Malcolm asked Dr. Stevenson. "I never saw him at all," Dr. Stevenson confessed—an astounding limitation on Plath's official biographer![6]

David McCullough, a highly experienced writer and broadcaster, was more careful. McCullough would undertake the life of President Harry Truman, and, like Caro, would win the Pulitzer Prize—but, as he later confided, he had first intended to write a very different life.

"I'd started working [in 1982] on a book about Pablo Picasso," McCullough later revealed. "I quit that book. I stopped after a few months because I found I disliked him so. He was, to me, a repellent human being, and he didn't really have the story of the kind that interested me. He was instantly successful. He never really went very far or had any adventures, so to speak. He was an immensely important painter. He was the Krakatoa of modern art. But I found he wasn't somebody I wanted to spend five years with as a roommate, so to speak."[7]

Picasso's posthumous loss was Truman's gain—one that led, in the 1990s, not only to a Pulitzer Prize for McCullough but to a widescale reconsideration of the thirty-third president of the United States.

Poor Picasso (full name Pablo Diego José Francisco de Paula Juan Nepomuceno María de los Remedios Cipriano de la Santísima Trinidad Clito Ruiz y Picasso) had meanwhile to wait, like Whistler, for a biographer who *could* overcome personal distaste for his quirky character. Eventually that person came forward: John Richardson.

Here is Richardson being interviewed on publication of the second of his projected four volumes—the first having won Britain's Whitbread Award for Biography in 1991:

> *Interviewer:* The current myth of Picasso is very much along these lines—woman hater, bad guy, I mean, general no-goodnik.
>
> *John Richardson:* That's a lot of nonsense. Whatever you say about him—you say he's a mean bastard—he was also an angelic, compassionate, tender, sweet man. The reverse is always true. You say

that he was stingy. He was also incredibly generous.
You say that he was very bohemian, but also he had
a sort of up-tight, bourgeois side. I mean, he was a
mass of antitheses. And that is one of the sort of
amazing things about him, that he was able to contain these totally different qualities, defects, what
have you.

Asked if he had ever challenged Picasso over his bad behavior, Richardson admitted he hadn't. "Nobody dared con-
front him. If you ever confronted Picasso over anything
like that, over any personal matters, if you were critical of
him, you were out." Asked if he had any other such demanding friends, Richardson acknowledged he hadn't,
but explained that he had put up with Picasso's strange
personality because "he's a genius, and you don't want to
offend him."

I mean, I liked the man, and I wanted access to him.
And I wasn't going to, you know, say something
dumbly critical and have the door barred in my face
in the future. I mean, I used to spend a lot of time
with Picasso in the 50's and early 60's, and he was a
marvelous, funny, nice guy to be around. But you'd
find by the end of the day, even if you'd just had

lunch with him and gone to the beach with him, had dinner with him, somehow by the end of the day that you had—were totally nervously exhausted; that everybody around him had suffered from nervous exhaustion; and he, at the age of eighty or eighty-five, would go off into his studio, strutting off into his studio, and would work all night on your energy.

The point here is that Richardson knew his subject, indeed was a devoted friend to Picasso, while remaining fully aware of the artist's complex personality, both good and bad. Such tolerance, moreover, was rewarded. After Picasso's death, Richardson was not only motivated but uniquely situated to explore Picasso's life, head-on, as the story not simply of a man but of modern art.

Confronting Critics

Richardson's perseverance was admirable—but even that was not enough. He accepted that Picasso's character was deplored by many, and that he could overcome such reader prejudice only by maintaining superlative standards of research and writing—as well as by keeping his equanimity in the face of media hostility when his work was published. You must accept the fact that your agenda will not necessarily be that of others.

For example, Robert Caro's initial Johnson volume, subtitled *The Path to Power,* caused a firestorm of controversy in 1982. Eight years later, Brian Lamb interviewed Caro on his TV program *Booknotes.* He quoted a hostile newspaper cutting in which a former Johnson aide, Jack Valenti, "accused Caro of being passionately bent on destroying the late president's reputation." Not content with quoting one critic, Lamb quoted another: Bob Hardesty, a Johnson speechwriter who'd helped Johnson write his memoirs. Hardesty went further still, labeling Caro's biography "dishonest." "I don't think it pretends to be fair," Lamb quoted Hardesty's diatribe on the air. "I think it is the work of a man with a burning unnatural hatred for his subject." Somewhat in the manner of a public prosecutor, Lamb then asked Caro how he wished to "answer those charges."[8] Caro was not in the least taken aback:

> Well, I don't think there's any truth in them at all. I think I let the facts speak for themselves. I'm taking people through Lyndon Johnson's life as he lived it, chronologically. Nobody disputes that these are the things that he did. Nobody has challenged really,

anything that I know of. . . . As for disliking him, that's not really true. The Johnson loyalists really dislike, as you can tell, even hate my books. That, however, does not mean that I disliked Lyndon Johnson. I think that the story of his life, to me, is a very sad and poignant story; it's not a question of liking and disliking. I'm trying to understand and make people understand.[9]

More than that, Caro added, he *himself* was "trying to learn how political power worked, as he [Johnson] used it, and I'm trying to portray that. Now, that's very unpleasant, in some of this volume. It's a very unpleasant story, but that doesn't mean it didn't happen. That doesn't mean that my portraying it means I dislike Lyndon Johnson."[10]

Memorably put—and worth remembering not only when you consider undertaking a biography, but when you are attacked for having done so.

Psychology—and Cohabitation

We've noted how biography builds upon the investigation of an individual life to evoke lasting insights. That potential to connect with the reader can be reassuring, as in McCullough's *Truman*, or disturbing, as in Caro's *Johnson*. Sigmund Freud was fascinated by this revelatory power—

indeed, it was the primary reason for his Leonardo da Vinci monograph, which was as much a squib aimed at cowardly conventional biographers as an exploration of Leonardo's sexuality. Biographers who indulged in mindless hero-worship were doing life-writing a grave disservice, Freud maintained. Such biographers were "fixated on their heroes in a quite special way. In many cases they have chosen their hero as the subject of their studies because— for reasons of their personal emotional life—they have felt a special affection for him from the very first. They then devote their energies to a task of idealization, aimed at enrolling the great man among the class of their infantile models—at reviving in him, perhaps, the child's idea of his father." To gratify this wish, Freud claimed, biographers "smooth over the traces" of the subject's "real life struggles," and "tolerate in him no vestige of human weakness or imperfection." The result was "regrettable, for they therefore sacrifice truth to an illusion, and for the sake of their infantile phantasies abandon the opportunity of penetrating the most fascinating secrets of human nature."[11]

A truthful life-study, Freud recognized, is a courageous undertaking. Indeed, it was one that exceeded his own limited ambitions in the realm of biography, for he had, he apologized, suffered from "insufficient material" to do more than posit a possible psychosexual explanation of

Leonardo's scientific and artistic creativity—knowing how offensive it would be to admirers of Leonardo's genius.

Intellectually, financially, practically, and psychologically, then, the task of serious biography is a challenge that you must carefully appraise before committing yourself. As David McCullough realized when rejecting Pablo Picasso as a bedfellow, the task of biography will involve a veritable cohabitation. And while cohabitation may be less daunting than marriage, and permits you (in theory, at any rate!) to part company without hard feelings (or legal punishment) if the relationship doesn't work, it is a major undertaking which you should not embark on lightly.

Cohabitation requires you to have some prior conviction as to why you think this is the right person for you to spend years of your life with. You must also be confident that you can measure up to your subject's expectations. For some, mutual respect will be enough for the partnership to prosper; but for most of us, genuine love and affection, on both sides, are a prerequisite—and this is as true in biography (notwithstanding Freud's skepticism) as in real life.

Many relationship therapists request that, before couples arrive for counseling, the two individuals set down on a piece of paper the positives and negatives that come to mind when they think of their partner. This is a very good exercise to perform before encountering relationship problems, not just after! Certainly it's one you might well adopt in deciding whether to tackle a specific biography you have in mind. You are proposing to *live with* this person, after all—and to find out *everything* about him or her! (Leo Tolstoy insisted on showing his fiancée, Sonya, his personal diary before they married—recording, in particular, the sowing of his wild oats in shocking detail. Sonya almost called off the proposed union, she was so disgusted. Although the revelations did not make for an easy marriage, they did enable her to anticipate and accept the vivid portrait of Anna Karenina when Tolstoy came to write his titanic novel of adultery.)

When you draw up the list of positives and negatives that come to mind in thinking of your proposed partner, make sure you have the humility to put yourself in his or her shoes! You must ask whether your subject has the requisite qualities and assets (a wealth of life-events, documents, friends who can be interviewed) that promise to make the cohabitation a success. But you must also ask: Have *you* the qualities and assets that augur well for success?

Respect, love, affection, even hatred have to go pretty

deep, in my experience, not simply to engage the eventual reader, but to ensure that you and your subject both survive the cohabitation.

The more, then, that you can review in advance your motivation—and your *level* of motivation (your aims, the feasibility of the project, your suitability for the task)—in selecting the subject of your biography, the more you'll be able to tackle the subject maturely when you settle down to work. And as any practicing biographer will tell you, moving in with your partner is precisely when the challenge truly begins!

THREE

Defining Your Audience

The play was a great success, but the
audience was a disaster.

—OSCAR WILDE, quoted in Hesketh Pearson,
The Life of Oscar Wilde

*F*or whom are you producing your biographical
work?

Biography is not just a conversation with oneself and
one's subject—it's a three-way communication. At one level,
yes, it's a private dialogue between you, as portrait painter
in words, and your sitter (dead or alive) whose story you're
attempting to record, illuminate, interpret. But—like Saint
Augustine's famous *Confessions,* which were ostensibly written down as an extended, private conversation with God

but which were published to be read by others—it's public. It will be your work, but produced for a third party: the reader.

Both for your proposal and for your own good, ask yourself: "Who will be interested in my subject?" Without an audience, your work has no use, save to you. So somehow you, the prospective biographer, *have* to take the audience into account, not only in proposing your work but in executing it. Like Vermeer's famous canvas *An Allegory of Painting,* in which an empty chair takes the visitor's eye to an inner scene in the artist's studio (where the artist is painting a beautifully dressed model of Clio, the muse of history), you need to ask yourself: "How can I fill that empty chair?" (Vermeer didn't; the painting was never sold in his lifetime, and he died penniless and despondent. The picture now hangs in Vienna, not Holland.)

Who is your potential audience, and how can you make your biography sufficiently compelling that it will attract one? What is it about the portrait that will prove of interest to readers: that will inform, entertain, educate, and *move* them?

The significance of the audience is different for biographers than, say, for novelists. Very few novelists can obtain an advance against royalties or an investment from a publisher before their novel is completed, or at least partly written. With biographers, it's the other way around—few biographers can undertake the years of work required to produce a worthwhile biography without a publisher's monetary advance. As a would-be biographer, then, you must craft a proposal that gives publishers a good idea of your intended audience.

Doing some research on the potential audience for your biography may vastly repay the time and expense it entails. To my surprise and delight, Harold Evans, director of Random House, was willing to take on the first volume of my biography of John F. Kennedy when my contracted publisher rejected my decision to make it a multivolume work. I found out later that he'd asked his chief assistant to go to the New York Public Library and find out what biographies were being borrowed most frequently. At the top of the list were lives of JFK! Evans was leaving nothing to chance when he accepted *JFK: Reckless Youth.*

Go in search of facts, figures, and indications which will convince prospective publishers that there is truly a market for the book you propose. (The publishers, too, will do their own checking, believe me.) It may help to think of this as seeking a financial loan—which, in effect, it is, as the publisher will be acting as your bank manager, advancing you money against your eventual royalties. He will run your credit report—in other words, determine what previous work you have done, and how it has been received and sold. He'll want to know what sort of work you're intending to write, how you're proposing to do it, and above all whether there is an audience for it.

The proposal has an audience of one, yet the book must have an audience of thousands to be commercially viable, let alone successful—and you have to show you're comfortable with that. "As far as I'm concerned, what makes this book a success," David McCullough said of his biography of Harry Truman, "is that it reaches readers." McCullough had reason to crow. "It's already a best-seller. It became rapidly a best-seller within a matter of weeks. For a 922-page serious biography to go right to the top of the best-seller list in the summertime—I won't say it's unprecedented, but it's certainly rare," he said with understandable pride.[1] He gave various possible reasons, such as the appeal of a man of principle as his subject, in the critical post–World War II years. But there was, too, the fact that he'd written the huge book with an essential aim always in mind: to inform, enlighten, and entertain an *audience.*

E. M. Forster, author of *A Passage to India,* once said, apropos of audiences, that he wrote for himself and a few friends. I'm sure Forster meant "friends" figuratively: friends as reliable stepping stones to that hopefully larger audience, whose highest standards of expectation he thereby disciplined himself to fulfill. Conversely, if he had reason to fear an audience's hostility, he shelved his work. The manuscript of *Maurice,* his novel of same-sex love written in 1913, has the words "Publishable, but worth it?" scribbled across the top. Uncertain of an audience for a book about a homosexual character in a homophobic age, he wisely *didn't* publish it in his lifetime—and thereby gave no one the opportunity to subject him to the same fate as Oscar Wilde.

Asking yourself who, ultimately, will be interested in, or willing to read, the life you're recounting should be your constant concern. When biographies fail to spark interest, become tedious or unsatisfying, it is usually because the biographer has lost his commitment to engage the reader and is taking the audience for granted, by getting too self-absorbed in the life he is depicting. Never forget or neglect the reader!

Perhaps the most vivid recent example of the need to remember your audience is that of Edmund Morris. A Pulitzer prizewinner for *The Rise of Theodore Roosevelt,* his wonderful biography of the young twenty-sixth president, Morris was asked to set aside his second Roosevelt volume in order to tackle the life of the fortieth president, Ronald Reagan, who was still living—indeed, was still president when Morris began his work. The story of the subsequent "fiasco," as Morris himself called it, is instructive, for it goes to the very heart of what the biographer wants to do, as opposed to what the audience wants him to do.

Commissioned in 1985 as President Reagan's official, authorized biographer, Morris found himself, after seven years, simply unable to write the same sort of "conventional" biography of Reagan that he had written of Theodore Roosevelt. And so, in 1992, like Virginia Woolf (who had thought she could "revolutionize biography in a night" by writing the life of her lover, Vita Sackville-West, as a fictional spoof-biography, *Orlando*), Morris realized that he, too, could do something "revolutionary." "I had spent a couple of years trying to write about Reagan in the orthodox fashion," he afterward confessed, "and he simply eluded conventional description. So I came upon this device, more or less, in a moment of inspiration."

Standing under an elm tree in Eureka, Illinois, where Reagan had been to college, Morris came up with an unusual device: he would enter the past *himself*, as a fictional narrator. "I knew what it was like," Morris explained. "I'd studied that period intensely. I'd read all the documents and interviewed people. So I decided to give a physical, fleshly presence to this biographical presence, this [authorial] mind, and I created a narrator, who throughout the book observes Ronald Reagan in action, but of whose scrutiny Reagan remains unaware."[2]

Interviewed in 1999, when the biography was released to widespread criticism and condemnation, Morris was unrepentant. "I understood that it was going to be controversial. I knew the moment I began to write it in the fashion in which it's now been published. So in a sense," he confessed, "I courted the controversy because I think that biography needs expansion, an adaptation to the values of a new century. So I knew this was going to happen."[3]

Dutch was, then, a form of professional suicide—followed, it may happily be said, by professional resurrection two years later, in 2001, when the second volume of Morris's life of Theodore Roosevelt, *Theodore Rex,* was published to universal acclaim.

Dutch, by contrast, remained a blot on the biographical landscape—not because people abhorred Morris's hubris in inventing himself as a participant-observer in Reagan's life, but because he had rejected the expectations of the audience for an official biography.

To Conform—or To Challenge?

There are, of course, differing audiences for biography—general and specialist—and each one will alter its expectations according to the cultural moment. This can be difficult to know in advance—especially when your planned biography may not appear for several years, by which time the social context may have changed. One thing you can do, however, is check to see whether biographies of your subject already exist, and, if so, what sorts of works they are. If, for example, a good conventional biography of a certain figure has already been published, there may be little point in replicating it, whereas readers may well be receptive to a different, fresh, perhaps more imaginative "take" on the individual—since no single biography can ever be definitive.

At the point in time when Morris was commissioned to write his biography of the fortieth president, for instance, there had been no scholarly account of Reagan's life. As official biographer, Morris had been given unique access to the president, his staff, his friends, and—most important of all—Reagan's unpublished documents, which remained inaccessible to other biographers and scholars. As a consequence, general readers, who expected a straight, solid, substantial account based on unprecedented access to sources, found it galling that, after fourteen years of waiting, the Reagan who appeared in *Dutch* was almost double-Dutch: Morris's eclectic, unconventional vision, in which fact and fiction were indistinguishable. Meanwhile, specialist readers—particularly historians of the period—were outraged at having been denied access to vital documents merely so that Morris could produce a profoundly personal, essentially dramatized-documentary version of Reagan's life.

Had there already been a conventional "official biography" of Ronald Reagan, Morris's biography would probably have been lauded for its innovativeness, its copious insight, its wit, its sheer descriptive narrative power. But there was no such book—and the public felt betrayed. Morris had misjudged his audience and their needs.

Expectations and Obligations

One way to think about audience expectation is to see it as a contractual obligation you must fulfill. Although others may offer advice, and act as legal intermediaries in the production and selling of your work, the audience is your ultimate *client*. What must you do in order to earn, and keep, the respect of that client? What is the nature of the biographical pact between you?

These are important matters. The journalist Janet Malcolm, in her 1994 book about Sylvia Plath's biographers, *The Silent Woman*, made the point that in a postmodern, relativistic world, the roles of fiction and nonfiction have reversed: we can no longer trust the truth which a nonfiction work purports to provide (since it is always debatable), whereas we have to accept the truth of what a fictional artist writes. This is true in a philosophical sense, but as an argument relating to biography it is utterly specious—for although we may never know the *whole* truth, biographers are nevertheless *trying* to attain it, via the skills and methods we've developed over centuries of civilization: that is to say, evidence in documents and testimony that are the mainstay of our research.

The English littérateur Desmond McCarthy once referred to the biographer as the "artist on oath," meaning a writer with integrity. Trust between yourself and your audience is essential, so that the reader will credit what you are presenting, arguing, claiming about your subject. Somehow you, the biographer, must learn how to create and develop a compact with your unseen audience: a compact based on acceptance of your agenda and a bond of trust in your integrity, as well as confidence in your mastery of detail and literary style (rhetoric). It's no good making unsubstantiated claims which you intuit, but cannot prove, and which the audience cannot credit! It's no good inundating your audience with minutiae that will tax the patience of the reader to no purpose! Constantly reminding yourself to respect your audience and earn its trust is a strategy that *will never fail you*. Being responsive to the high expectations of your audience is not a sin, but rather a bracing constraint that you, as a biographer, must learn to bear with pride and dignity.

Let's look more closely at these audience expectations. An audience expects a biography to be a work, usually of nonfiction, that records and investigates the known (or knowable) aspects as well as the mystery of a real life. A biography is also expected to portray, by implication, how that individual's life connects with more universal aspects of the human condition: the common themes and preoccupations that fascinate us about life—from family to career, from loves to wars, from childhood to old age and death. Behind the record of an actual individual, there is thus a broader, *symbolic* focus that constitutes a work of life-depiction: a focus that must resonate with the reader and with his or her interests and concerns.

Robert Graves understood readers' curiosity about real lives extraordinarily well. In 1929 he dictated, in a few weeks, his famous early account of his life, *Good-bye to All That*—and the next year candidly explained, through one of the characters in a stage play, the secret. Though he was being cynical, he was also being realistic: his character explains how, in writing a best-selling work, he has given "frank answers to all the inquisitive questions that people like to ask about other people's lives. And not only that, but I have more or less deliberately mixed in all the ingredients that I know are missed in other popular books." These include "food and drink . . . murders . . . Ghosts . . . kings. . . . People also like reading about other people's mothers. I put in mine." Name-dropping was *de rigueur:* "T. E. Lawrence . . . the Prince of Wales . . . racing motorists and millionaires and pedlars and tramps and adopted children and Arctic explorers. . . . I have met most of the best-known ones in England . . . Prime Ministers," he boasts. Beyond people are places: "foreign travel . . . Sport . . . commerce . . . school episodes, love affairs (regular and irregular), wounds, weddings, religious doubts, methods of bringing up children, severe illnesses, suicides. But the best of all is battles, and I had been in two quite good ones. . . . So it was easy to write a book that would interest everybody."[4]

Still suffering, in 1930, from the First World War's traumatic effects, Graves could be forgiven for being sarcastic. Yet his point remained fair. He *had* taken into account his audience's curiosity while writing *Good-bye to All That,* and had been rewarded with not only abundant sales but impressive stature. His autobiographical work, with its myriad themes, would become one of the landmark texts of the twentieth century—whereas his play was never performed! It had taken *no* account of the audience's lack of interest in his fictionalized authorial self-scourging!

The Stepping Stone

Respecting your audience means a willingness to give potential readers, listeners, or spectators what you know they *want* to know—with the added bonus that, if you are skillful, you can use that interest to explore *further* and *more deeply* what the audience may be willing to learn about human nature and even, perhaps, about themselves. Amid the madding crowd of lives chronicled, then, your job is to find a key first to unlock, then *extend* the reader's curiosity about your chosen individual—and how that individual can provide other insights.

One of the great virtues of Michael Holroyd's 1968 biography of Lytton Strachey, for example, was not simply that it allowed Strachey's true homosexual orientation (and the private lives of the entire Bloomsbury group) to be opened to public view for the first time, following the legalization of homosexuality in Britain, but that it used such revelations as a stepping stone for the reader to enter the intellectual, artistic, and political world of Lytton Strachey—one of the greatest English-language biographers.

Holroyd recounted in wonderfully researched detail the

genesis of Strachey's *Eminent Victorians*—including the way in which Strachey used his Bloomsbury friends as stand-ins for his future readership: his audience. Amazingly, Strachey had begun his book in 1912 without any other agenda than recording twelve notable personalities of the Victorian age. Yet by 1917, three years into World War I, he was so angry at the appalling loss of life in the war that his whole agenda had changed: instead of twelve figures, there would now be but four. Strachey read a draft of his first two lives—those of Cardinal Manning and Florence Nightingale—to a group of friends at the country house of Virginia Woolf's sister, Vanessa Bell. "The response within this Bloomsbury sanctum varied enormously," Holroyd described. "Duncan Grant fell asleep and Vanessa Bell was rather critical, not of Lytton's treatment of his subjects, but of the prose style, which she thought too brim-full of clichés. Clive Bell was more generously appreciative." It was the writer David Garnett who sensed the magnitude of what Strachey was doing. Highly impressed, he realized (as he later wrote) "that Lytton's essays were designed to undermine the foundations on which the age that brought war about had been built."[5] Such a reaction fortified Strachey's belief in his evolving project.

Don't be afraid, then, to try out your agenda and your draft manuscript on potential readers in the course of your researching and writing. Moreover, don't listen solely to your own voice expounding your thoughts (though this may well help you articulate your approach, selection, and so on). Listen also to your audience's responses: to what *they* have to say! For it is on the basis of that continuing dialogue—on your sensitivity to what works in gaining and holding an audience's attention—that a successful biography is fashioned.

As Holroyd so perceptively noted about Strachey's *Eminent Victorians,* the work was not biography in the traditional sense of lifelikeness, but biography with an agenda: biography with a devastating human and political purpose which Strachey had rehearsed with his colleagues and friends, and which, when the book was published in the spring of 1918 in Britain and the United States, caused Strachey, like Byron, to become famous overnight.[6] None of his later books—though superbly crafted—ever achieved that same intense level of dialogue between author and audience.

Respect your audience. Think of them; meet them; measure constantly their curiosity. Whether you are succeeding in arousing their curiosity or putting them to sleep, be aware of them!

I often think, in this respect, of a TV interview I once saw, in which Groucho Marx explained to viewers of the

Dick Cavett Show the genius of Irving Thalberg, the young production supremo of Universal and MGM studios. Thalberg never issued a film without first having it shown to an unsophisticated audience in a small community—and, in the case of *A Day at the Races* (1937), he encouraged the Marx Brothers to rehearse and test the skits *for two years* on the vaudeville stage before they began filming. Well, perhaps it shows: the film's narrative thread is very thin and disjointed at times. But the slapstick scenes are as wacky, subversive, and outrageous as anything the Marx Brothers ever did.

The fact that Thalberg insisted on previewing films before unsophisticated audiences does not mean that he pandered to simplistic audience expectations. He built a Hollywood reputation for consummate production craftsmanship, yet never wanted his name listed in the credits. If his preview audience didn't respond well to the draft film, he would have scenes recut, even reshot. Soliciting the opinion of unsophisticated viewers represented his search for an honest response, rather than an occasion for small-town residents to dress up and feel honored, as at a premiere—when by definition it's too late to make any changes in the work. It was a sign that he would take nothing—not even the Marx Brothers—for granted. And neither should you.

FOUR

Researching Your Subject

Research! A mere excuse for idleness; it has never achieved,
and will never achieve any results of the slightest value.

—BENJAMIN JOWETT, Regius Professor of
Greek, Oxford University, 1855–1893

He must comb every library, large and small, every archive,
every institution where manuscripts may be kept. . . . He
must try to communicate with every single person.

—RICHARD ALTICK, *The Scholar Adventurers*

*R*esearch may be optional for other disciplines, and
other arts. But it is the core of biography—the criterion
that most distinguishes the practice of life-writing from
that of fiction.

A novelist, by conducting research, may seek more detailed information to increase the *semblance* of veracity in his work. The search for *verifiable* truth is, however, the very wellspring of the biographical endeavor. It is the current that makes biography electrifying for the audience, continually prompting us to ask: Is this true? Was this really so? How do we know?

Is biographical research more or less the same as historical investigation? Yes—and no. The methodology is identical, certainly: the biographer works in the same archives and libraries as the historian, trawls among the same documents, invokes the same Freedom of Information Act or rules of bequest to view restricted papers, seeks verifiable evidence. Yet the two types of research are *not* quite the same. Historians sift through masses of evidence in search of that which will advance their understanding of an event, an issue, a development in history. In that quest, people's roles and personalities are subordinate to the main agenda: what happened, when, and how. In biography, however, it's the other way around.

Yes, biographers will wish to see evidence that helps them understand and describe the context, the environment, the social and political forces and wider developments that serve as background to their portrait of an individual. But in the end it's the *personal foreground,* not the background, that will ultimately be their *locus vivendi,* so to speak.

In due course, as part of our survey of the composition stage, we'll explore the sorts of selection that biographers make *from* their evidentiary research. For the moment, though, let's look more closely at the difference between historical and biographical inquiry—in fact, let's look again at Vermeer's *Allegory of Painting.* The beautifully dressed model holds the correct accoutrements for Clio, the Muse of History, as set out in Cesare Ripa's *Iconologia* (1593), written in Italian and translated into Dutch in 1644. Gowned in shimmering blue and yellow, she wears a crown of laurel. In one hand she holds a trombone; in the other, a book by the great Greek historian Thucydides. Behind her is a detailed 1592 wall map of the Netherlands by Nicolaes Visscher, as well as other icons of contemporary history and political/military power. All very interesting, historically. But who *is* the pretty model? Is she the baker's daughter? How was she chosen to pose? Is the painter paying her? Does he expect other favors? What does she think of him and his work? What happened to her after the painting was finished? What is her life-story? (These are not impertinent questions to ask of an old master. Tracy Chevalier devoted a whole novel to the conundrum in Vermeer's painting *Girl with a Pearl Earring,* and a feature film starring

Colin Firth and Scarlett Johansson was made of the novel.[1]
Simultaneously, a major art exhibition entitled "The Artist's Model" was presented in four English cities and was
the basis for a book published under the same title.)[2]

Biographical research, in other words, is impelled by curiosity about individual human nature, not the more impersonal forces of society and politics.

Since the days of the ancient Greeks and Romans, in
fact, biographers have grumbled about the superficiality of
historians' understanding of the *individuals* who people
their chronicles, as well as the way in which historians often manipulate individuals to suit their narrative analytical
aims and objectives. Not the least of biography's many du-
ties in Western society is thus as a *corrective* to the work
of historians (as well as novelists, dramatists, filmmakers).
The success of that task will depend on good research, allied to the depth of the biographer's insight.

The Earthly Pilgrimage of a Man

How deeply you choose to explore the historical background, and how tenaciously you research the biographical foreground, will depend on a number of factors: time,
cost, priority, access, motivation. What is important to note,
here, is that the biographical research will be a journey of
discovery for yourself, but on behalf of others. It's vital to

keep curiosity and skepticism running in tandem. Research is not something you undertake to carry out a preconceived agenda, nor should you delude yourself that there is ever a single (let alone simple) truth. The key to fulfillment as a biographer is to proceed always with honesty and intellectual humility. What will you do, for example, if your biographical research turns up material that runs counter to your initial thesis, bias, or predisposition? How will you stop yourself from seeking only evidence that supports a conviction, rather than evidence that might not?

This is—as it is with historians—perhaps the greatest test of a biographer—and no biographer, if truth be told, comes off with a perfect score. We have all erred on the side of complacency, or worse. How could we not, given that we are as human as our subjects? Historians have an advantage, in that they are taught from the start to keep their distance and, for the most part, their comparative objectivity. They may suffer from ideological prejudices (Marxist, Whig, postmodern), but they'll always be less emotionally invested in their portrayal of individuals than will biographers, whose *personal* relationship with their primary subject is crucial to the success of their enterprise.

More than a century ago, Thomas Carlyle, the English biographer of the German king Frederick the Great, gave a fine description of the biographer's task:

The biographer has this problem set before him: to delineate a likeness of the earthly pilgrimage of a man. He will compute well what profit is in it, and what disprofit; under which latter head this of offending any of his fellow-creatures will surely not be forgotten. Nay, this may so swell the disprofit side of his account, that many an enterprise of biography, otherwise promising, shall require to be renounced. But once taken up, the rule before all rules is to do *it,* not to do the ghost of it. In speaking of the man and men he has to deal with, he will of course keep all his charities about him; but all his eyes open. Far be it from him to set down aught *untrue;* nay, not to abstain from, and leave in oblivion much that is true. But having found a thing or things essential for his subject, and well computed the for and against, he will in very deed set down such thing or things, nothing doubting,—*having,* we may say, the fear of God before his eyes, and no other fear whatever.[3]

Courage, in other words, is required of biographers when they cast their net. For persons willing to become the fishermen of biography, in fact, the enterprise has all the challenges of deep-sea trawling. You must go out in clement or inclement weather. You know you must be patient. You know the fish you seek may not be found, or may be overfished, or may not bite straightaway. Or they may bite yet not be landed, if illegal. But out you must go.

The wise researcher begins by consulting existing authorities on where good sources may be found, and on what steps must be taken to access them. Read carefully the bibliographies, footnotes, and endnotes of existing biographical works on your topic, and make a list of the names mentioned—especially in other authors' acknowledgments. Then check archival reference books. Contact relevant libraries and archives which may have material pertinent to your subject, and find out their precise holdings under those and other writers' names. There are many guides to the methodology of good research in science, history, anthropology, and most of the humanities—even in biography.

Though the scholarly purpose to which research is put may vary, the essential methodology or investigative process remains largely the same across the different disciplines. Good research (as opposed to spotty, inadequate, or superficial investigation) requires energy, prioritization, perseverance, honesty, careful recordkeeping, and an open mind. It also requires hunches—as James Watson showed in his autobiographical memoir *The Double Helix,* which told the story of how he and others discovered the molecular structure of DNA and which we'll look at later.[4]

The Three Graces

In the realm of biography, when all is said and done, there are only three possible fields of information you will be required to investigate.

If we take these in order of ease-of-access, the first is material that is already *published* or previously broadcast, which we call "secondary" sources (so called since they were primary until published).

The second kind of material comprises *unpublished* or archival documents, which we call "primary." These require that the biographer make contact with, and personal visits to, archival institutions or private repositories.

Finally, there's interview or *oral* evidence, which is also primary until published, when it, too, becomes secondary material.

For academic reasons, this third tier of evidence was for many years considered by historians to be the least valuable of the three research graces—indeed, the most suspect. Previously published information was ranked according to the status of the scholar who published it. For example, writings by the great Oxford educator and prolific writer Benjamin Jowett carried substantial weight.

Professor Jowett despised primary research and researchers, on the grounds that, though they might industriously ferret out information from original sources, it was the job of the real historian, philosopher, jurist, and teacher to *interpret* evidence, not produce it. Fresh, primary archival evidence was therefore considered *infra dig:* something professors got their graduate students to obtain for them, just as barristers and courtroom lawyers got minions to look up the relevant statutes and cases. If primary research was beneath such Oxonian dignity, however, interview evidence or oral history was considered simply beyond the pale: subjective, based upon fallible memory, and demanding actual (heaven forbid!) personal *contact* between historian and source. Cambridge University, where I did my degree, was pretty much the same as Oxford. Training there as a historian in the early 1960s under professors such as Sir Harry Hinsley, I well remember the "Cambridge antipathy" toward interview evidence—which made my research methodology, once I began to write biography, a *terra nova.* None of my teachers had ever taken oral history seriously, let alone taught us *how* to interview, including the use of a tape recorder. Thus, for my first project—a dual biography of the brothers Heinrich and Thomas Mann, which I began in the late 1960s—I only made handwritten notes of my "background" interviews with Mann-witnesses, critics, archivists, and aficionados, relying in my text almost entirely on the Mann brothers' supremely articulate written correspondence, all of which had been preserved in specialist archives in cities ranging from East Berlin to London and Zurich. These I trawled, and the results made for a well-documented literary-historical draft manuscript—but not one that had much vivid *life* in it.

Fortunately a childhood friend of mine, Elizabeth (Sissy) von Scheel-Plessen, *had* done extended, recorded, and transcribed interviews for South German television with Thomas Mann's widow, Katia Mann—interviews which Sissy shared with me. Suddenly the past came to life! Here was a flesh-and-blood woman: a widow with real opinions, prejudices, likes, and dislikes—including such a strong dislike of Thomas's elder brother, Heinrich, that she refused to meet me when, at the invitation of her distinguished historian son, Golo, I visited the family home in Kilchberg, outside Zurich. Thanks to Sissy, I began—belatedly—to recognize the value of oral evidence in researching a human life: not as objective evidence, but as *subjective* testimony. Armed with that perception, I was able to approach my next work—the official biography of Field

Marshal Montgomery—with a completely different attitude toward the value of oral testimony. Indeed, I became determined to make interviewing a sort of *sine qua non* of modern military biography. The next question was how I should proceed.

Polychromatic Portraiture

There was another reason I was eager to use oral evidence, beyond live-liness: namely, the chance to get away from the mono-perspective, which leads ultimately to monochromatic portraiture, if not hagiography. Everyone knows that two or more witnesses in court will give two or more different versions of the same event. So, in biography, I wanted to use the different lenses of multiple observers to emphasize the diversity of truths about a human being.

By switching between Thomas and Heinrich in *The Brothers Mann,* I'd been able, despite the paucity of interviews and my reliance on Sissy von Scheel-Plessen's work, to avoid the mono-perspective. In 1977, as official biographer of Field Marshal Montgomery, I not only had unique access to his private as well as official papers (diaries, memos, telegrams, letters, manuscripts), but also obtained introductions to all his surviving family, colleagues, and subordinates. It was through them, I hoped, that I could arrive at a multifaceted portrait of military greatness.

I was by no means the only biographer who relied on oral evidence to enrich modern biography; I instance this merely to demonstrate how the absolute refusal of universities and colleges to teach biography meant that biographers of my generation (and still today) were self-taught, indeed had first to *un*-teach themselves in order to advance the genre. From colleagues and subordinates (and their spouses), from friends to enemies, from members of the House of Lords to domestic staff, I contacted and sought interviews with as many people as I could. By gathering their subjective testimonies, I was determined, alongside my archival work, to achieve a fresh degree of critical perspective, veracity, and vividness in my portrait—more so, ironically, than a portrait painter, who, after all, is painting in some ways in monochrome, even when he is using the entire palette of colors, for it is always via *his own* brush that we are seeing the subject. A biographer who is willing to seek out and interview a host of possibly competing witnesses can, by contrast, offer a multifaceted picture of the subject through diverse insights and contributions: a *collage* rather than a single-perspective painting.

For the next ten years, I devoted my energies to the documentary research, the interviewing, the reading, and finally the composition necessary for the three volumes of *Monty.* Alongside the official biography of Winston Chur-

chill (for which, sadly, almost no new interviews were conducted), it was the longest biography ever undertaken of a
British World War II commander. In the course of preparing it, I clashed with many historians—including my old
professor, Sir Harry Hinsley.

Pas de Héros

Harry Hinsley had been a brilliant lecturer on the history
of international relations. Having worked for Britain's wartime code-breaking establishment, Bletchley Park, he had
in due course been chosen as the official historian of British Intelligence and its influence on field operations in
World War II. Like my own work, it appeared in a number
of volumes.[5]

To my mind, Hinsley's opus was a misfortune: a Jowett-
like history rendered almost completely useless to the modern public because Hinsley, backed by a team of research
assistants, and amply funded, had adamantly refused to
conduct a single interview for inclusion in his multivolume text. A Cambridge-trained historian, he simply
could not abandon his disdain for oral history—obstinately
refusing, volume after volume after volume, to mention
even one name of anyone who had served in British or An-
glo-American Intelligence, let alone anything they might
have said.

To add insult to modern injury, Hinsley defended his scholarly complacency with the words of a French nineteenth-century *novelist!* Gustave Flaubert, Hinsley declared at the start of each and every volume, had once given as recipe for the perfect realist novel the injunction, "Pas de monstres, et pas de héros" ("No monsters, and no heroes"). In an age of cheap tape recorders and even video cameras, this excuse for failing to name names or conduct personal interviews was a wretched justification for impersonal history, which proved intensely disappointing. And now that most of the Bletchley team has passed away, it seems quite tragic.

Clearly, Hinsley had never actually read *Madame Bovary.* The irony is that, in misusing a phrase from Flaubert, Hinsley missed one of the most exciting elements of modern research—one that has, in fact, spread across every academic discipline, as the status of the *grand récit* has been undermined. Today, the very *subjectivity* of individual perspectives is seen as rich, valuable, and illuminating in many disciplines of the humanities and social sciences, especially biography.

Interviewing more than a thousand sources for the three volumes of *Monty,* I certainly learned many lessons—from the need to use a good, simple, sturdy, and reliable tape recorder, to the need to prepare well for the interview.

Written notes should be made either at the time, or immediately after, in case of mechanical malfunction. Tapes need to be properly labeled and dated. Transcriptions need to be checked carefully, unless you do the transcribing yourself.

No one methodology, however, can govern the conduct of the actual interview. Each interview demands its own rules of engagement. Reel off lists of questions, and the interviewee may balk, take offense, or feel manipulated; allow the interview to run its own course, and vital information may not get addressed. Somewhere between the two is a dialogue that permits you to learn what the interviewee has to offer in the way of insight and perspective. Moreover, an interview can often reveal an additional pointer on the complicated trail of documentary and other evidence. An interviewee, for example, if convinced of my sincerity and fairness, would show me unpublished letters, diaries, or photographs, and often pass me on to another witness. That witness might also turn up documents which had never been seen before.

I wondered, for instance, how Montgomery—a man of almost superhuman self-control in combat, and whose relations with women were, at best, cordial—had reacted to his wife Betty's painful death in 1937 from septicemia, occasioned by an insect bite on the beach while she was swim-

ming with their young son. I asked one of Betty's sons by
her first marriage, Brigadier Richard Carver. Richard had
gone into the army, encouraged by his stepfather, and had
been stationed in India at the time of his mother's death.
Upon my question, he brought me a folded, handwritten
letter Monty had written him on the day she passed away,
and which he had added to immediately after her funeral
several days later. It was deeply, almost hysterically emotional, and very moving.

After dinner, while Richard was out of the room, his
wife remarked what a cold man Monty had been. I begged
leave to differ, and instanced the letter her husband had
earlier shown me, on the death of Monty's wife, Richard's
mother. "What letter?" she demanded. *He had never shown
it to her.* Overcoming his reticence, he allowed me to quote
from it.

On another occasion, I drove up to the north of England, to interview the son of the headmaster who had
looked after Monty's son David on school holidays during
World War II (since David had no mother after 1937). "Ah,
Hamilton, you're in luck!" the major shouted, as I pulled
into the yard where he was stabling his favorite hunter. "I
looked in the attic, and found two hundred letters from
Monty to my mother!"

In sum, interviews with living relatives, friends, even enemies, are unpredictable, but invaluable to the serious biographer—especially when they open further doors.

Research and Agenda

Day by day, week by week, month by month, year by year the cumulative fruits of research—oral, archival, secondary—offer the dedicated biographer a cornucopia of evidence, education, and insight. Plutarch once wrote that it is "above all things most necessary" for a biographer "to reside in some city of good note, addicted to liberal arts, and populous; where he may have plenty of all sorts of books, and upon inquiry may hear and inform himself of such particulars as, having escaped the pens of writers, are more faithfully preserved in the memories of men, lest his work be deficient in many things, even those which it can least dispense with."[6]

By the end of *Monty*, I knew exactly what Plutarch meant. I had begun with a mere acorn of very personal, imperfect information about a man; I ended feeling that I was standing beneath a vast oak of knowledge. It was the very trunk of this tree, moreover, that most surprised me. I had expected to delve deep into the Field Marshal's strange psyche, but I had not expected to find so much evidence of his self-preparation for military leadership—indeed, it was this research that caused me to alter my plan for the work. Not having served in the military, nor having previously specialized in military history, I had thought to write a study of Montgomery the man and to leave the record of his military career to someone more expert. It was my disappointment with the work of so-called military historians, as well as my own realization that I could never disentangle the professional from the personal in Monty's long life, that made me reconsider—and led me to tackle both. First in his private letters to his parents during World War I, then in a variety of regimental and other World War I archives, as well as in my interviews, I started to discover the true origins of his greatness as a general: namely, his absolute devotion during and after World War I to the art of training and preparation—an art that would help win World War II for the Allies.

Such a simple perception seemed to have been missed by most previous historians, but the evidence mounted, month after month, so that I wholly recast my agenda. Why had millions of Allied soldiers put their trust in the beaky-nosed, egotistical, boastful, and bombastic "little man on the make," as Churchill once called him? How had he reversed years of defeat, retreat, and military fiasco when taking over command of the British Eighth Army, ranged against Field Marshal Rommel at Alamein, outside Alexandria, in mid-August 1942? Was he hugely "overrated," as most American historians and a growing chorus of British historians were claiming in the 1970s? Gradually the evidence came together: Monty wielded battlefield command not as strategy or tactics—though both were important—but as the culmination of two decades' dedication to the art of making effective soldiers from volunteers and conscripts, by first training a cadre of professionals who could train *them* in time of war. The story of that dedication—how near to dismissal it brought him, and how reluctant Churchill was to appoint him to field command even at the nadir of Britain's military fortunes in 1942—made it a drama of exceptional significance.

By assembling hitherto unseen primary sources and the transcripts of my interviews, I was able to demonstrate Montgomery's nation-saving military professionalism, while never sparing the reader the truth about his quirky, difficult, and peremptory personality, which continually got him into hot water with superiors, colleagues, and allies. In this sense, the biography was a once-in-a-lifetime opportunity, at a time in my life when I was young and energetic enough to do the necessary research in Britain and America, before the crucial witnesses passed away. My status as official biographer was a vital—though not always effective—passport to obtaining the interviews I needed. I remember feeling disappointed after General Matthew Ridgway, the great Airborne Corps commander in World War II, declined my request—having fallen out with Montgomery when he was Monty's boss at NATO in the early 1950s. To my despair, General Joseph Collins, the American infantry and Armored Corps commander from D-Day to the end of the war, also declined—until General Alfred Gruenther, Supreme Commander of NATO in the 1950s, called Collins at his Washington home. "He's in the shower?" General Gruenther queried when Mrs. Collins answered the telephone. "Well, *get him out!* I've a young British historian here who wants to talk to him—*today!*" Collins saw me.

Doors were likewise opened by generals Maxwell Taylor, James Gavin, Mark Clark . . . Later, I would wonder at my good fortune in getting such legendary World War II commanders to talk with me and give me their unique perspectives and memories of Monty, as well as grant me access to their papers. Each one had his own point of view, and insofar as possible I attempted to illustrate the subjective, personal nature of their testimony by quoting them verbatim, so that their very syntax reflected the way they thought and spoke. Interlacing their testimony with the documents I assembled was a huge task, and I was often counseled to hire a research assistant. But I persisted in going it alone, out of a sense that I was making my own journey through the material and the past, and that this would be important once I came to write up the research in the book itself. I felt connected, involved, committed. An initially modest undertaking had become a sort of life's work, as I realized that I was not only writing Montgomery's lifestory, but contributing to the military history of World War II in Europe and the Mediterranean—and that *research* was the key. I could not be impartial, but I could make sure my narrative was based upon good authority.

The zeal to know, the rush of excitement when discovering "new" documents, the sense of exploration, the willingness to see the negative as well as the positive, the compassion you feel for your subject (and your subject's "victims"), the pride over your subject's accomplishments: these are the rewards of deep and attentive research into a subject's life. How well I understood my colleague, Philip Ziegler, who was appointed official biographer of Monty's younger contemporary, Admiral Lord Louis Mountbatten. Ziegler's biography ends with a confession: namely, of how Ziegler constantly struggled with his own desire to laud a charismatic, aristocratic English lord (the last viceroy of India), but was put off by Mountbatten's lifelong efforts to burnish his own image and reputation to the point of deceit and prevarication. "The truth, in his hands, was swiftly converted from what it was to what it should have been,"

Ziegler berated Mountbatten. "He sought to rewrite history with cavalier indifference to the facts, to magnify his own achievements. There was a time when I became so enraged by what I began to feel was his determination to hoodwink me that I found it necessary to place on my desk a notice saying: REMEMBER, IN SPITE OF EVERYTHING, HE WAS A GREAT MAN."[7]

That authorial awareness made for a justly celebrated biography.

Misuse of Research

What happens if biographical research is used not to discover and present to the public the truth (however varied), but as a means to deny it? Perhaps the example of British historical and biographical writer David Irving will best illustrate the problem. Irving's father was an English World War II veteran—a brave naval commander who survived the sinking of his submarine by the Germans, but an unreliable family man who abandoned his wife and children. Young Irving grew up with a decided chip on his shoulder. He matriculated at Imperial College, University of London, to study science, but never completed his degree. He seems to have had, beginning in his schooldays, another agenda in mind: devoting himself throughout his life to a rehabilitation of the Nazis—thus, by extension, perhaps wreaking a sort of vengeance on his father. He went to Germany and took a job as a steelworker in the Ruhr, where he learned to read and speak German fluently. Aware that most British and many American historians were too lazy, complacent, or busy to do original research in Germany, he began to sift German archives—private as well as public—for unpublished World War II material.

Finding no documentary evidence that Hitler had ordered the extermination of the Jews in Germany and Nazi-occupied Europe, and eager to make his mark, Irving literally made (that is, fabricated) history by maintaining over a number of years that Hitler was not responsible for the Holocaust. Indeed, Irving achieved the dubious distinction of becoming a star among neo-Nazis: their best-selling proponent (or "prostitute," as the Austrian judge would later say when imprisoning him for deliberate incitement of neofascists, a criminal offense under Austrian law). By the 1990s, Irving had begun to question whether there had been a Holocaust at all—preferring to believe that six million Jews had mostly died of disease. Yet when an American Jewish professor named Deborah Lipstadt labeled him a "Holocaust denier" in print in 1994, he denied it and retaliated by suing Lipstadt for libel, or defamation of character, in the English High Court.

The case put "history on trial," as the newspapers

phrased it. Under British law, any person who can afford to is permitted to sue for large sums of money if he feels his "reputation" (his standing among his peers) has been damaged. Irving was able to keep his own legal costs to a minimum by dispensing with a lawyer and representing himself in court; by contrast, Professor Lipstadt (who was living in the United States and Israel) and her English publishers, Penguin Books, not only had to pay huge legal fees to defend themselves but were compelled (on pain of punitive libel damages) to prove that they had *not* libeled him— since, unusually under the British system, a libel-defendant is guilty until proved innocent.

Mercifully, after years of litigation that cost Penguin and Lipstadt more than £5 million ($9 million) in legal fees,[8] they won their case—for Lipstadt's defense went to the heart of historical and biographical research methodology in today's postmodern world. Lipstadt's legal team persuaded her that they should avoid calling upon Holocaust survivors to testify, since they feared that oral evidence would be insufficient in a court of law to prove, for example, deliberate genocidal extermination by gassing, given that the Nazis had destroyed much of the evidence. In addition, the lawyers feared that Irving, indulging in courtroom antics as a *faux* prosecutor, might subject the survivors to humiliation and mental anguish, ridiculing their age, their frailty, their allegedly unreliable memories. At a single stroke, this decision to forgo eyewitness testimony eliminated the strongest proof of Nazi atrocities from the courtroom—a tremendous gamble.

I was teaching history and biography in London at the time, and took a group of my students to the High Court to observe "history on trial." Capitalizing on British ignorance, Irving had carved out quite a career as an archive worm, unearthing *tens of thousands* of documentary sources no British historian had ever seen—as well as tracking down everyone he could find connected with Hitler, from secretaries to chauffeurs, and requesting access to their diaries, correspondence, and memorabilia. This, in itself, was admirable research; it was his *misuse* of the research that was so troubling.

Anyone sickened by genocide could not but be disappointed by the way Irving's libel trial against Professor Lipstadt appeared to be going. At a publisher's gathering in London, I was "reliably" informed that the directors of Penguin Books despaired of achieving a successful verdict; and failure would have dire consequences for anyone attempting to challenge deniers of the Holocaust. Had six million Jews perished in vain? Once the few remaining survivors died, or became too infirm to appear in court, would historians be able to claim that the Holocaust was a

.figment of the Jewish imagination? That the deaths of so many unarmed, innocent civilians had merely been "collateral damage" and isolated mistreatment in the East?

Fortunately Penguin Books hired Richard J. Evans, professor of history at Cambridge University, for two years to draw up a report on Irving's work as a historian and biographer. Under legal rules of "discovery," Professor Evans and his two doctoral-student assistants were permitted by the judge to examine Irving's voluminous records—including Irving's own diary and correspondence.[9] In this way, not Deborah Lipstadt but David Irving wound up on trial—for Evans and his two assistants were fluent in German and were able to check out the research Irving had conducted for his many books.

They came to the conclusion not only that Irving could legitimately be called a "Holocaust denier," but also that, as Evans reported to the High Court, he did not even deserve the title "historian." "Not one of his books, speeches or articles, not one paragraph, not one sentence in any of them, can be taken on trust as an accurate representation of its historical subject," Evans told the court. "All of them are completely worthless as history, because Irving cannot be trusted anywhere, in any of them, to give a reliable account of what he is talking or writing about." Evans's conclusion was unforgiving. "If we mean by 'historian' someone who is concerned to discover the truth about the past, and to give as accurate a representation of it as possible, then Irving is not a historian."

Evans's explanation bears repeating in the larger context of historical methodology and biographical research.

Reputable and professional historians do not suppress parts of quotations from documents that go against their own case, but take them into account and if necessary amend their own case accordingly. They do not present as genuine documents which they know to be forged just because these forgeries happen to back up what they are saying. They do not invent ingenious but implausible and utterly unsupported reasons for distrusting genuine documents because these documents run counter to their arguments; again, they amend their arguments if this is the case, or indeed abandon them altogether. They do not consciously attribute their own conclusions to books and other sources which in fact, on closer inspection, actually say the opposite. They do not eagerly seek out the highest possible figures in a series of statistics, independently of their reliability or otherwise, simply because they want for whatever reason to maximise the figure in question, but rather, they assess all the available figures as impartially as possible in order to arrive at a number that will withstand the critical scrutiny of others. They do not knowingly mistranslate sources in foreign languages in order to make them more serviceable to themselves. They do not wilfully invent words, phrases, quotations, incidents and events for which there is no historical evidence in order to make their arguments more plausible.

"At least," Evans concluded, "they do not do any of these things if they wish to retain any kind of reputable status as historian."

Irving duly lost his libel case, as well as his subsequent appeals—and was bankrupted. In his Austrian prison cell, several years later (having deliberately courted arrest by slipping into the country to address a neofascist group), the biographer of Hitler, Rommel, Goering, and Gehlen, would have cause to reflect upon Evans's harsh denunciation. But he had only himself to blame. He had initiated the court case in an effort to silence a world authority on the subject of the Holocaust by exploiting British libel law, and had deliberately targeted a non-British historian, whose daily life would thereby be enormously disrupted. He had reaped as he had sown, opening himself up to a meticulous examination of his own unsatisfactory research methods.

The saddest aspect of Irving's approach is that good research forms not only the core content of history and biography, but is unquestionably the most rewarding part of the authorial journey. Had Irving not become trapped in his own willful agenda, he could have gone down in historiography and the history of biography as a distinguished self-made historian and biographer of World War II figures. For by his energy and determination, he had traveled far and wide, interviewing prominent and ordinary Nazis, and could have reported back the most fascinating of anthropological stories: how such individuals had come to support Hitler, how they saw the world in the heady days of German conquest, and how they rationalized that world in its aftermath—insights such as Hannah Arendt provided in *Eichmann in Jerusalem* (1964), or Gitta Sereny in her magisterial *Albert Speer: His Battle with Truth* (1995), or Ray Müller in his documentary film *The Wonderful, Horrible Life of Leni Riefenstahl* (1994). But Irving didn't. Instead he squandered his talents to feed a deeper desire for fame—even if this turned out, in many people's reckoning, to be infamy.

Biographical research, then, is the effort you make not to prove an ideological conviction to the exclusion of other views and evidence, but to follow, document, and verify the results of genuine, open-minded curiosity: exploring, with honesty and humility, the mystery, myths, and realities of a human life.

That is the challenge which the biographer seeks to meet—and which holds out untold delights, frustrations, and rewards.

FIVE

The Shape of a Life

Those two fat volumes, with which it is our custom to
commemorate the dead—who does not know them, with
their ill-digested masses of material, their slipshod style,
their tone of tedious panegyric, their lamentable lack of
selection, of detachment, of design?

—LYTTON STRACHEY, *Eminent Victorians*

You're clear about your agenda; you've identified
your prospective audience; you've done the preliminary
research that tells you what is (and isn't) available in terms
of material and access. Now you're thinking about "composition."

It's an appropriate word. In music you might be con-
templating forms such as a symphony, concerto, chamber

piece, oratorio, choral work, sonata, tone poem, and so forth. In biography, too, you have an almost limitless choice—though, unlike the field of music, biography has few terms to describe its different genres. Is your work to be a biographical essay, a monograph, a psychoanalytic study, a profile, a critical biography, a full-length portrait, or a composite portrait of the individual and his or her circle? Will it be one volume, two, or a triple-decker?

Of course, you cannot know this for certain in advance (I certainly didn't, when embarking on what I thought would be single-volume studies of Montgomery, JFK, Nehru, and Bill Clinton)—but believe me: the prospective publisher will want to know, beforehand, how many words you're intending, or are agreeing, to write. Don't promise more than you can reasonably take on. And don't underestimate what you think will be an "appropriate" size—a word I use advisedly, since I strongly believe that the size and shape of a biography should conform to the intrinsic subject matter and the nature of your agenda.

If, for example, you are the official or authorized biographer, with unique access to unpublished, hitherto private or secret material, you are almost duty bound (as Edmund Morris learned, to his cost) to set a length and detail commensurate with that undertaking and with the audience's expectation.

If, by contrast, the subject is already well covered, you should find a design or form that plays to the strength of your particular agenda. Each form bears with it certain conventions—conventions which change over time.

Take, for example, three biographies of the novelist Edith Wharton. R. W. B. Lewis, her first official biographer, wrote a 548-page life addressed to a wide readership, the sort of book that in those days (1975) had no footnotes, though Lewis was an academic.[1] By contrast, Millicent Bell, not being the official or authorized biographer, chose to write a study of Wharton through Wharton's relationship with the great American man of letters (and fellow expatriate) Henry James: a 341-page work subtitled "The Story of Their Friendship." It was addressed to a much smaller, more specialized audience, with footnoted references to help literary scholars.[2] Over the years, however, even general readers demanded more evidence for biographers' assertions and quotations. By the time Hermione Lee came to write a major new life of Wharton, in 2007, she was able to merge the two approaches, yet create her own, highly distinctive, quasi-symphonic biography. It had copious footnotes and used thematic prisms—depicted as "rooms" in Wharton's house—thus allowing Lee to apply analytical, thematic study even as she wove an overall chronological narrative through the 762-page tome.[3]

Deciding on the scale and architecture of your book, then, is important—even though, as every architect knows, the finished product will probably look almost unrecognizably different from the design that was submitted in the initial proposal.

Input and Output

As we saw in Chapter 2, the proposal is a mythical offering, an initial sacrifice to the gods of commerce. Yet that first articulation of the design, however speculative, is crucial to the publisher or funding institution. It gives an outline of the life you propose to tackle and states why that life is of interest, to whom it will be of interest, what is available to be learned on the chosen subject, how you propose to relate the life, on what scale, and how long you will take. It is the opportunity to hone your aim, scope, and point of view in such a way as to convey the excitement and rewards that the story of an individual life holds for the potential reader. Publishers will check off each of these items, and if they are impressed by the way you've presented them (your articulateness, your use of examples, your tone), then you stand a good chance of being backed. The rest will be up to you.

Be warned: the "rest" will be the opposite of rest! Once the project is greenlighted, you have shareholders in your enterprise who must be satisfied in terms of output, quality, and delivery time. From a mere idea, the biography becomes a commission.

Few authors, of course, undertake the actual process of biography—the planning, the research, and the writing—sequentially. Instead, you'll find yourself simultaneously juggling the different component aspects—agenda, audience, investigation, drafting—as you struggle constantly to produce a *design*.

The historian E. H. Carr put the matter very well nearly half a century ago. "The commonest assumption appears to be that the historian divides his work into two sharply distinguishable phases or periods. First, he spends a long preliminary period reading his sources and filling his notebook with facts: then, when this is over, he puts away his sources, takes out his notebooks, and writes from beginning to end." To Carr, this was nonsense.

> For myself, as soon as I have got going on a few of what I take to be the capital sources, the itch becomes too strong and I begin to write—not necessarily at the beginning, but somewhere, anywhere. Thereafter, reading [for Carr, research at Oxford and Cambridge] and writing go on simultaneously. The writing is added to, subtracted from, re-shaped, can-

celled, as I go on reading. The reading is guided and directed and made fruitful by the writing: the more I write, the more I know what I am looking for, the better I understand the significance and relevance of what I find.

Moreover, Carr added, "I am convinced that, for any historian worth the name, the two processes of what economists call 'input' and 'output' go on simultaneously and are, in practice, parts of one single process. If you try to separate them, or to give one priority over the other, you fall into one of two heresies. Either you write scissors-and-paste history without meaning or significance; or you write propaganda or historical fiction, and merely use the past to embroider a kind of writing that has nothing to do with history."[4]

Or with biography.

Biographical Design

What *is* biographical design, you may ask? Certainly most people who read biography—and almost all who don't—assume there is no architecture to a written life. They think it is simply a matter of form following function, as in building a modest house.

How wrong they are! Design is the shaping of the biographical work, so that it not only compels attention but fulfills your developing agenda. As in any art, from architecture to sculpture, it is difficult to define, yet unless you strive toward it, your biography will be stillborn. It will be not a life, but—as Lytton Strachey saw it—a coffin.

We will come to the chief elements of composition, but I would ask you to be patient and read this chapter carefully, for it goes to the very heart of biography—a secret that is invisible to the outside world, and almost never discussed in reviews or critical literature. As Strachey pointed out, however, "design" is the key to modern biography: the feature that separates life-depiction today from the formless "cortèges" of Victorian biography.[5] Thus, you may, if you wish, write a life-chronicle without concern for its form and shape—but if you do, you will be joining the ranks of "funereal barbarism" that Strachey complained of.[6] Why do so, when biography offers such exciting opportunities in its components and its forms—its *design?* As I see it, after decades of trial and much error, biographical design has five main strands, each of which contributes to its success.

The Life-Line

First, there's the inherent structure of any life you may choose to address. In comparison with writers of fiction, who have no such "given" format, the biographer is accorded one priceless asset: namely, the life-story or life-line, so familiar to palm readers and fortune tellers.

The life-story is biography's most prized possession. No other art, no other science has such a simple, such an inexorable, such a *given* format—as Jaques, attending on the banished Duke, so wonderfully evokes in Shakespeare's *As You Like It* (II, viii):

> At first the infant,
> Mewling and puking in the nurse's arms.
> Then the whining school-boy, with his satchel
> And shining morning face, creeping like snail
> Unwillingly to school. And then the lover,
> Sighing like furnace, with a woeful ballad
> Made to his mistress' eyebrow. Then a soldier,
> Full of strange oaths and bearded like the pard,
> Jealous in honour, sudden and quick in quarrel,
> Seeking the bubble reputation
> Even in the cannon's mouth. And then the justice,
> In fair round belly with good capon lined,
> With eyes severe and beard of formal cut,
> Full of wise saws and modern instances;
> And so he plays his part. The sixth age shifts
> Into the lean and slipper'd pantaloon,

With spectacles on nose and pouch on side,
His youthful hose, well saved, a world too wide
For his shrunk shank; and his big manly voice,
Turning again toward childish treble, pipes
And whistles in his sound. Last scene of all,
That ends this strange eventful history,
Is second childishness and mere oblivion,
Sans teeth, sans eyes, sans taste, sans everything.

Those seven ages of man form the fundamental map of every life. Use them! In terms of design, they offer you the basic routes of the map which you'll have to incorporate: childhood, education, relationships, apprenticeship, success, aging, and the end. At the very least, your biography can present them in turn. It will be a simple house, a straightforward construction, but it will stand. And yet, as Strachey sniffed, such a plain approach will not, in itself, answer the higher challenge of biographical design.

Plot

If the seven ages of man form the first, essential backbone of design, the second element is plot.

Aristotle, in his *Poetics,* was the first to claim that, in order for a story to be "whole," it must have a beginning, a middle, and an end—or resolution. Since then, a thousand writers have sought to define or describe the art of fictional narrative. Robert Penn Warren, for example, characterized storytelling as "the presentation of characters moving through their particular experiences to some end that we may accept as meaningful." To achieve this, he asserted, the novelist uses an age-old fictional device: he causes his characters to face "a problem, a conflict. To put it bluntly: no conflict, no story."[7]

Christopher Booker, who founded the British satirical journal *Private Eye,* agreed. Fascinated by the mystery of great storytelling, Booker spent the last part of the twentieth century—almost three and a half decades—researching and writing in deadly earnest. What finally emerged was a 700-page tome without a single gibe. *The Seven Basic Plots: Why We Tell Stories* was a deeply researched Jungian investigation into the repertoire and raison d'être of storytelling across world literature and cultural expression. Booker concluded there were only seven basic "plots": inherent patterns insatiably demanded and devoured so early in human infancy and childhood that they had to bespeak an almost evolutionary development—thereby serving "a far deeper and more significant purpose in our lives than we have realized; indeed one whose importance can scarcely be exaggerated."[8] His seven distillations were "Overcoming the Monster," "Rags to Riches," "The Quest," "Voyage and Return," "Comedy," "Tragedy," and "Rebirth." The late twentieth-century tendency to veer away from those seven basic designs Booker felt to be mistaken, since it placed fiction in danger of losing the plot.

Despite being known for his satirical weekly, Booker in this case wasn't joking. Using our minds to experience, in our imagination, examples and variants of those seven basic plots, he insisted, was and remains psychologically vital to our growing sense of identity and satisfaction, from infancy onward. "Not only are our heads full of stories all the time; we are each of us acting out our own story throughout our lives," he wrote. "Outwardly male or female, we are each of us, like David Copperfield, cast as the hero of the story of our own life—just as we are equally its heroine. And the aim of our life, as we see from stories, is that those two should become one, 'to live happily ever after.'"[9]

Does the same hold true for the biographer? More than you might at first recognize. You are setting out to tell the story of a life. For what purpose? It cannot simply be to provide information, since even the barest information presumes an interpretation of what is important in a life. The biographer may not necessarily subscribe to a notion of seven possible plots from which to choose—but plot there must ultimately be! In doing your research, in mapping the terrain of a human life, you are observing, analyzing, recording, representing—and thus setting down the *pattern* of an individual's life. Cumulatively, its threads will add up to something, namely an overall portrait: your portrait of the subject—one that can be, and will be, compared with others.

The biographer's plot, then, may not be as archetypally constructed as a work of fiction or drama, ranged around conflict and resolution, but it still aims to move us by its record of the basic life-experiences through which all of us go. It does not need to follow a linear, chronological progress through them. It does not even need to have a beginning, middle, and end. Nor does it require the catharsis which Aristotle believed to be the great contribution of Greek drama: the purification of the audience's soul through the imaginative psychological identification with a hero or heroine through conflicts and travails. And yet, beyond the information you provide, you are responsible for the plot of a life-story, the unfolding of a human life: the shape it took, in your eyes, that will convey a cumulative, representative meaning and moral insight to the reader.

The precise design or plot-line will probably emerge only gradually in the course of your research and writing—long after completion of your proposal, or preliminary design, and well into the process of composition.

That doesn't matter. Yet behind the cogs and wheels of composition, you must develop a plot if the life is to amount to more than the "eminently practical" facts espoused by Dickens's Mr. Gradgrind. It must have an intrinsic message or cumulative meaning that will move the reader—your reader.

An example will be useful here. Let's look briefly at how Lytton Strachey actually achieved his "design" purpose in *Eminent Victorians*.

Cardinal Manning was the first of Strachey's four Eminences—and gave the lie to the way he would treat his other victims. Manning's apostasy, his switch from the Church of England to that of Rome, his elevation to Catholic archbishop of Westminster and a cardinal, his un-Christian treatment of Cardinal Newman . . . Each segment drives the story inexorably toward a cumulative conclusion. "As his years increased," Strachey wrote of Manning, "his activities, if that were possible, increased too.

> Meetings, missions, lectures, sermons, articles, interviews, letters—such things came upon him in redoubled multitudes, and were dispatched with an unrelenting zeal. But this was not all; with age, he seemed to acquire what was almost a new fervour, an unaccustomed, unexpected, freeing of the spirit,

filling him with preoccupations which he had hardly
felt before. "They say I am ambitious," he noted in
his Diary, "but do I rest in my ambition?" No, assur-
edly he did not rest; but he worked now with no
arrière pensée for the greater glory of God. A kind of
frenzy fell upon him. Poverty, drunkenness, vice, all
the horrors and terrors of our civilization, seized
upon his mind, and urged him forward to new fields
of action and new fields of thought. The temper of
his soul assumed almost a revolutionary cast. "I am
a Mosaic Radical," he exclaimed; and, indeed, in the
exaltation of his energies, the incoherence of his
conceptions, the democratic urgency of his desires,
combined with his awe-inspiring aspect and his venerable age, it was easy enough to trace the mingled
qualities of the patriarch, the prophet, and the dem-
agogue.[10]

By the time Strachey comes to Manning's death and funeral, we have seen Manning at his best—*and at his worst.*
Moreover, we know the author's deeper view. "The Cardinal's memory is a dim thing today," Strachey wrote. "And
he who descends into the crypt of that [Westminster] Ca-
thedral which Manning never lived to see, will observe, in
the quiet niche with the sepulchral monument, that the

dust lies thick on the strange, incongruous, the almost impossible object which, with its elaborations of dependant tassels, hangs down from the dim vault like some forlorn and forgotten trophy—the Hat."[11]

Published early in 1918, at a time when readers in Britain and America were sickened by the seemingly endless slaughter on the Western Front, *Eminent Victorians* became one of the seminal texts of the twentieth century in its representative exposé of a generation. What had been intended as a dozen conventional, informative, nicely written "lifelets" had become four serious studies in Victorian hypocrisy, ambition, fundamentalism, and craziness—aspects which he then laid at the door of his supposed elders and betters, for all their fine brass hats, bowler hats—and cardinals' hats. Form had grown out of changed function, which was not merely to record events but to puncture myths, at a moment when patriotism and blind zeal had resulted in one of the most devastating wars in human history.

Few biographers, of course, are called upon to assume such a cathartic role as Strachey did in his *Eminent Victorians*—a sort of *J'Accuse* of its era. Even Strachey's own later biographies, of Elizabeth I and Queen Victoria, never approached the power of controlled outrage that characterized the plot of his World War I masterpiece. But the lesson, for those who wish to embark on biography, is important. *Design matters.*

Let me repeat: don't worry if your authorial design doesn't emerge or manifest itself immediately. Rather, take comfort from the fact that Strachey needed *five years* of research, reflection, drafting, and iteration to decide on his overall structure and motifs.

The Search for Truth

Beyond the use of the life-course and development of plot, you shouldn't be coy in using, even celebrating, the notion of quest—the third important design element. Relentless truth-seeking may be less impressive than Strachey's measured, polished, ironic, almost Olympian narrative, but the insistent beat of the search for truth can give your biography a base rhythm: one that can either underpin the plotline, or even, at times, become the very plot itself—as it did in A. J. A. Symons's famous biography, *The Quest for Corvo*.

Symons, initially drawn by the lure of an unacknowledged genius, Frederick Rolfe (author of *Hadrian the Seventh*), gradually learned the sad truth about his subject, over many years of investigation. In the end, Symons decided to use his own quest as the shape of his biography, thereby producing an unforgettable study not of success but of failure—a subject most authors and readers naturally shy away from. In Symons's hands it became a literary masterpiece.[12]

Leon Edel, the authorized biographer of Henry James, also considered the search for truth to be one of the *raisons d'être* of good, and potentially great, life-writing. For Edel, biography was exciting because it enabled one to peer behind the mask of an individual's life, in order to discern the *true* individual. His metaphor—"the figure under the carpet," playing on Henry James's novella *The Figure in the Carpet*—was a trifle fusty, but his point was well argued. "In an archive, we wade simply and securely through paper and photocopies and related concrete materials. But in our quest for the life-myth we tread on dangerous speculative and inferential ground, ground that requires all of our attention, all of our accumulated resources. For we must read certain psychological signs that enable us to understand what people are really saying behind the faces they put on, behind the utterances they allow themselves to make before the world." Biographical portrayal thus necessitates, as part of its design—and sometimes as the very mainstay of the design—the constant striving to discern the true person behind the myth: "the 'psychological evidence' the biographer must learn to read, even as he learns to read the handwriting of his personality and the slips of his pen."[13]

As a prime example of this investigative imperative, Edel cited the *über*-manly image which the novelist Ernest Hemingway presented to his contemporaries, both in his *machismo* writings and in his actions—including shooting himself to death in 1961. Looking behind Hemingway's mask, Edel proposed that "somewhere within resides a troubled, uncertain, insecure figure, who works terribly hard to give himself eternal assurance. Where there seems to be immense fulfillment, we discern extraordinary inadequacy—and self-flagellation and high competitiveness; also, a singular want of generosity toward his fellow artists, since he must always proclaim himself the champ."[14]

"Life reduced to the terms of the bullring and the prize fight is a very narrow kind of life indeed," Edel commented. "The biography of Hemingway that captures the real portrait, the portrait within, still needs to be written. And what is important in Hemingway's archive, which is large, are the answers to the questions that will relate his doubts, his failure, his struggles, and not the answers to his successes that are written in the public prints."[15]

The search for the truth behind the mask, then, is the challenge that faces every biographer in today's post-Freudian age—the X-ray machine through which you must slowly pass your subject's profile, before you can make your own work into a work of true art. Edel constantly drew people's attention to the similarity between sculpture and biography. By "sculpture" he did not mean prettification; he meant *artistry*—whose beauty lay in the uncompromising effort to artfully review, reveal, and represent the truth of what the artist divines *behind* the façade or exterior. It was a case not of search and destroy, but of search and reveal—artfully. When the bust or the portrait "comes from the hand of a master," he once wrote, "it is certainly more than a mask, it is an essence of a life, and it captures—when painterly eyes and shaping hands have looked and seized it—certain individual traits and features and preserves them for posterity."[16] He wanted no less from good biography.

Selection

If we accept that the design of modern biography—in contrast to that of the Victorians' overly respectful portraiture—demands not only the following of a life's course but the finding of the plot-line or meaning, which in turn involves a quest for truth, a peering behind the mask of an individual (or at the "reverse of the tapestry," in Edel's analogy), the next question becomes: How can that best be accomplished?

The simple answer is: by selection—the fourth essential aspect of biographical design. Choosing, extracting, glean-

ing: the selection process in composition is absolutely crucial, as Strachey stated when excoriating his Victorian predecessors. As your plot becomes clearer to you, you must
keep asking yourself: What does the reader wish to know,
and what does the reader need to know? Is a particular detail really germane to the shaping of your portrait? Just
as the sculptor decides which features to emphasize and
which ones to ignore when working at a clay or plaster
model of a bust, so too must you decide what aids your
story and what distracts, even detracts, from it.

Selection is the biographer's chisel, which he must keep
sharp. It is a constant challenge; perhaps only 10 percent of
your research, at most, will ever get into print, the rest being consigned to the proverbial cutting-room floor. Nevertheless, until you actually draft your work and arrive at
your general design, you cannot know for certain what
will be of ultimate value or relevance. Even the tiniest
behavioral detail may come in handy as you strive to give
the reader a sense of the true, essential, living individual—
"the minute details of daily life," as Johnson wrote[17]—
thereby endowing your portrait with human credibility.
When gathering information, then, you would do better to
err on the side of possible utility than to stint on it. I've regretted my failure to make note of something on countless
occasions, when I've had to return to an archive or source

"for want of a nail" I knew was there but hadn't jotted down!

You will need patience, and ever more patience, as you engage with a chosen life through its extant remains. Try, nevertheless, to keep in the manuscript only that which works in the overall development of your plot. I remember, for example, charting the history of Arkansas as a sort of extended prelude or overture to the first volume of my life of Bill Clinton. In those hundred pages I described in detail the fascinating (to me) story of the landlocked Southern state where Clinton was born and raised, and elected governor five times. My editor, however, was of a different mind. He estimated that the history of Arkansas would cost me three-quarters of my audience, who wouldn't have the patience to wade through so much background material. And with that—though the research undoubtedly helped *me* to understand my subject—five months' work went out the window!

Storytelling

The fifth and final element of biographical design that raises life-writing above mundane recordkeeping is narrative or storytelling technique. In the next chapters we are going to explore this aspect in more detail, with examples of distinguished biographical composition. Here I merely

wish to note the importance, indeed the imperative, of using narrative methods to bolster your overall design or
plot. And the most basic of those techniques, as in all good
storytelling, is the use of suspense.

A life-story plays deeply upon human curiosity. Use that
curiosity! Even when the reader knows the final outcome
in advance, he or she does not know the details of the life,
or the minute contours of its development. Ultimately the
reader wants to know the meaning of that life, what it
amounted to; but to merit that meaning, the reader knows
he or she must follow its course, be convinced by the quality of the narrative that it was so—and yet be sufficiently
curious about what comes next to keep reading. For that,
you must employ suspense.

Suspense can be created in many ways—and you
shouldn't flinch in using techniques drawn from other arts.
After all, novelists shamelessly borrow from the stuff of biographies. Don't be shy about returning the compliment!

Storytelling is universal, in fiction *and* nonfiction. "It is
not easy for the most artful writer to give us an interest in
happiness or misery, which we think ourselves never likely
to feel, and with which we have never yet been made acquainted," Dr. Johnson acknowledged. Yet somehow, if
you, as biographer, are to fulfill the role Johnson envisaged
for modern life-writing, you must be bold and "enchain

the heart by irresistible interest."[18] Avoid giving away in advance either the guts of your story, or your ultimate message; this is a crucial part of maintaining suspense. As novelists know, the art of storytelling consists as much in *withholding* information as in giving it! Your readers will be prepared to follow your story only if, consciously or unconsciously, they become seduced by the need to know more—and that need will grow only if you tell your story right. "The story promises us a resolution, and we wait in suspense to learn how things will come out," Robert Penn Warren explained. "We are in suspense, not only to learn what will happen, but even more about what the event will *mean*. We are in suspense about the story in fiction because we are in suspense about another story far closer and more important to us—the story of our own life as we live it."[19] As in fiction, so in biography: the biographer focuses on those aspects of the life that enable the reader to identify with the subject and to draw moral lessons from the life—both good and bad.

Oliver Goldsmith tells a revealing story about a wise man who was asked, "What is the best lesson for youth?" The wise man replied, "The life of a good man." And the next best? "The life of a bad one."[20] As Goldsmith expresses it, biography holds up a mirror to life, providing a reflected image that we use in an "oblique manner" to see into humanity itself—something which "renders biography as well as fable a most convenient vehicle for instruction."[21] Maintaining suspense, in that cause, is a cardinal technique that makes both biography and fiction possible.

The distinguished novelist A. S. Byatt, author of the novels *Possession* and *The Biographer's Tale,* once wrote that narration "is as much part of human nature as breath and the circulation of the blood. Modernist literature tried to do away with storytelling, which it thought was vulgar, replacing it with flashbacks, epiphanies, streams of consciousness. But storytelling is intrinsic to biological time, which we cannot escape." And she added: "Stories are like genes, they keep part of us alive after the end of our story, and there is something very moving about Scheherezade entering on the happiness ever after, not at her wedding, but after 1001 tales and three children."[22]

No primer can provide a formula for achieving the enchantment of Scheherezade. But by looking at the way various modern biographers have gone about their task, we can get some idea of the techniques available—and draw inspiration, perhaps, for our own work.

II

COMPOSING A LIFE-STORY

SIX

The Starting Point

> "Where shall I begin, please your Majesty?" he [the
> White Rabbit] asked. "Begin at the beginning," the
> King said, very gravely, "and go on till you come to
> the end: then stop."
>
> —LEWIS CARROLL, *Alice's Adventures in Wonderland*

Though not a true biography, Orson Welles's *Citizen Kane*—a thinly disguised life of William Randolph Hearst—has always seemed to me the finest example of imaginative biographical design, right from its brilliant opening.

Beginning with a prologue filmed outside the castle of Xanadu, the narrative then moves inside, and we see the dying John Foster Kane, a fabulously wealthy media mogul, as he whispers his last enigmatic word: "Rosebud."

The movie then dissolves into a fast-rolling newsreel obituary, recounted by a stern, unseen narrator racing through Kane's controversial life with the aid of archival film, interview clips, and weighty words. In a darkened projection theater, we meet the figures watching the newsreel: an editorial team, under Mr. Rawlston, owner of a media chain. He asks his staff for their reaction. They are hesitant, explaining how difficult it is to summarize a whole life—prompting Rawlston to give his own view. He tells his journalists he's dissatisfied—and orders them to try again.

"You see, Thomson," Rawlston says to one of the reporters, "it isn't enough to show what a man did—you've got to tell us who he was."[1] And for the next 101 scenes we are treated to a biographical quest to unravel the mystery of Kane's last word—via interviews with surviving colleagues and family members, flashbacks, visits to archives, newspaper headlines—mostly set out in the chronological order of his life, yet brilliantly, tantalizingly narrated through the use of scene changes and points of view, sometimes through the eyes of the reporter Thomson, sometimes via interviewees' memories. Each enhances our knowledge and brings us a bit closer to solving the enigma of Charles Foster Kane.

First Words, Last Words

The question of where to begin a biography is far from straightforward. That actual starting point—the first paragraph of the very first page—is seldom something you get right until your vessel is substantially built. It's as if, until you truly feel you have the measure of the whole story, you cannot make that decision—and the same is true of the book's title. (For this reason, all publishing contracts refer to the "working title" of a project.)

The opening of a biography should, if possible, be as seductive as the first line of a good novel. "It is a truth universally acknowledged," goes one of the most famous first lines in the history of the English novel, "that a single man in possession of a good fortune, must be in want of a wife." The opening sentence of Jane Austen's *Pride and Prejudice* is hard for any other novelist, let alone biographer, to match. But take heart: if biographers do not have the first word, they still have the last! From Julius Caesar's remark to Brutus, as he collapsed beneath his assassins' many dagger-thrusts ("You, too, my child?"), to Marie-Antoinette's apology for stepping on the foot of her executioner ("Pardonnez-moi"), biography is the chief repository of famous last words—as Herman Mankiewicz and

Orson Welles, the screenwriters of *Citizen Kane,* were well aware. Make sure you include them—and if necessary, begin your book with them!

First words don't have to be dramatic, of course. Many of the finest recent biographies begin mysteriously, or gently, like a Mahler composition. Let's instance two that take one's breath away by their haunting, quasi-symphonic tone:

> In the cold, nearly colorless light of a New England winter, two men on horseback traveled the coast road below Boston, heading north. A foot or more of snow covered the landscape, the remnants of a Christmas storm that had blanketed Massachusetts from one end of the province to the other. Beneath the snow, after weeks of severe cold, the ground was frozen solid to a depth of two feet. Packed ice in the road, ruts as hard as iron, made the going hazardous, and the riders, mindful of the horses, kept at a walk.
>
> Nothing about the harsh landscape differed from other winters. Nor was there anything to distinguish the two riders, no signs of rank or title, no liveried retinue bringing up the rear.[2]

Descriptive, intriguing, compelling: this is the start of David McCullough's *John Adams,* his wonderful biography of the second U.S. president. You know, from these first words, you are in the hands of a master storyteller.

Edmund Morris's account of the twenty-sixth president, *The Rise of Theodore Roosevelt,* opens right in the subject's home—in the "historical present," as the verb tense is called:

> At eleven o'clock precisely the sound of trumpets echoes within the White House, and floats, through open windows, out into the sunny morning. A shiver of excitement strikes the line of people waiting four abreast outside Theodore Roosevelt's front gate, and runs in serpentine reflex along Pennsylvania Avenue as far as Seventeenth Street, before whipping south and dissipating itself over half a mile away. The shiver is accompanied by a murmur: "The President's on his way downstairs."
>
> There is some shifting of feet, but no eager pushing forward. The crowd knows that Roosevelt has hundreds of bejeweled and manicured hands to shake privately before he grasps the coarser flesh of the general public. Judging by last year's reception, the

gate will not be unlocked until one o'clock, and even then it will take a good two hours for everybody to pass through. Roosevelt may be the fastest handshaker in history (he averages fifty grips a minute), but he is also the most conscientious, insisting that all citizens who are sober, washed, and free of bodily advertising be permitted to wish the President of the United States a Happy New Year.

This was Washington on January 1, 1907—on the "best and fairest day President Roosevelt ever had," as one newspaper recorded. Again, we are right inside the story before it even starts, chronologically—and we have a fair idea of the gentle tone of amused admiration and irony that will be our guide's narrative timbre.[3]

The moral? Don't be afraid to assert your own individuality through your choice of narrative perspective, focus, shutter-speed, frame—right from the start. Some writers on biography have sought to identify the voice of the biographer, even prescribe or proscribe it. My own view is that you should follow your own instinct and inclination in terms of narrative voice. Orson Welles was only twenty-five when he began making his masterpiece, *Citizen Kane*—his first film, yet one in which he employed many new camera and lighting techniques. Don't be self-conscious!

Draw inspiration and stimulation from others, but don't try to squeeze into their straitjackets. Poor Virginia Woolf, toward the end of her career, disciplined herself to tell Roger Fry's life as if she were her father. It became, as she wrote in a letter, "a question, how far to intrude, and how far to suppress oneself."[4] By the end she was complaining, "I've never done anything so devilishly difficult"[5]—whereas, had she let herself go, as she did in her fiction, she might have written a great interpretive biography.

Your voice will emerge as you write; it cannot be prepackaged. Obviously, the more lucid and readable your prose, the easier it is for the reader to become absorbed, even entranced—but there is no rule. Indeed, if you believe in Brecht's alienation-effect theory, entrancement may be the opposite state from the one you wish to induce! Start with the subject matter and your narrative design, and let your voice find itself—that's my advice. Biography is storytelling. And to tell the story well, in your own way, stamped with your own individuality, you need to be willing to work hard and to experiment, accepting that biography is a process of trial-and-error and of iteration. As you yourself age, so will your focus and your interpretation, both of events and of people. Seize the day, as Welles did—but don't be afraid to employ a different voice, or different narrative techniques, according to the different lives you subsequently tell. Even the same life, should you choose to retell it later.

Consider, for example, Michael Holroyd's pioneering biography of Lytton Strachey, himself a biographical pioneer. In the first edition of his life, in 1967, Holroyd began not only with a seventeenth-century reference, but in almost seventeenth-century style:

> "Strachey—an old family, small in numbers, but of a marked and persistent type. Among its characteristics are an active interest in public matters, and an administrative aptitude." So wrote the geneticist Francis Galton defining the essential disposition of the Strachey family. With the majority of writers a survey and assessment of their antecedents is unnecessary. In the special case of Lytton Strachey some knowledge of his family and its inherited culture is fundamental to the understanding of his development and the individual nature of his contribution to critical and biographical literature.[6]

Three decades later, when publishing *Lytton Strachey: The New Biography*, Holroyd decided to open in a very different style. First, he ditched the opening chapter title, changing it from "The Ancestral Treadmill" to the more metonymic

"Papa and Mama." Then he reopened his narrative with a quotation from one of Strachey's relatives. "The Stracheys are most strongly the children of their fathers, not of their mothers," Amy St Loe Strachey had once written. "It does not matter whom they marry," insisted another relative, emphasizing the persistent family character through the ages. As Holroyd noted, however, "This was not obviously true of St Loe's cousin, Lytton Strachey [his subject]. 'You'd never think he was a general's son,' the head porter at the Great Gate of Trinity sighed to Clive Bell, as Lytton's drooping silhouette moved across the quadrangle."[7]

This time we are inside the story—and instantly contradicting family lore.

Enter the Biographer

Strachey's friend Virginia Woolf had predicted biographers would eventually be upgraded from the tradesman's entrance to the front door—yet even she could not have anticipated the changes that would overtake biography in the late twentieth century. Hermione Lee put the whole matter of biographical openings under the microscope in a major new life of Virginia Woolf in 1996. She opened with a quote from Woolf herself: "My God, how does one write a Biography?" Virginia Woolf's question "haunts her own biographers," Lee commented—beginning with the very question: "How do they begin?"

Answering, Lee quoted various predecessors' openings:

> "Virginia Woolf was a Miss Stephen." "Virginia Woolf was a sexually abused child: she was an incest-survivor." "Was Virginia Woolf 'insane'? Was Virginia Woolf 'mad'?" "Virginia Woolf said that 'if life has a base' it is a memory." Or: "Yet another book about Bloomsbury."

The different openings suggest some of the choices for Virginia Woolf's biographers. They can start at source, with her family history, and see her in the context of ancestry, country, class. They can start with Bloomsbury, fixing her inside her social and intellectual group and its reputation. They can start by thinking of her as a victim, as someone who is going to kill herself. They can start with her own words about her own sense of the past. They can start with a theory or a belief and see her always in terms of it, since, like Shakespeare, she is a writer who lends herself to infinitely various interpretation. What no longer seems possible is to start: "Adeline Virginia Stephen was born on 25 January 1882, the daughter of Sir Leslie Stephen, editor of the *Dictionary of National Biography,* and of Julia Stephen, née Jackson."[8]

Hermione Lee was right on the mark. Three years later, Edmund Morris would not only be opening his next biography of a U.S. president (Ronald Reagan) with a description of the White House, but he himself would be *in* the narrative! Here Morris describes Reagan's reaction to a leaf he's been handed.

> He holds the speckled leaf in his hand, caressing its green patches with his sharp, scarred thumb. The Oval Office is so silent I hope that the dry whisper of that caress will register on my tape recorder. "Direct from Lowell Park," I say. "Remember that big oak tree you used to sit under, when you were a lifeguard?"
>
> He tilts his head at me, mildly amused but wary. Most public yet most private of men, he does not welcome undue familiarity with his past. I have never forgotten the blue anger that came into his eyes (no aquamarine flash like Jimmy Carter's, but a sort of dark flicker, like the inner flame of a candle) when I boasted that I had tracked down his first fiancée. "Oh, you found out about her, huh." It was a state-

ment rather than a question—Ronald Reagan hardly ever used the interrogative form—signaling, for all its tone of polite interest, his resentment at being surprised, and his disinclination to hear another word about the preacher's daughter he once wanted to marry.[5]

As we've earlier noted, Morris came under fire for defying audience expectations of an official biography of President Reagan—but for his mastery of the craft and style of modern biography, he was rightly lauded.

Openings, in other words, seldom launch a book with the birth of the subject, or even an account of his or her family. The role of an opening is, as Orson Welles understood when he was a mere twenty-five-year-old making his first film in Hollywood, to intrigue the audience.

Stuck for a start?

Don't worry! As E. H. Carr explained, the process of writing is messy and illogical, and it may take a while before you get the design right. Only very rarely will you know where to start at the commencement of your labors. I remember reaching the very last section of the first volume of my life of John F. Kennedy. I still had neither a title, nor an incisive opening for an extraordinary tale, which incorporated so many hitherto unknown and unpublished documents and interviews. And then it dawned on me that although the book would chronicle only Kennedy's early years, before he entered politics, it should start with the scene that was imprinted most vividly on readers' memories: the November 1963 funeral cortège, which had been filmed and broadcast across the world.

The saga of the president's state funeral seemed an intriguing approach, a way of beginning the life both with a known event—and a provocative challenge. The moment I wrote it, I knew it would infuriate the Keepers of the Flame. But I had a unique and profoundly touching story to tell, if only I could compel readers to sit up and take note—to alert them that this was no rehash of received opinions and sentimentality. "At nine-thirty A.M. on November 25, 1963, the doors to the great rotunda of the U.S. Capitol were closed," I began the prologue (which I entitled "The Birth of Camelot"):

> Over a quarter of a million people had paid their last respects to the slain president, John F. Kennedy. At eleven o'clock the coffin, draped by the Stars and Stripes, would be carried outside and borne first to the White House, then to St. Matthew's Cathedral, and from there to Arlington Cemetery, the confiscated estate of the Confederate general Robert E.

Lee, where a special underground vault had been prepared.

There had been much dispute about the burial site. "We're all going to be buried around Daddy in Boston," Eunice, sister of the dead president, had insisted. Her brother, the attorney general of the United States, had agreed, as had the Irish "mafia"— the thin-lipped contingent of hangers-on, body-guards, pimps, and court jesters who had been paid over the years by the father of the slain president. Even the new president, Lyndon Johnson, had as-sumed the burial would be in Brookline, the suburb of Boston where Kennedy was born.

The secretary for defense, however, had favored Arlington: a national, rather than a parochial resting place for the first president to be killed in office since President McKinley in 1901. Although Robert McNamara's suggestion was ridiculed by the White House staff, the State Department, and the dead president's immediate family, it was welcomed by the president's widow, Jackie. Unable to tame her husband's rampant sexual appetite in his lifetime, she was determined to shape his memory in death. Thus, at Jackie Kennedy's insistence, Arlington be-came the choice, complete with a hastily assembled

Eternal Flame copied from that of the tomb of the
Unknown Soldier beneath the Arc de Triomphe.[10]

The only question that remained, once the prologue had
been written, was the overall title. Calling the book *JFK:
Reckless Youth*—against protests from the publisher's office—
was another contentious gambit, but though it further outraged the flame-keepers, it helped sear the book into the
national consciousness—"an antidote to both the treacle
about Camelot and the backlash biographers," as one reviewer kindly wrote.

Openings, then, *matter* in the writing of a biography.
They are your passport through Customs and Immigra-
tion, assuring the reader you are in control of your documents, your luggage, and your destination, as you start
your journey.

Remember, too, that you may not be the sole traveler to
that destination. A dear, older friend of mine, the World
War II poet John Pudney—famous for the poem "For
Johnny," which he wrote during a German air raid on London in 1941—became a biographer later in his writing career. He'd been stationed as an air force intelligence officer
in the Mediterranean through much of the war, and had
spent time in Egypt. He suggested to his publisher that
he write a biography of the French engineer Ferdinand

de Lesseps and the story of the Suez Canal, to coincide with the centenary of its construction in 1969. Duly commissioned, he was researching in an antiquarian Egyptian bookstore one day, asking for old topographical works, including prints and drawings, when the bookseller remarked how interesting it was that two Englishmen should be writing about the same subject at the same time. Pudney was crestfallen. On his return to England he told the publisher he had a rival, and offered to ditch the book and give his publisher back his advance.

Unfazed, the publisher said it was quite normal for two or more people to have the same idea for a book simultaneously. This concomitance, the publisher explained, merely demonstrated people's interest in the subject, and would actually help the books garner *more* attention—guaranteeing that they would be reviewed.

Multiple Openings

No two biographies are ever alike—as their varied openings demonstrate. Let's look at just two, published simultaneously in 2003–2004, recording the life of one of the founding fathers of the United States, Alexander Hamilton.

Ron Chernow's account begins quietly, long after Hamilton's death:

In the early 1850's pedestrians strolling past the house on H Street in Washington, near the White House, realized that the ancient widow seated by the window, knitting and arranging flowers, was the last surviving link to the glory days of the early republic. Fifty years earlier, on a rocky, secluded ledge overlooking the Hudson River in Weehawken, New Jersey, Aaron Burr, the vice president of the United States, had fired a mortal shot at her husband, Alexander Hamilton, in a misbegotten effort to remove the man Burr regarded as the main impediment to his career. Hamilton was then forty-nine years old. Was it a benign or a cruel destiny that had compelled the widow to outlive her husband by half a century, struggling to raise seven children and surviving almost until the eve of the Civil War?

Elizabeth Schuyler Hamilton—purblind and deaf but gallant to the end—was a stoic woman who never yielded to self-pity.[11]

Immediately we are taken back to a long-ago period, a time of different manners, occupations, and worldviews, before we meet Hamilton and his nemesis, Burr. The book, deservedly, won the first George Washington Book Prize.

Yet, like Hamilton himself, Chernow had a rival: Willard Sterne Randall, who was also a prizewinner for his biographies and who had previously written a life of Thomas Jefferson. Under the chapter title "The Wish of My Heart," Randall commenced his work on a strikingly dramatic note:

> Alexander Hamilton realized instantly that he would die. Before he even heard the shot, the oversize lead ball had torn into his right side just above the hip, crashed through a rib, sliced through his liver, shattering a vertebra. Pitching forward on his face, Hamilton, the first secretary of the treasury of the United States, the author of the *Federalist Papers*, George Washington's strong right hand, the financial genius who had created Wall Street, and, as inspector general of the U.S. Army, launched the U.S. Navy, fell to the ground, clutching his dueling pistol. His friend and second in the duel, Nathaniel Pendleton, rolled him over, cupped him in his arms, and held him, half sitting, under a cedar tree, away from the glaring July sunlight.
>
> "Dr. Hosack!" Pendleton yelled. "Dr. Hosack!" Waiting with the oarsman below by the Hudson shore, Dr. David Hosack rushed up the narrow path toward the dueling place atop a small granite out-

cropping of cliff below the waking village of Weehawken, New Jersey, that steaming Thursday morning of July 11, 1804. He brushed past Aaron Burr, vice president of the United States, shielded by his second's umbrella to conceal his face as he hastened toward a rowboat that would hurry him across to New York City.[12]

Biography, then, is a challenge—and like all composition, competitive. You may have assembled wonderful information and may have developed wonderful insights during your research. But you must design and fashion that subject matter into a "work," just as a composer does when writing a musical piece. Whether you begin with a preface, prologue, or introduction or jump right into the main text, the opening sets the tone, sows the seed of suspense—and thereby assures the reader your journey has begun, and is worth following.

Bon voyage!

SEVEN

Birthing Your Subject

It is hard to have patience with people who say "There is
no death" or "Death doesn't matter." There is death. And
whatever is matters. . . . You might as well say that birth
doesn't matter.

— C. S. Lewis, *A Grief Observed*

*D*eath is, *pace* cryogenicists, the end that awaits
us all—causing us to review life, and retrace its course.
Where did it begin, how did it begin, and as a result of
what or whom?

Though at some point you will fashion your book's
opening or overture, and though you can thereafter ar-
range the order of your narrative to suit your agenda,
you'd be daft to ignore the seven ages of man. It's what the

reader wants to know, intrinsically: the beginning, the middle, and the end of the life-cycle.

The order in which you tackle those seven ages is another matter. Asked about her new life of Franklin and Eleanor Roosevelt, *No Ordinary Time,* Doris Kearns Goodwin recalled her first major biography, that of Lyndon Johnson, whom she'd found infinitely "sad in his retirement, while he was at the ranch, that it was almost like he had nothing else left in his life once politics was taken from him. That whole experience, I think, seared into my mind forever."[1]

In retrospect, Goodwin wasn't satisfied with her biography. "Surfeited with such rich, dramatic material [Johnson had treated Goodwin as his literary secretary and confidant during the writing of his memoirs], I wish I could have waited to write the book for ten or twenty years, so that I could really understand and convey its human value." Given the opportunity to do it again, "I would have written the book backwards rather than forwards, starting with his last years on the ranch, then going back to the Senate and House years, and finally to the sources of his character in childhood. In other words, following the tale in the order in which he presented it to me." As she acknowledged, this would have made it impossible build up "the pattern of traits shown in his childhood and early adulthood and later in his leadership. And it might have made the narrative telling more personal and difficult. But it would have allowed me to accompany Johnson on his search for his own past, to go with him, backwards in time, as he tried, in the last years of his life, to understand who and what he was. And that journey, however difficult to describe, would have been, I believe now, a richer tale."[2]

Goodwin was being too hard on herself, since her book still reads wonderfully well three decades later—but her reflection illustrates the many different ways of narrating an individual's life. Retelling an individual's "adventures through life" is the alpha and omega of biography—but it doesn't have to be linear! A person's lifeline gives you an immutable chronology: an indelible map, a clear frame of reference—but you can sail into any harbor and make your own course, just so long as you stay in contact with your base: the reader's interest.

Often out of envy, nonbiographers—especially novelists—have sniffed at the biographical life-course paradigm. The "first duty" of a biographer was, Virginia Woolf mocked in *Orlando,* "to plod, without looking to right or left, in the indelible footprints of truth; unenticed by the flowers; regardless of shade; on and on methodically till we fall plump into the grave and write *finis* on the tombstone above our heads."[3]

As we've seen, poor Woolf was the one who plodded

through her friend Roger Fry's life, and all too soon ended, herself, under the tombstone—when, with her incomparable intelligence, her wry, elastic, seemingly effortless prose, she might have written a serious biographical masterpiece. Far from being tied by straitjacket and blinkers, forbidden to look left or right or to acknowledge the flora, fauna, and landscape surrounding the figure whose life is being told, modern biographers are permitted, *encouraged* in fact, to wield their linguistic paintbrush no differently from portrait or landscape painters. Moreover, this is as true of film biographies as of print biographies today. Consider film critic A. O. Scott's review of a biopic dealing with the life of the French chanteuse Edith Piaf:

> So if you have seen *Ray* [a film based on the life of Ray Charles] or *Walk the Line* [based on the life of Johnny Cash], you will hardly require a summary of *La Vie en Rose,* which flings its subject back and forth in time, simultaneously charting her rise from the tough streets of Paris and her decline into drug abuse and ill health. There are tearful confrontations, moments of bliss and betrayal, tantrums and onstage collapses, love affairs and business deals, all of it punctuated by the big, expressive, unmistakable singing of Piaf herself. . . .

La Vie en Rose, which Mr. [Olivier] Dahan wrote
as well as directed, has an intricate structure, which
is a polite way of saying that it's a complete mess.
Resisting the habit of starting at the end and flashing
back to the beginning, it begins at the late middle,
goes back to the beginning, comes back to the near-
end, jumps around in the early and middle middle
and then noodles around between a bunch of al-
most-ends and the really absolutely final end, with a
quick baffling detour into an earlier part of the early
middle. Clear enough?[4]

Marking the Birth

Whichever course you choose—that of a backward quest
through a life (chronologically, thematically) or that of a
forward-moving detective investigation via clues—the
reader will seldom be content, nevertheless, unless you
show evidence, somewhere in your narrative, that you've
been present at the creation. So let's look at the way writers handle one of the major aspects of the life-journey:
birth.

Wystan Hugh Auden was born on the twenty-first
of February 1907, in the city of York in the north of

England, the third and last child of George Augustus Auden and Constance Rosalie Bicknell.

He was the youngest of three boys. Later in his life he liked to point out that in fairy-tales it is the youngest of the three brothers who succeeds in the quest and wins the prize. "I, after all, am the Fortunate One," he wrote in a poem, "The Happy-Go-Lucky, the Spoilt Third Son."

He had hazel eyes, and hair and eyebrows so fair that they looked bleached. His skin, too, was very pale, almost white. His face was marked by one small peculiarity, a brown mole on the right cheek. He had big chubby hands, and soon developed flat feet. He was physically clumsy, and took to biting his nails.[5]

Such was Humphrey Carpenter's vision of W. H. Auden at the outset—with his distinctive birthmark.

James Atlas pictured Saul Bellow's arrival on Planet Earth—actually the town of Lachine, near Montreal—in a less physical, more social way. Lachine was a melting pot: "Ukrainians and Russians, Greeks and Italians, Hungarians and Poles were packed in side by side, drawn there by its thriving industries."

The Bellows moved into the cramped ground-floor apartment of a two-story brick house at 130 Eighth Avenue, just a block from Notre Dame, the main commercial thoroughfare. Upstairs lived the Gameroffs with their four children, Lena, Sam, Louis, and Meyer. In the summer of 1915, two years after their arrival in Canada, Abraham and Liza had a fourth child of their own: Solomon Bellow, known as Shloime or Shloimke and later as Saul. He was the first—and last—of their children born in the New World—an accident of fate that was to shape his life. It gave him a huge advantage, enabling him to harness the raw cultural power of this world to his own developing genius, but it also made him different. "I never belonged to my own family," he lamented in later life. "I was always the one apart."

The circumstances of the birth were contested, by Bellow himself and by his relatives.

On the morning of his birth—or so Bellow later claimed—one of the Gameroff boys was dispatched to find the bibulous obstetrician. "Sam made the rounds of the saloons until finally he found him, slumped over the bar counter, dead drunk. He dragged the doctor outside, cranked up his Model T, and drove him home to my poor mother, who'd been in Canada two years and couldn't speak a word of English or French. There she was, in the midst of labor, being tended to by a dead-drunk French-Canadian who could barely stand up." (Ruth Gameroff, Sam's wife, told a less scandalous version of this episode: The doctor, named Dixon, was "not a drinking man," she maintained. But Bellow's made a better story.)

Even the date of Bellow's birth was the subject of controversy. "On Bellow's birth certificate, the date of birth is listed as July 10," Atlas pointed out, "but subsequent biographical and reference works list his birth date as June 10, 1915." Bellow's mother sided with the June date, Bellow with that of July. Amused, the biographer concluded his account of Bellow's birth: "Thus did a writer renowned for his elusiveness, his resistance to biography, throw into question even the first, most basic fact about his life."[6]

Place

Other biographies focus on the *landscape* of birth. An example is Joanna Richardson's life of Stendhal, in which you sense, at the start, the push-and-pull of place and genealogy:

> Grenoble is some 400 miles southeast of Paris; it is not far from the borders of Switzerland, and it is very close to the northwest border of Italy. It was the native town of Hugues de Lionne, the statesman who negotiated the Treaty of the Pyrenees for Louis XIV. It was the birthplace of Cardinal de Tencin, Bishop of Lyons (and uncle of d'Alembert). It was in Grenoble, in 1715, that Etienne Bonnet de Condillac was born: philosopher, chief of the sensualist school and author of the *Traité des sensations* and the *Logique*. It was in Grenoble, in the rue des Vieux-Jésuites, that Marie-Henri Beyle, later known as Stendhal, was born on January 23, 1783.

"All his life he was to show the warmth of nature, the dilatory manner of the south; [but] all his adult life he was to look beyond the frontiers of France," Richardson commented—noting that Stendhal himself considered himself a Milanese, an Italian. If so, it was an assumed identity.

> He came of bourgeois stock. His paternal great-great-grandfather, Jean Beyle, had been a draper in

Lans. His great-grandfather, Joseph Beyle, and his grandfather, Pierre Beyle, were *procureurs* at the Parlement at Grenoble. On his mother's side, his great grandfather, Antoine Gagnon, had been an army surgeon; his grandfather, Henri Gagnon, was a doctor. The ancestors of Henri Beyle were respectable, solid Dauphinois.[7]

Already, then, we can see how good biographers quote and challenge details, anecdotes, heredity, and environment, as well as the future of the individual as adumbrated in birth. Far from plodding, they tease and pivot on our curiosity, our defective knowledge as readers—asking, indirectly, how much we may, by inference, know about our own name, our own provenance. Above all, they *question* fact, they play with fact—appreciating that play is something which, far from being absent from biography, is the privilege of biographers: their poetic license, so to speak.

Unacknowledged by critics or (sadly) by university educators, biography not only offers an opportunity to express ideas and tell stories in prose, but is a veritable treasure-house of fine writing. Go into any public library, take down almost any modern biography, and the quality of the narrative, the intelligence of the author, and the architecture of the account are likely to expose the mediocrity of most of the novels, detective yarns, thrillers, sci-fi tales, romances, and "chick lit" that pass today for Fiction. Fiction is, after all, largely escapism—punctuated occasionally by great works of art, from Bellow's to Stendhal's. By contrast, biography today is for the most part skillfully chronicled, serious, exploratory life-literature, with only an occasional dud or disgrace.

When conceiving the birth of their subject, biographers are thus seeking to unravel a puzzle—or at least begin that process. "In the middle of the last century," begins Judith Thurman's life of Colette (1999), "the village of Saint-Sauveur-en-Puisaye was a rustic backwater despite its proximity to Paris, three hours by train to the nearest station followed by a rough cart ride."

> The Puisaye was called "the poor Burgundy" to distinguish it from the rich Burgundy of the great vineyards. The landscape was dotted with ponds which bred malaria and smelled of caltrops and marsh mint. Coppice grew thickly in the ravines, where the wild strawberries and lilies of the valley were guarded by pitiless brambles. Game abounded in the woods. There were ancient stands of pine, which Colette loved for their scent. The spongy paths she followed when she gathered wild mushrooms or hunted for

butterflies with her brothers were carpeted with vi-
olet heather. It was a secretive, inbred region of
casual morals, hard winters, poaching, and poor
farms. Wet-nursing was, as late as the fin de siècle, a
lucrative sideline for the farmers' wives.[8]

We know, from the start, with this description of the rough,
sensual landscape into which Colette was born, that we're
in good hands: we will not necessarily know everything for
certain, but we can *trust* this narrator. Colette's mother,
Sido, was born in Paris on August 12, 1835. Thurman tells
us that Sido "never knew her mother, née Sophie Chatenay,
who died of puerperal fever two months later"—thus leading us not only to the nurse who raised Sido, Madame
Guille, but to the errant father who didn't: Henry Landoy,
"the first of the unfaithful and profligate men in her own
life and in her daughter's. He was 'ugly but well-built!'
Sido told Colette, with 'pale, contemptuous eyes and a
long nose above the thick Negro lips that had inspired
his nickname,' the Gorilla. At the end of her life, in a pass-
ing phrase, Colette describes her mother's antecedents as
'cocoa harvesters' from the colonies, 'colored by island
blood,' with frizzy hair and purple fingernails."[9]

Birth, in other words, contains a cornucopia of secrets
that will be explored as the life-story unfolds. Consider Ted

Morgan's version of Somerset Maugham's beginning—in the British Embassy in Paris. "Maugham's birth in an embassy was the result of France's defeat in 1870," Morgan explained.

> Concern about manpower led to the proposal of a law that would give all children born on French soil automatic French citizenship, so that they might be conscripted in the next war. The embassy, a mansion with gardens on the Champs-Elysées which had once been the residence of Napoleon's sister, Pauline Borghese, was British soil, and the ambassador, Lord Lyons, had turned the second floor into a maternity ward. Although the law was never passed, three children were born in the embassy during its imminence, all in 1874: Violet Williams-Freeman, daughter of the second secretary; Emily Lytton, daughter of the first secretary, the Earl of Lytton; and William Somerset Maugham.
>
> William Somerset's father, Robert Ormond Maugham, born in 1823, was a lawyer in England who had gone into partnership with a friend named William Dixon. In 1848 they had established an office in Paris.[10]

In this account we not only witness the beginning of a named individual, but become acquainted with the milieu—professional, attached to grandeur, situated in a foreign land—that will play such a vital role in Maugham's life and work.

Even the names given to an individual are subject to the magnifying glass of the biographer's curiosity—demonstrating the endless quirks of real, rather than invented, human experience. Take, for example, one of the most famous American composers and conductors of the twentieth century, Leonard Bernstein—who wasn't born Leonard. As Humphrey Burton related, when opening the lid of Bernstein's metaphorical music box:

> He was almost born on the kitchen floor. Jennie Bernstein, age twenty, had gone back to her parents' house in Lawrence, Massachusetts, for the final days of her pregnancy so that her mother could look after her. When she awoke with her labor pains at three in the morning on August 25, 1918, her mother telephoned the family doctor; before he could arrive, her water broke. Her mother slipped old newspapers under Jennie's straining body to help soak up the birthing fluids. Shortly afterward the doctor ar-

rived and drove Jennie in the throes of labor to the Lawrence General Hospital, where around one in the afternoon (she remembered the clock on the delivery ward wall) she gave birth to a rather sickly baby boy.

He was registered as Louis Bernstein. The name Louis was a potentially confusing choice, since Jennie's recently deceased *zayde*—or grandfather—had been named Louis, as was her twelve-year-old brother. But Louis was the name Carol and Samuel Resnick, Jennie's parents, wanted, and so Louis he became, at least on the register.

At sixteen, Bernstein changed his name to "Leonard" at City Hall. His surname he decided to keep—indeed, for the born musician it had special significance, being the German word for "amber." "Leonard Bernstein would later call himself 'Lenny Amber' when he needed a pseudonym for the popular piano transcriptions he published in his mid-twenties, and his business affairs would be organized within a company called Amberson Enterprises."[11]

Alert to the ironies of real life, then, modern biographers make clear from the start that they have a right to be intimate, critical, and collegial in their accounts, even when—like Boswell—they may be recounting the life of a veritable genius.

Isaiah Berlin was nothing if not a genius. Undaunted, his biographer Michael Ignatieff captured in the story of Berlin's birth in Riga, Latvia, the very essence of Berlin's Johnsonian character, even deformity:

> His memory of his birthplace was framed by two sphinxes, standing guard at the entrance to the Albertstrasse apartment, reclining plaster figures with paws, breasts and a pharaoh's head-dress. They are still there—mossy with damp and chipped with age—guarding the entrance to the Art Nouveau apartment block where he was born, on the fourth floor, on 6 June 1909. In his parents' bed, in all likelihood, with a German doctor and nurse in attendance, his father pacing up and down the parquet outside, chloroform oozing beneath the door.
>
> He may have been lucky to survive. After many hours of labour, the German doctor delivering the child—"Do you want his name? It was Hach"—placed forceps on the infant's left arm, and yanked him into the world so violently that the ligaments were permanently damaged.

Isaiah was not the first-born. His mother had had a stillbirth in 1907 and been told she would never be able to have children again. His parents greeted his arrival with the astonishment reserved for miracles. These facts—the stillborn sister, the longed-for realisation of his parents' wishes, the injury at birth, an only child—are vitally important, though interpreting their significance is not easy. He himself never liked interpreting them at all. But there is a story in the Bible that might be taken as an oblique fable about his own beginnings. It is the story of Hannah, the barren woman who goes to the temple to pray for a son, and who is so distraught that the high priest takes her for mad.[12]

In other words, though every life commences with a birth that holds significant clues to the individual's future, every birth will be different—as will be the clues. That beginning can be told in any number of ways. But in tackling it, you have a great opportunity to establish the familial and physical circumstances in which your subject is brought to life. Use it!

EIGHT

Childhood and Youth

The fact is that anybody who has survived his childhood has enough information about life to last him the rest of his days.

—FLANNERY O'CONNOR, "The Nature and Aim of Fiction," in *Mystery and Manners*

*O*nce you've successfully written the first ten pages of a biography, its narrative style and level of detail are pretty much set. These will determine how the rest of your story unfolds. As you progress, you'll see that, within the overall scheme, narrative is like a revolving Chinese buffet: a choice of episodes and themes, through which and into which you can weave your evolving interpretation of the life.

Even if you choose the thematic approach—as, say, Hermione Lee did in her *Edith Wharton*—the life's progression will still serve as the underlying current that takes you and the reader from the beginning to the end, the flow (or plot) that is the basis of all storytelling. The same will be true of flashbacks and flashforwards, which are simply techniques that permit you to tackle the subject in your own way. In whatever order you tackle it, however, the inherent life-story, from birth to death, remains the same. For that is how the subject *lived* it.

The Life-line

Let's look more closely at the early part of the human life-line. Roman biographers tended not to spend much time on childhood, beyond a few anecdotes or omens, but in our post-Freudian Western world a biographer who does not record and reach deeply into the childhood of his subject will be viewed as being in denial. It is in childhood that the individual's character and potential take shape. Mine it!

By this I don't mean you should attempt to psychoanalyze your subject. Biography is not psychoanalysis—though it can furnish psychoanalysts with interesting material. Your job is to draw the reader into the warp and weft of a person's developing character—and where better than in those formative years, when nature and nurture combine to mold a unique personality?

We earlier touched on Freud's *Leonardo da Vinci*. The book focused on an early daydream Leonardo remembered, in which a bird inserted its tail in Leonardo's mouth—a memory which (together with court documents relating to alleged homosexual activity in the artist's youth) convinced Freud that the archetypal "Renaissance man" was gay.

In the autobiography that Freud wrote in the same year (1910), he paid surprisingly little attention to his own childhood (a total of one page) and was notoriously unwilling to be analyzed by others at the time—refusing, for example, to allow his protégé Carl Jung to do so—since he felt it would diminish his own authority as the father of psychoanalysis. Yet if one of Freud's greatest contributions to human understanding was his focus on childhood, how can his biographer not investigate Freud's own early years and childhood memories?

Peter Gay's biography of Freud, for example, gives short shrift to Freud's father, describing him as "a small merchant with insufficient resources to cope with the industrializing world around him." In contrast, Freud's mother loomed all too large in Freud's childhood memories, which present a pattern of family tensions: mother against father, and child against child in the struggle for loving attention.

The appealing youthfulness and striking good looks of his mother did not make the young Freud's emotional task any easier. Later he would recapture a childhood experience, one of those "significant details" that he rescued from the pervasive amnesia which mantles everyone's earliest years. The memory came back to him in October 1897, in the midst of his self-analysis, while discoveries about his unconscious life were tumbling out at him with dizzying profusion. Sometime between the ages of two and two and a half, he told his close friend Wilhelm Fliess, his "libido toward matrem had awakened" on an overnight railway journey from Leipzig to Vienna, a trip on which he had the "opportunity of seeing her nudam." Immediately after unpacking this tantalizing recollection, Freud remembered that he had welcomed the death of his infant brother Julius, born some seventeen months after him, with "malevolent wishes and genuine childish jealousy." This brother, and Freud's nephew John, a year older than himself, "now determine what is neurotic, but also what is intense, in all my friendships." Love and hate, those elemental forces struggling over human destiny, forces that were to loom large in Freud's mature psychological writings, were confronting one another in this recall.

Immediately, via an account of Freud's childhood, we are entwined in Freud's own struggle to make sense of his emotions. Moreover, the author is not taking Freud's version as gospel, but stitching it intriguingly into his biographical record, acting as our guide and not as Freud's apologist:

> Whatever the exact nature of the episode, it would be his doting, energetic and domineering mother, far more than his pleasant but somewhat shiftless father, who equipped him for a life of intrepid investigation, elusive fame, and halting success. . . . In the end, Freud never fully worked through the meaning of his passionate unconscious ties to that commanding maternal figure. While many of his patients were women and he wrote much about them, he liked to say all his life that Woman had remained a dark continent to him. It seems most likely that some of this obscurity was self-protective in origin.[1]

Parents and Children

As a biographee's childhood gives way to puberty and ado-
lescence, of course, the life-line becomes less obscure and
more adventure-filled, as personality meets, and begins to
have a real impact on, the outside. A struggle with authority, parental and institutional, becomes a testing ground
that the biographer—*you*—must not pass over hastily, since
it is, in effect, the individual's first battlefield.

The relationship between Wolfgang Amadeus Mozart
and his father is a case in point. Leopold Mozart recognized very early that little Wolfgang was a genius—and
given his ambitions for the boy, a clash of wills was perhaps inevitable. Isn't it natural to suppose that such a
struggle would have influenced the music of the young
composer? Stanley Sadie, editor of the *Grove Dictionary of
Music,* wrote a biography of Mozart, subtitled *The Early
Years, 1756–1781.* It climaxes with the creation of one of Mozart's greatest early commissions, written for the Elector
of Bavaria. This was his opera *Idomeneo,* the story of a father caught in a situation in which he is called upon to sacrifice his own child.

Mozart's own father acted as intermediary during the
composition of the libretto and music. Sadie thus had not
only wonderful material in Leopold's correspondence with

his son and with the librettist, but also an opportunity to chronicle the opera's true genesis and assess the father's practical and possibly psychological role. Five hundred pages into his reconstruction of Mozart's early years Sadie concluded:

> Mozart was twenty-five years old two days before the opera's premiere. *Idomeneo* is, however, a fully mature work, and it represents the peak of his achievement in serious opera, the field of music that mattered to him most of all. Not until the very end of his life, more than ten years later, did he have the opportunity to return to serious opera, and by then the genre was a different one. Some writers have sought to explain the depth of his involvement in the work with some pseudo-Freudian explanation: it is an opera about father and son, Idomeneo and Idamante, and so struck a special chord in a composer whose relationship with his father was so central. This is specious and unnecessary, and in any case the opera is unconcerned with the father-son relationship, which is normal, uncomplicated and predictable. The crucial relationship, the one that governs Idomeneo's actions, is that between himself and the gods, or more broadly between the society

of ancient Crete and its gods. Idomeneo stands as a masterpiece because Mozart was able to forge what is essentially a new language, in which he could portray so strongly in his music the stark inevitabilities of Greek tragedy while at the same time drawing us deeply into the predicaments and the fates of its principal characters.

Whether right or wrong in his assessment, in tackling the musical climax of Mozart's early life Sadie was alert to the *possibility* of a Freudian interpretation of the father-son theme. And he rejected it, preferring to see the opera as the intensely moving culmination of Wolfgang's precocious talent—nurtured, prodded, challenged, defended, and advanced by his adoring dad. The chronicle of Mozart's youth ends on March 14, 1781, as Leopold returns with his daughter Nannerl from the Heiligkreuz monastery to Salzburg, while Wolfgang, summoned to Vienna, "arrived in the imperial capital, where the next and the most dramatic chapters in his relations with the Salzburg court were to be conducted and where he was to spend the rest of his life."[2]

Very different is Christopher Sawyer-Lauçanno's treatment of the tumultuous early years of E. E. Cummings—culminating in the poet's extraordinary confrontation, at age twenty-one, with his own doting father, after a night out with a drunk friend, Tex Wilson. The visit to a seamstress, Marie Hayes—"a good-natured whore," according to detailed notes Cummings kept—had gone horribly wrong. Not only was Wilson too drunk to perform, but while Cummings went off on "an errand of mercy" to buy oranges to revive him, the police towed away his illegally parked Ford—belonging to his father, a clergyman! Worse still, Miss Hayes, "thinking she was doing a good deed, had rung the Reverend at three in the morning to tell him his car had been seized by the Boston Police."

Somehow Cummings got Wilson home, then arrived at 104 Irving Street as dawn was breaking. His father was waiting for him on the steps. Before Cummings could even offer an explanation, his father, staunch supporter of the Watch and Ward Society, launched into a tirade, accusing his son of having disgraced the family, particularly his mother. Cummings countered by noting that Jesus had also associated with prostitutes. The argument grew more intense and heated, culminating in his father threatening to evict his son from the house. "Go ahead," replied Cummings. At that his father began sobbing. Through his tears he cried out, perhaps to God or

Estlin or Rebecca, who had by now joined the scene, or maybe just to himself: "I thought I had given birth to a god."

The effect of this statement on Cummings was profound. In autobiographical notes written thirty, even forty years after the event, Cummings occasionally mulled over the phrase, pondering his father's terrible moment of realization that his son was, in fact, a mere mortal.[3]

According to Sawyer-Lauçanno, this was a turning point in the poet's early life, since "Cummings in no way regarded himself as a god or even approaching godliness." He "drank, he caroused, frequented burlesque shows at the Old Howard, fantasized about sex, and masturbated almost daily."[4] In this way, the poet of mundane reality was seeded and took root, as the opposite of a paternal ideal.

Interpreting the early years of your subject is thus an intrinsic part of modern biography. You cannot assume there will be a filial struggle in the youth of your subject, but as a conscientious biographer you would be remiss if you did not at least keep an eye open for such trials as a stepping stone to a better understanding of an individual's development—especially that of an artist.

Noël Riley Fitch's biography of Anaïs Nin portrays an

even crueler childhood "education"—at the hands of an abusive rather than adoring father. Fitch opens her book with an introduction:

> Famous for her erotica and her passionate affair with Henry Miller, Anaïs Nin (1903–1977) was an artist of life. And of her life she made a book, a diary of some 35,000 pages in 150 volumes, from which she spun poetic novels and short stories. "Like Oscar Wilde," she said, "I put only my art into my work and my genius into my life. . . . I play a thousand roles."

One of those roles was that of the sexually abused child:

> The title of her first novel, *The House of Incest,* and scenes in four pieces of fiction say it all. Señor Joaquin Nin y Castellanos, a distinguished Spanish composer and concert pianist, seduced his daughter. This fact is impossible to prove conclusively, but it is borne out by her subsequent behavior, which fits the classical patterns of a child who has been seduced. She only remembered that he was sadistically cruel to his children, that he told her she was ugly, and that the only affection she received from him

before he deserted the family when she was ten was
when she posed naked for his photographs: "He always wanted me naked. All admiration came by
way of the camera." She learned to seek approval in
a sexual way. She sat for "countless pictures" in a
prefiguring of the literary disrobing in her diary.
In her first childhood diary she pasted one of the
nude photographs, apparently unaware that the
photograph revealed unusual behavior on her father's part. In a fragmentary entry in a later diary
she writes: "Guilt about exposing the father. Secrets.
Need of disguises. Fear of consequences."[5]

At the center of Nin's childhood world, in Noël Fitch's account, was a father whose affection and validation she
wanted more than that of *le Bon Dieu,* to whom, as a Catholic, she prayed. Page by page, Fitch peels back the layers
of Nin's diaries, letters, and interviews, along with memoirs by Nin's contemporaries, to reconstruct the life. By
the time she was eleven Nin had lived in several countries,
including the United States, but it was always her father's
abandonment of the family in France in the summer of
1913, when Nin was ten and recovering from an appendec-
tomy and peritonitis, that would torment her. Her fifty-
year journal, published only in abridged versions, would

make her the "High Priestess of diary writing" in the latter part of the twentieth century.[6] It amounted to a nonfiction *Bildungsroman* of feminine artistic consciousness, and yet was infuriatingly fictional for a self-styled diary. "The one virtue she does not practice" in childhood, Fitch wrote, "is truthfulness"—since the truth was in many ways unbearable: "Lying becomes a lifetime habit that she excuses by saying that lies for the sake of a beautiful illusion do not taint the soul. They are like costumes. But one of her adult friends calls her a "monstrous liar or prevaricator or fabulator" who could not tell the truth because she could not bear reality: "She had to alter reality to suit her own view of the world. She admits as much: 'If I had not created my whole world, I would certainly have died in other people's.'"

The famous diary that Kate Millett once called the "first real portrait of the artist as a woman," Fitch writes, was "itself a work of fiction, an act of self-invention. Untrue confessions." In short, Fitch concludes, "her diary is not to be trusted." Yet, however fictional the diary may be, how can one's heart not go out to an abandoned daughter who, at age thirteen, wrote to her father: "I am nothing but dust. . . . I want to spread myself on a lot of paper, turn into lots of sentences, lots of words, so that I won't be walked on."[7]

There are of course many ways to tell Anaïs Nin's life-story. But Fitch's "plot"—using the broken childhood of an acutely sensitive daughter of an abusive musician as the ground on which to chart the life-course behind the celebrated diary—is at once touching, elegiac, compassionate, and relentlessly honest.

The Role of Youth

Clearly, the childhood and early years of any individual are the repository of many clues to the later character and achievement of the individual whose life you wish to relate. Whether or not you choose to openly interpret those clues in relating those early years is your own call—but somehow you will have to resolve, in your own mind, the role of your subject's childhood in that life-story. In most cases you will probably not know in advance, before you do your research, just how much of the life-story will be prefigured in those years, or whether you can find the material necessary to make the connections with your character's later development—yet that very process of discovery and disclosure will be the fuel that propels your mission. If, that is, you are ready.

You yourself, I must emphasize, must be prepared in your own mind and being for the themes you choose to tackle, if you are to do justice to them! If you feel the early years of your subject are of little importance, compared with the later years, you can skip over them; but if you feel—as did the biographers whom I've quoted—that the childhood and early years allow the reader to penetrate the soul, the creativity, the distinctive worldview of your subject, then you must follow your instinct. Certainly, when embarking on the life of President Kennedy, I had no idea Kennedy's childhood and youth would so engross me that I would write a *900-page* biography devoted solely to his early years!

I'd drawn up a proposal for a one-volume reappraisal of President Kennedy's life in 1988, and, having moved to Boston to be close to the JFK Library archives, I began interviewing surviving childhood friends, then those from JFK's college years—people at the London School of Economics, Princeton University, Harvard University, Stanford University, and Northwestern. I began to turn up a vast new trail of unpublished documents, and realized that the image of a playboy son transmogrified by an ambitious father on the death of the eldest son was a myth.

The documents told all. The father, Joseph P. Kennedy, had been appointed U.S. ambassador to Britain, where he pursued a relentless policy of appeasement with Hitler and

Mussolini to keep America out of World War II. His eldest son, Joe Jr., turned out also to be an American isolationist, and mouthpiece of the frightening, millionaire father. By contrast, JFK emerged from my interviews and the collected documents as a second son of high intelligence, roguish good looks, self-deprecating wit, ebullient energy, subversive behavior—and unending illnesses. The saga of the young JFK was gripping: a kid so engaging, so brave in the face of so many medical trials, and who, as a Navy lieutenant, would demonstrate enormous courage when called to battle in the Solomon Islands in 1943.

I learned that JFK's most important battle had taken place long before he captained his legendary PT-109 in the Blackett Strait, fifty miles behind Japanese lines. That struggle, I discovered, had been with his own father, in December 1940, a year before America's entry into World War II.

Asked to help his father draft a letter of resignation as U.S. ambassador to Britain, the twenty-three-year-old had tried to defend his father against charges of appeasement and defeatism, but recognized, unlike his older brother, that what needed to be defended even more than his father's reputation was democracy—and the only country left defending it at that moment was Britain. "As England failed from September 1938 to September 1939 to take advantage of her year of respite due to her feeling that there would be no war in 1939, we will have failed just as greatly," JFK began a handwritten letter he sent his father from California.

> Now as this affects your position. I realize that aid for Britain is part of it but in your message for America to stay out of the war you should not do so *at the expense of having people minimize aid to Britain.* The danger of our not giving Britain enough aid, of not getting Congress and the country stirred up sufficiently to give England the aid she needs now—is to me just as great as the danger of our getting into war now—as it is much more likely.
>
> If England is defeated America is going to be alone in a strained and hostile world. In a few years, she will have paid out enormous sums for defense yearly—to maintain armaments—she may be at war—she even may be on the verge of defeat or defeated—by a combination of totalitarian powers.
>
> Then there will be a general turning of the people's opinions. They will say "Why were we so stupid not to have given Britain all possible aid. Why

did we worry about money etc. *We should have put in more* legislation. We should have given it to them outright."[8]

The letter—lost for fifty years, but which I found misfiled at the JFK Library—worked. The following month, in a national radio speech in January 1941, Ambassador Kennedy—to everyone's astonishment—dropped his opposition to the Lend-Lease Bill before Congress. Britain—and America—*did* survive.

I lost my first publisher, partly because the publisher feared my portrayal of Joseph P. Kennedy would upset the Kennedy family, and partly because I insisted on making JFK's early years the sole period covered by my biography. Yet of all the books I've written, it remains the one in which I felt the most invested—emotionally, intellectually, and artistically—in terms of its narrative construction. I concluded my portrait of JFK's youth with words that today sound a little sentimental, but at the time I wrote them (1992) came from the heart:

> Above all, Jack had, by his performance as a student, his ability as a writer, his courage in war, and his honorable conduct in electoral combat, single-handedly reinvented the Kennedys. By his self-

deprecating wit, his love of history, curiosity about others, and reckless spirit of adventure, Jack Kennedy had escaped his father's and his elder brother's narrow, selfish Boston-Irish bigotry and found a pluralist, idealistic, and yet internationally committed liberalism, a liberal spirit that would, one day, define a whole generation of Americans.

He had not, however, found true love—or if he had, he had not been able to hold on to it. That search would go on for the rest of his days.[9]

No prizes, then, for guessing the theme of our next chapter!

NINE

Love Stories

Had we never lov'd sae kindly

Had we never lov'd sae blindly,

Never met—or never parted,

We had ne'er been broken hearted.

—ROBERT BURNS, "Ae Fond Kiss, and Then We Part"

Love stories fuel much of biography—though you wouldn't believe it from the things biography critics say. Janet Malcolm, a brilliant journalist, spoke for many a fault-finding snob in her 1994 magazine articles describing Sylvia Plath's life-chroniclers, later published in book form as *The Silent Woman*. "The biographer at work," she claimed, "is like the professional burglar, breaking into a house, rifling through certain drawers that he has good reason to think contain the jewelry and money, and triumphantly bearing his loot away." The "voyeurism and busybodyism that impel writers and readers of biography," she sniffed, were only thinly veiled by the mask of serious research—"an apparatus of scholarship designed to give the enterprise an appearance of blankness and solidity." In truth, she wrote, the "transgressive nature of biography" was "the only explanation for biography's status as a popular genre." For this, she blamed "a kind of collusion" between the life-reader and the biographer, "tiptoeing down the corridor together, to stand in front of the bedroom door," where they attempted to "peep through the keyhole."[1]

Coming from a journalist who was being sued for libel by one of her own victims, this was a clear case of the pot calling the kettle black. But is it true?

Compared with the ratio of sex to text in fiction (highbrow and lowbrow), the proportion of sex in biographies is infinitesimal! Yet because we've been conditioned to accept voyeurism along with the Nude in fiction but not in real-life chronicling, reviewers and critics often complain of a surfeit of sex in biography and seldom give up their Victorian protests.

I've certainly suffered my share of such attacks. Some critics welcomed *JFK: Reckless Youth* as "the central and authoritative reference on Kennedy's early life,"[2] but others were disgusted. "Despite the author's credentials," wrote one *New York Times* reviewer, the biography "often reads like a trashy novel."[3] The same reviewer slammed my next biography of a U.S. president, Bill Clinton, as a "sleazy new low in the chronicling of presidential lives. It regurgitates the most scurrilous and unsubstantiated rumors about Mr. Clinton and his wife; dwells, with voyeuristic fascination, on his sex life [and adopts] the same sensationalistic approach he used in his 1992 biography of John F. Kennedy (*JFK: Reckless Youth*)."[4] "Kinder and more insightful biographies have been written about Stalin, Hitler and Jack the Ripper," a Chicago reviewer sneered. "*Bill Clinton* is a sleazy, snide, cynical and very dirty book, contemptuous of its subject and its readers. It should be wrapped in dark plastic and shelved at the back of the bookstore with *1001 Nights in a Sheik's Harem* and *The Cruel Lessons of Miss Harriet Birch, Governess*."[5]

For a biographer who had spent four years researching and recording the lives of the brothers Heinrich and Thomas Mann, ten years researching and recording the life of Field Marshal Montgomery, four years researching and recording the early years of John F. Kennedy, and another four years researching and recording the early life of Bill Clinton, such criticism was tough to take. But deserved or undeserved, it illustrates a real problem for the biographer publishing in the United States. "Does he know the national sport is baseball, not adultery?" asked the Chicago reviewer.

How, then, should you tackle the business of love, marriage, relationships, and sex in a society where, in order to shame the biographer into silence, the inevitable accusation will be made that, if you include sex, you are larding such material merely in order to sell your book? No one really doubted my credentials as a research historian. The question for me—and my editor—became: How much of that authentic material could I include without incurring the wrath of censorious reviewers?

It is a question almost every biographer meets—and that you yourself will have to tackle. I'm not sure, though, that I have found the perfect answer—beyond confining oneself to the biographies of saints! How can any biographer be expected to write a truthful biography of John Kennedy or Bill Clinton that does not address their lifelong struggles with desire and infidelity, even sexual addiction? It cannot be done. But the bigger challenge for the biographer is: How to relate that *faiblesse* to the individual's career and life-course?

Sex and Truth

The finest model for the link between love and life, to my mind, is a work written almost two thousand years ago in Latin: *The Twelve Caesars,* by Suetonius. Writing in 125 A.D., the great Latin scholar and biographer recorded the lives of Rome's greatest emperors, from Julius Caesar to Domitian. Each was a masterpiece of concision—and frankness. Emperor Tiberius' tremendous early achievements as a warrior in subduing the German tribes, for example, and his initial display of tolerance and wisdom were chronicled with respect. Tiberius was, according to Suetonius, "quite unperturbed by abuse, slander, or lampoons on himself or his family, and would often say that liberty to speak and think as one pleases is the test of a free country." Tiberius' accession to Roman caesar seemed therefore, at the start, to augur well.

> Very gradually, Tiberius showed that he was the real ruler of the Empire, and though at first his policy was not always consistent, he nevertheless took considerable pains to be helpful and to further the national interest. At first, too, he intervened in matters of state only when abuses had to be checked; revoking certain orders published by the Senate, and sometimes offering to sit on the tribunal beside the magistrates, or at one end of the dais, in an advisory capacity. And if it came to his ears that influence was being used to acquit a criminal in some court or other, he would suddenly appear and address the jury either from the floor or from the tribunal, ask-

ing them to remember the sanctity of the Law and their oath to uphold it, and the serious nature of the crime on which their verdict was required. He also undertook to arrest any decline in public morality due to negligence or licence."[6]

Thus far, so good. Yet the greatness of Suetonius as a *biographer* is that, unlike Tacitus and other Roman historians, Suetonius wanted to understand the man whose life he was chronicling. He wanted to learn how—and why—Tiberius' life, so noble at the outset of his reign, degenerated into filth and cruelty. Suetonius did so by recounting the story of Tiberius' marriage, and the divorce forced upon him by his adoptive father, Caesar Augustus.

Tiberius had married Vipsania Agrippina—daughter of Augustus' admiral Marcus Agrippa, and granddaughter of Caecilius Atticus, a Roman knight to whom Cicero addressed many of his letters. "It proved a happy marriage," Suetonius recorded, "but when Vipsania had already borne him a son, Drusus, whose paternity he acknowledged, and found herself pregnant again, he was required to divorce her and hurriedly marry Augustus' daughter Julia." Now the trouble really began.

Tiberius took this very ill. He loved Vipsania and strongly disapproved of Julia, realizing, like everyone else, that she had felt an adulterous passion for him while still married to his father-in-law Agrippa. Tiberius continued to regret the divorce so heartily that when, one day, he accidentally caught sight of Vipsania and followed her with tears in his eyes and intense unhappiness written on his face, precautions were taken against his ever seeing her again.

This is the turning point in Suetonius' biography of Augustus' heir. We read with mounting sadness and psychological concern the consequences of Tiberius' sacrifice, made to please (and obey) his adoptive father, the emperor: "At first he lived on good terms with Julia and dutifully reciprocated her love; but gradually conceived such a loathing for her that, after their child had died in infancy at Aquileia, he broke off marital relations."

How venomous and ultimately evil that unhappiness became was the meat of Suetonius' biography—an account that has never been rivaled for its intimate portrait of human degeneracy. The unhappy tyrant Tiberius, haunted by the threat of assassination and overthrow, and by visions of his own death, attempted to allay his fears by engaging in ever more extreme perversions on the island of Capri: "Having found seclusion at last, and no longer feeling himself under public scrutiny, he rapidly succumbed to all the vicious passions which he had for a long time tried, not very successfully, to disguise. I shall give a faithful account of these from the start." Incipient alcoholism had marked Tiberius' military service. To this was added lechery on an increasing scale. After he became emperor, this tendency grew to epic proportions when, at his retreat on Capri, Tiberius ordered "sexual extravagances" that became legendary.

Some aspects of his criminal obscenity are almost too vile to discuss, much less believe. Imagine training little boys, whom he called his "minnows," to chase him while he went swimming and get between his legs to lick and nibble him. Or letting babies not yet weaned from their mother's breast suck at his breast or groin—such a filthy old man he had become! Then there was a painting by Parrhasius, which had been bequeathed him on condition that, if he did not like the subject, he could have 10,000 gold pieces instead. Tiberius not only preferred to keep the picture but hung it in his bedroom. It showed Atalanta performing fellatio with Meleager.

The story goes that once, while sacrificing, he took an erotic fancy to the acolyte who carried the incense casket, and could hardly wait for the ceremony to end before hurrying him and his brother, the sacred trumpeter, out of the temple and indecently assaulting them both. When they jointly protested at this disgusting behaviour he had their legs broken.

What nasty tricks he used to play on women, even those of high rank, is clearly seen in the case of Mallonia, whom he summoned to his bed. She showed such an invincible repugnance to complying with his lusts that he set informers on her track and during her very trial continued to shout: "Are you sorry?" Finally she left the court and went home; there she stabbed herself to death after a violent tirade against "that filthy-mouthed, hairy, stinking old man."[7]

Were it not one the greatest works of Roman literature, history, and biography, would *The Twelve Caesars* be published today? And if it were, would reviewers accuse the publisher of deliberately appealing to the public's base interest in salaciousness? Yet salaciousness was clearly not Suetonius' purpose in recording the lives of the great caesars. Suetonius wanted the truth to be known and, in the case of the tyrants Tiberius, Nero, and Caligula, he strove to understand the genesis and development of such documented behavior.

The fact is that, if you are to be a serious biographer, affection, desire, love, distaste, hatred, and sex must feature at the center of your work, in tandem with the events that punctuate the life. The ideal of love is what we—both writers and readers—are interested in, for although many animals show symptoms of altruistic nonsexual bonding, as in maternal, parental, pairing, sibling, and collegial attachment, love is an emotion we think of as distinguishing our species from others. It is one of our most powerful instincts, and, in terms of our life-line, the one we are most eager for soothsayers to divine.

Love, not sex per se, is thus far more important as a theme for biographers than for novelists, who must pander to man's need for escapism (sex, violence, horror) to satisfy modern readers. Tracing the course of love—unrequited, requited, tangled, delayed, lost, suppressed—is at the heart of almost all serious biographical storytelling, because that is what, as human beings, we are seeking to obtain and maintain. History offers only "the pomp of ornament, and grandeur of ideas"; but biography, as Dr. Johnson recognized, offers the reader "pains or pleasures" that we recognize as our own, as we identify with a well-researched, credibly reconstructed life—hopefully a life so well recounted that it can enchant even the "man whose faculties have been engrossed by business, and whose heart never fluttered but at the rise or fall of stocks," and who "wonders how the attention can be seized, or the affections agitated by a tale of love."[8]

Love: A Universal Concern

Scratch any serious modern biography and love will be the predominant motif, behind the information given about stocks, or strikes, or screen roles. Chekhov and Olga Knipper, Gustav and Alma Mahler, Einstein and Mileva Marić, Gertrude Stein and Alice Toklas, Katherine Mansfield and Middleton Murray, H. G. Wells and Rebecca West, Modigliani and Jeanne Hébuterne, Karen Blixen and Denys Finch Hatton, Virginia and Leonard Woolf . . . Each love story of the early twentieth century intrigues us, not because it necessarily lasted, or because it was intensely sexual, but because we wonder about it—just as we wonder about our own affections, and disaffections.

From childhood to the grave, love, not simply sex, will be a major part of your tapestry—and you will have to learn to research, interpret, and navigate its various expressions, not only to help the reader understand the character of your subject, but—if possible—to see where and how love fits in with the rest of the business of living; for this represents, symbolically, the concern of everyman. As Dr. Johnson cautioned, however, it is no straightforward challenge.

Let me give some instances of biographies that have, to

my mind, succeeded remarkably well in recounting the link between love and career.

The first is Martin Stannard's two-volume life of one of the greatest satirists of the twentieth century, Evelyn Waugh. Neither sentimental nor flowery, Stannard charts the novelist's life with scholarship and compassion. His account of Waugh's disastrous first marriage to the Honorable Evelyn Gardner, "She-Evelyn," is as quietly, tragically moving as Waugh's own work is movingly comic. Following his marriage, Waugh had just begun work on what would be one of his most celebrated social satires, *Vile Bodies*. For the writing he needed seclusion; but his wife, after a year of unexciting marriage, wanted company. The result was catastrophic.

"During June Waugh had left for Beckley, and to keep She-Evelyn company her closest friend, Nancy Mitford, had moved into the spare room in Canonbury Square," Stannard related. The Honorable John Heygate, son and heir of the third Baronet Heygate, "and the other unattached men of their circle could be relied upon, Waugh thought, to chaperone his wife through the visits to nightclubs and parties for the six weeks or so of his absence."[9]

> During those weeks of seclusion in June and early July he had been working to a fixed routine. As each section was written, he would send it to his wife

who would have it typed and passed on to [his literary agent] Peters for his criticism. Shortly after he had written to [his friend Harold] Acton, a letter (dated 9th July) arrived from She-Evelyn which had nothing to do with the book. She was in a desperate confusion of happiness and misery. She had, she said, fallen in love with John Heygate and did not know what to do about it. She begged forgiveness, even help; emotionally, it seems, she had plunged beyond her depth.

Waugh was devastated. "Evelyn's defection," he later wrote to his parents, "was preceded by no kind of quarrel or estrangement. So far as I knew we were both serenely happy." The foundations of their trust had seemed to him deep and permanent. His first reaction was to think that his wife had lost her senses. It could not be true. There had to be a more reasonable explanation.

Abandoning the novel, he returned to London immediately. The situation was intensely embarrassing. Nancy Mitford was still in the flat though she knew nothing of the affair; his wife was racked with guilt and more than a little afraid. But she could only repeat what she had said in the letter. Heygate and she were not only "in love" but lovers. Waugh was appalled but, in this desperate situation, prepared to simulate liberality. He had never been able to take sexual passion altogether seriously. Their relationship was too precious to be destroyed by hurt pride over a casual affair. If she would give up Heygate, he said, he would forget the whole business and they could go on as before. Out of loyalty to him, she agreed. It was the sensible, logical thing to do.

Waugh stayed in London for a fortnight and neglected his novel in an attempt to repair the marriage.[10]

Thinking that her adultery was the consequence of marital neglect, Waugh accompanied his wife from party to party. It was, after all, the Roaring Twenties—at least for upper-middle-class and aristocratic young people who had been spared service in World War I.

Waugh's close friend and first biographer, Christopher Sykes, had suggested that "this interlude" was happy. "It was not," Stannard corrected—quoting a letter from Waugh's wife, more than half a century after the painful episode: "The following fortnight was a very unhappy time with E. [Waugh] even saying that I was trying to poison him!'" Although they did not speak of Heygate, "neither was able to forget about him," Stannard wrote. "She cannot have escaped the impression that she was being watched or, at least, guarded. Disguising their embarrassing secret made the situation all the more awkward. Waugh no doubt felt saddened that even his marriage was now 'shop soiled and second hand.' Compromise did not come easily to him."[11]

Breaking her promise, She-Evelyn began seeing Heygate again—and told her flatmate, Nancy Mitford, that she "had never loved her husband. She had married only to escape parental opposition and now she regretted it."[12]

No reader who admires or loves Evelyn Waugh's work can fail to be moved by Stannard's patient, caring account of love inspired and love betrayed—which in turn helped to make Waugh such a brilliant caricaturist and trenchant satirist, if also such a flawed father and human being for the rest of his unhappy life. As Stannard recounted, what had been a "gently malicious" look at the contradictions of the disoriented modern world turned into "bitter satire— the satire of someone deeply, profoundly betrayed." Quite suddenly, Waugh "found his subject and 'point of view.' More correctly, it was forced upon him by events which nearly cost him his sanity."[13]

The Second Sex

Being alert to the intimate context of your subject's life, and the links between private life and work, is thus essential if you are to produce a moving biography. It requires patience and almost unceasing devotion. Those biographers who cut the corners, and attempt thereby to go straight to the meat of the human drama, seldom succeed in the long run, for the trust you must build up with your reader has to be based upon gradual, painstaking detail that establishes your bona fides. Then, having earned the right, you can explore the relationship between love-life and work-life with confidence—accepting always the fallibility of the enterprise.

Deirdre Bair, in 1990, wrote a biography of Simone de Beauvoir that I also treasure—particularly for its evocation of de Beauvoir's awkward but creatively inspiring love triangle, in the late 1940s.

Beauvoir had suffered deeply when her partner, Jean-Paul Sartre, fell in love in 1945 with a married Franco-American, Dolores Ehrenreich, whom he'd met while on tour in the United States. Then, at a moment when Beauvoir felt that her sex-life was finished, she herself fell madly in love, with an American, the writer Nelson Algren.

Angry at "losing" Sartre sexually and emotionally (though not intellectually, thanks to their editorial partnership at Les Temps Modernes) to another woman, Beauvoir had considered writing an autobiography, but in order to do so she felt she had to analyze her position as a woman in the modern world. An invitation in 1947 from the Alliance Française to visit the United States had meanwhile arrived. It was during her first tour of American universities to preach existentialism that a friend, who had been a lover of Nelson Algren, suggested she meet the rising novelist of Chicago low-life. It took several phone calls before the notoriously "difficult" Algren would even answer his phone, but when he did, her life was turned "upside down," as she later acknowledged.[14]

Rather as Virginia Woolf had been one of the century's most prolific literary minds and the doyenne of Bloomsbury, Beauvoir was the superstar of French bohemia, the "high priestess" not only of existentialism and "No. 2 to Sartre," but already in her thirties a well-known philosopher, playwright, novelist, and literary figure. Certainly she was as difficult (moody, self-centered, intellectually snobbish, ravenous for knowledge that she could use) in her own way as Algren was in his. "How could they have fallen—whamo!—so hard, so fast?" Algren's former lover reflected. "Easy—each was the most exotic thing the other had ever seen."[15]

Algren was known to play the role of anti-intellectual: hard-drinking, tough, no-nonsense. In Beauvoir the intellectual, he had met the greatest challenge of his life. "I wanted to show her that the U.S.A. was not a nation of prosperous bourgeois, all driving toward ownership of a home in the suburbs and membership in a country club. I wanted to show her the people who drove, just as relentlessly, toward the penitentiary and jail. I introduced her to stickup men, pimps, baggage thieves, whores and heroin addicts. Their drive was downward, downward. I knew many such that year. I took her on a tour of the County Jail and showed her the electric chair."[16]

De Beauvoir, the spoiled daughter of upper-middle-class French Catholic parents, was shocked and disturbed. Afterward Algren took her to his small apartment and made love to her—"initially because he wanted to comfort me," she later confided, "then because it was passion."[17]

The friend who had given Algren's phone number to Beauvoir was stunned by the unlikeliness of such a *coup de foudre.* "Scratch a bum like Nelson," she later said, "and you will find a snob somewhere. I guess he was sort of impressed with her, and he—well, for her he was virility incarnate, and those of us who had lived and worked in Paris knew she didn't get much of that with Sartre."[18]

Beauvoir would not have contested this view. Deirdre Bair interviewed Beauvoir many times in the final years of her life, and had access to the correspondence between the unlikely lovers. With Algren, Bair recorded, Beauvoir "had her 'first complete orgasm' and she learned 'how truly passionate love could be between men and women.'"[19]

The Second Sex, which Beauvoir took up again on her return to France, would become the bible of feminism—yet it would not have achieved its extraordinary international success had its author not had her world turned upside down by Algren, the man she called her "husband" (though they never married) and "the only truly passionate love in my life."[20] "It was Algren with whom she first discussed her 'essay on women,' and it was he who initially encouraged her to think about expanding it into a book," Bair revealed. "They had discussed the situation of women when they were in New York in May [after Algren had flown to meet her there], sitting and smoking in the twin beds of their hotel room after they made love; he was curious about the lot of French women and how she differed from most of them, and she wanted to know what he thought of her observations about American women."[21]

Gradually, "women's status throughout the world" became the theme he steered her toward—while into his own fiction he injected a renewed intensity. They traveled together, wrote together, wrote to each other, translated and criticized each other's work. Energized, loved, Beauvoir would never be Greta Garbo's Ninotchka, who melts into feminine fluff; but in her own way, she was—

and Bair's biography details both the creative inspiration and the heartache the affair brought them.

Algren, head over heels in love, even moved to Paris, since Beauvoir felt she could not leave Paris, or her life's work as Sartre's literary and philosophical partner. On the Left Bank, however, with only a smattering of French, Algren was out of his depth. Divided by two opposing cultures, their love affair was doomed. Though Algren begged her to marry him and live in America, the relationship ended, causing lasting grief for both of them.

The moral is that you are privileged, as a biographer, to do what no historian or novelist can ever achieve: to research and tell the true love-stories that not only give color to people's lives, but profoundly influence them. Even those "who seem wholly busied in publick affairs, and elevated above low cares," in reality spend "the chief part of their time in familiar and domestick scenes," wrote Dr. Johnson. Moreover these "domestick scenes" are neither trivial nor unrelated to a person's public life. "To be happy at home is the ultimate result of all ambition," Johnson asserted; in his opinion, it is "the end to which every enterprise and labor tends."[22]

You may well be castigated, then, for focusing on your subject's private life. But be of good cheer, knowing the Great Doctor stands behind you!

TEN

Life's Work

Whatever your life's work is, do it well. A man should do
his job so well that the living, the dead, and the unborn
could do it no better.

—MARTIN LUTHER KING JR., "Facing the
Challenge of a New Age" (quoting an
unnamed college president)

*D*oing justice to your subject's personality, to his or
her capacity for love, passion, desire, hatred—this requires
sensitivity, the exercising of inevitable moral judgment
(however objective you try to be), and deep human understanding. Simultaneously, however, you are seeking to understand the nature of your subject's contribution to other
people's lives: to family and society, at an immediate level,

then upon the larger stage, as your subject embarks on a career. Narrating and assessing that career is the challenge which every biographer since Xenophon has had to face, and it will be yours too.

Never forget as you compose your work that the biographer is not a historian, recording facts for facts' sake. As Plutarch put it two thousand years ago, at the start of his comparative biography of Alexander and Julius Caesar:

> The careers of these men embrace such a multitude of events that my preamble shall consist of nothing more than this one plea: if I do not record all their most celebrated achievements or describe any of them exhaustively, but merely summarize for the most part what they accomplished, I ask my readers not to regard this as a fault. For I am writing biography, not history, and the truth is that the most brilliant exploits often tell us nothing of the virtues or vices of the men who performed them, while on the other hand a chance remark or a joke may reveal far more of a man's character than the mere feat of winning battles in which thousands fall, or of marshalling great armies, or laying siege to cities. When a portrait painter sets out to create a likeness, he relies above all upon the face and the expression of the

> eyes and pays less attention to the other parts of the
> body: in the same way it is my task to dwell upon
> those actions which illuminate the workings of the
> soul, and by this means to create a portrait of each
> man's life.[1]

Plutarch was, of course, exaggerating—for his biographies of famous Greeks and Romans, written at the same time as the biblical gospels of Matthew, Mark, Luke, and John, exhibited enormous scholarship in the accurate retelling of near-contemporary public lives and accomplishments. With enough will and humility, you too can reconstruct the life-course and character of your subject—remembering always it is the emergent, underlying pattern of a career, and the relationship between that and the growing character of your subject, that you are attempting to discern behind the factual data.

Earlier, we asked what the right credentials for a biographer might be. Do you, for example, need to be a fellow professional in order to undertake the biography, say, of a philosopher, musician, psychologist, or politician? Being a fellow warrior—as was Xenophon when recording the life of King Cyrus, or Roy Jenkins when writing his life of Winston Churchill—can certainly make for a profoundly insightful work, and sometimes a great biography. In most cases, however, it doesn't. All too often, the "expert" author loses sight of what is important to readers; or has too big an ego as a practitioner; or simply does not possess the skills of research and composition that make for an outstanding biography. The truth is, the best biographies of politicians today are written by biographers who are *not* politicians; of poets by biographers who are *not* poets; of film directors by biographers who are *not* filmmakers. The most adept write on behalf of readers who love biography as "the illumination of the workings of the soul," not simply as an adjunct to the individual's works.

Total immersion, dogged research, hard work, skilful narrative, deep respect for the task, illumination of the themes tackled, compassion for the human dimension of history and achievement: *these* are qualities you need. Also, an awareness of Dr. Johnson's "parallel circumstances, and kindred images." In the realm of a man or woman's career, this will entail a curiosity about the genesis of the subject's achievement, and its unfolding—for all of us are symbolically invested in the story of a child's dreams of the future, and then the enactment of those dreams, through apprenticeship and fulfillment, or failure.

An American Dreyfus

Let's look at some examples of enactment, starting with the life of Robert Oppenheimer, the father of the atomic bomb. While a fellow scientist can certainly record and evaluate the history of the Manhattan Project, especially the scientific challenge it posed, only a biographer can tell us how Oppenheimer himself saw that challenge, the way in which he met it, and the psychological, ethical, and moral consequences for Oppenheimer the man.

Neither Martin Sherwin nor Kai Bird is a scientist; yet in *American Prometheus* the distinguished historian and the brilliant biographer, working in the field of twentieth-century security and defense studies, decided to combine forces and set down the riveting story of an American genius—as well as the tragedy that followed Oppenheimer's signal contribution to the struggle between the democracies and the Axis powers in World War II. As the great physicist became more concerned about the ethics of nuclear weapons development—in particular the hydrogen bomb—so the U.S. government security agencies, in an ever-glaciating Cold War, became more concerned about him and his family. Ironically, the situation came to resemble more what was going on in the Soviet Union than in the America most Americans were aware of—a situation that grew steadily worse during the anti-Communist McCarthy witch hunt. It climaxed with the 1954 kangaroo-court hearings of the Atomic Energy Commission (AEC) to determine whether Oppenheimer, the founding architect of America's nuclear weapons program, should have his security clearance rescinded.

It was not that Oppenheimer had passed secrets to an enemy power, as Alger Hiss had done; it was a question of whether, given his moral qualms about the hydrogen bomb, he *might* do so. In an era of Cold War suspicion, he was no longer considered trustworthy and obsequiously loyal to the governing powers—despite having informed on many of his closest Los Alamos colleagues, at the McCarthy hearings.

Oppenheimer's "trial" forms the central episode of a justly prize-winning biography: one that combines painstaking scholarship, seamless narrative construction, complete candor in charting character flaws, profound insight into the many relationships described, great sensitivity to the nuances of fidelity and infidelity, and an appreciation not only of the extraordinary human drama but of the injustice and depredations of a police state operating within a great democracy. The authors never raise their voices or overstate their narrative case; instead, they chart the story of "Oppie's" life, piecing together many thousands of letters, interviews, FBI files, congressional testimonies, and contemporary accounts. They are alert not only to the pattern of success and failure at both the personal and public levels, but also to the historical analogy with the French military officer Alfred Dreyfus—another Jew who was scapegoated by fanatics in his own country.

Bird and Sherwin's account of the trial is heart-wrenching: five long weeks of testimony, interrogations, and cross-examinations, as well as the machinations of senior government figures, the FBI, and other agencies. "On May 23 [1954], the Gray Board returned its formal verdict," Bird and Sherwin wrote of the finale. The father of the atomic bomb would become an outcast from the atomic Establishment.

> Their reasoning was tortured. They did not accuse Oppenheimer of violating any laws or even security regulations. But his associations gave evidence of a certain indefinable ill-judgment. His studied lack of deference to the security apparatus was particularly damning in their eyes. "Loyalty to one's friends is one of the noblest of qualities," Gray and Morgan wrote in their majority opinion. "Being loyal to one's friends above reasonable obligations to the country and to the security system, however, is not clearly consistent with the interests of security." Among other deviations, Oppenheimer was guilty of excessive friendship.[2]

It was not a unanimous verdict. One of the three members of the AEC dissented. Like Emile Zola's famous "J'Accuse," Ward Evans's objection to his colleagues' verdict makes sterling—and stirring—reading many decades later. "Most of the derogatory information was in the hands of the Committee when Dr. Oppenheimer was cleared in 1947," Evans began his anti-verdict, which the authors quote verbatim.

> They apparently were aware of his associations and his left-wing policies: yet they cleared him. They took a chance because of his special talents and he continued to do a good job. Now when the job is done, we are asked to investigate him for practically the same derogatory information. He did his job in a thorough and painstaking manner. There is not the slightest vestige of information before this Board that would indicate that Dr. Oppenheimer is not a loyal citizen of his country. He hates Russia. He had communistic friends, it is true. He still has some. However, the evidence indicates that he has fewer of them than he had in 1947. . . . To deny him clearance now for what he was cleared in 1947, when we must know he is less of a security risk now than he was then, seems hardly the procedure to be adopted in a free country. . . .
>
> I personally think that our failure to clear Dr. Oppenheimer will be a black mark on the escutch-

eon of our country. His witnesses are a considerable segment of the scientific backbone of our Nation and they endorse him.[3]

Evans's dissent, however, only made the other two commissioners more intent on destroying "Dreyfus." They even released the transcript of the proceedings, despite all prior assurances that they would not do so, as a public document to the press, in order to feed "red-baiting" journalists like Walter Winchell and whip up ignorant support in the press. For Oppenheimer, although he continued to work at Princeton alongside Albert Einstein, the verdict meant ruin.

Matisse

From a genius of physics, let's move to a genius of art: Henri Matisse. Hilary Spurling was neither a painter nor French, but her award-winning multivolume life of Matisse provides another example of superlative biographical narrative, which no fiction writer's or historian's account can ever match.

Using traditional chronological narrative, Spurling—a former theater critic and literary editor, who had written a fine biography of Paul Scott (author of The Raj Quartet, later filmed as *The Jewel in the Crown*)—turned to the great post-Impressionist, revealing a Matisse behind his harmonious, serene paintings whom almost no one had imagined: perpetually subversive, often tormented, always innovating in his art, whatever his critics threw at him.

"Each felt isolated by his achievements," Spurling wrote of Picasso and Matisse in the aftermath of Cubism. "Each had reached the end of one experimental stage and was ready for the next." For Picasso, "next" was the invention of Cubist collage; for Matisse, however, it was something else, as he turned sharply away from "the dry cerebral aspect that contrasted so sharply with the passionate impulses of his own divided character."

> "Of course Cubism interested me," he said long afterwards, "but it did not speak directly to my deeply sensuous nature, to such a great lover as I am of line and of the arabesque, those two life-givers." In Morocco [from which he had returned in the spring of 1913] he had pushed that side of himself as far as it could go. Now it was time for a drastic change of course.
>
> The four major projects he worked on through the summer at [his house at] Issy looked to other

people like wilful exercises in human disfigurement and deformity. All but one were serial experiments started three or four years earlier. . . .

Matisse's third project was more worrying than either of the other two at this stage. He returned to a set of busts of Jeanne Vaderin, a model whose portrait he had also painted as the shy, charming *Girl with Tulips* of 1910. The first two busts were inoffensive, semi-impressionistic studies of a perfectly conventional young lady, but in two more, made a year later, he recklessly exaggerated the liberties he had taken in his painted portrait with her hair, nose and the tilt of her head. "The sculptor goes after the gargoyle in human nature," the *New York Evening Post* said reprovingly of *Jeannette III*, when it went on show at Stieglitz's gallery in 1912. In 1913, Matisse began to pummel the clay for a *Jeanette V* of such extreme distortion that even the most sophisticated customers found it hard to stomach. . . .

This was the provoking, punitive Henry Hairmattress hellbent on driving ordinary people wild. When bewildered onlookers protested that no human being resembled the creatures of his imagination, Matisse agreed, adding cheerfully that if he met one in the street, he would probably flee in terror. Meanwhile his house was booby-trapped with shocks for the unwary. First-time visitors, already rattled by the bulging forehead and staring eyes of the African carvings in the drawing room ("Wooden fetishes surround you and seem to follow you"), were nearly always floored, when they crossed the garden to his studio, by the *Bathers* or the *Backs* ("Vast neo-Assyrian bas reliefs which Matisse cuts out of enormous planks of plaster"), and what [Robert] Rey called "the bust with the tapir's nose." Again and again people who reached Issy in the years immediately before 1914 made it sound as if they had stepped into the future: a strange, scary, savage world that filled them with foreboding and disquiet.[4]

Spurling's patient record of the *pattern* of Matisse's creativity and output, alongside her account of his domestic life, travels, and travails, awes the reader. No psychoanalyst, such as Freud, could ever take us where Spurling does, marrying a command of so many sources with deep and engaging insight—so much so that we cannot but identify with the poor visitors who made their way to Matisse's home and studio in Issy in 1913, and found themselves facing the future of modern art.

Lawrence of Arabia

Suetonius would certainly have been intrigued, nineteen hundred years later, by John Mack's biography of the legendary desert warrior of the early twentieth century, Lawrence of Arabia.

A Prince of Our Disorder charts T. E. Lawrence's Shakespearean life up to his early death on his motor bike, when he swerved to avoid a cyclist. Far from being a warrior, John Mack was a psychiatrist at the Harvard Medical School, but became a superlative biographer of the complex archaeologist-turned-tribal-leader. (Mack, too, died in a traffic accident, when struck by a London taxi.)

As best he was able, working from various (often elusive or evasive) historical sources, Mack recounted T. E. Lawrence's childhood in Oxford as the illegitimate son of a minor Irish aristocrat who had run away with the family governess, changing his name from "Chapman" (he became the last Sir Thomas Chapman, baronet) to "Lawrence." Mack then charted Lawrence's passionate travels and involvement in the Middle East, and explored Lawrence's role in the Arab revolt against the Turks during World War I, including Lawrence's supposed "rape" at Der'a and the massacre of the Turks at Tafas. Entering the story himself, as Suetonius often did, the biographer addressed the ethical controversy over Tafas:

> I have dwelt at length upon the Tafas episode, and have taken particular pains to try to establish Lawrence's role in it, because it not only, I believe, is pertinent to the evaluation of his character, but raises at the same time issues pertinent to assessing the actions and personality of any public figure. A man who, with little provocation, orders, takes part in, and even enjoys killing helpless prisoners, while experiencing no guilt, is a sadist who invites little sympathy or interest. The film *Lawrence of Arabia* would lead us to believe this true of Lawrence. On the other hand a man who, after observing extreme atrocities committed against people with whose lives and suffering he has become overly identified, gives way to the impulse to order a retaliatory execution by the victims of these atrocities is a different, more complex person, who may be deserving of our compassion and understanding as well as our criticism.[5]

In defense of Lawrence, Mack quoted Lawrence's own description of his hysteria, when laughing at a medical major who reprimanded him for the terrible conditions in Damascus' main hospital. Lawrence had witnessed the massacre at Tafas only the day before—and the contrast had caused him to cackle like a chicken, "with the laughter of strain."

> The major had not entered the charnel house of yesterday [Tafas], nor smelt it, seen us burying those bodies of ultimate degradation, whose memory had started me up in bed, sweating and trembling, a few hours since. He glared at me, muttering "Bloody brute." I hooted out again, and he smacked me over the face and stalked off, leaving me more ashamed than angry, for in my heart I felt he was right, and that anyone who pushed through to success a rebellion of the weak against their masters must come out of it so stained in estimation that afterward nothing in the world would make him feel clean. However, it was nearly over.[6]

How truthful was Lawrence's account, in his own extraordinary autobiography, *Seven Pillars of Wisdom?* It is one of the tests of biographers that they must weigh their different sources, including those things written by their subjects, ranging from letters and diaries to memoranda and memoirs. The challenges of self-representation we shall address in another chapter, but we need to note here that no biographer should ever take such sources at face value—especially a text as beautifully wrought and "composed" as Lawrence's autobiography was. Equally, biographers should never shy from using such material as stepping stones into the mind, memory, manipulations, and personality of their subjects.

John Mack had no intention of writing a psychobiography. He did wish, however, to use his psychiatric skills to better interpret Lawrence's own version(s) of his life and the meaning of his experiences. "Lawrence was twenty-eight when he first took an active, personal part in the Arab Revolt," Mack informed his readers.

> Although he had seemed thus far to his friends and acquaintances an unusual, even odd, sort of genius, he had not given evidence of being deeply troubled, or even especially introspective. But his experiences in the Revolt, however his part in it is assessed, were personally shattering. The horrors he observed and took part in during 1917 and 1918 following the deaths of his two brothers [killed on the Western Front]; the political conflict; the disillusionment with the behavior of the Arabs; the multiple bouts of fe-

brile illness; the death of [his beloved Arab servant] Dahoum; and, above all, the traumatic assault at Der'a and the loss of control at Tafas, brought about profound changes in Lawrence's mental state and personality. . . .

Der'a and Tafas touched off in Lawrence—there seem to be no right words—or brought into his consciousness in an abrupt and devastating way, forbidden or unacceptable sexual, aggressive and vengeful impulses. Until this time, what he had felt as merely a strong attraction to renunciation and self-denial, a kind of idealistic puritanism not without its normal place in the England of his day, became exaggerated into a powerful need for penance through degradation and humiliation, a need that was accompanied by a permanently lowered self-regard. In addition, he was left with a compulsive wish to be whipped, attributable directly to the Der'a experience.[7]

Whether we agree with the biographer's evaluation or not, John Mack's patient, compassionate, humane quest to understand the mystery of T. E. Lawrence must be an example to all would-be biographers.

Truman Capote

One final text that illustrates the biographer's search for the keys to the work and achievements of a subject is Gerald Clarke's *Capote: A Biography,* published in 1988 after twelve years of research. In it Clarke addressed head-on the great short-story writer's switch from fiction to nonfiction, whereby Capote created one of the most influential nonfiction books of the twentieth century: *In Cold Blood.*

Obsessed with the adulteries and divorces of his rich society friends, and unable to make headway with the novel he had started (one that would be posthumously published as *Answered Prayers*), Capote had reached a turning point in his literary life. Norman Mailer had lauded *Breakfast at Tiffany's:* "He is tart as a grand aunt, but in his way he is a ballsy little guy, and he is the most perfect writer of my generation, he writes the best sentences, word for word, rhythm upon rhythm. I would not have changed two words in *Breakfast at Tiffany's,* which will become a small classic." With that quotation, Clarke reeled in his line:

> Although he still talked about *Answered Prayers,* Truman's mind was really on nonfiction. "I like the feel-

ing that something is happening beyond and about me and I can do nothing about it," he explained to a reporter. "I like having the truth be the truth so I can't change it." He was too restless to settle down to fiction, he told the now elderly Glenway Wescott. "I couldn't sit there to write," he said. "It was as though there were a box of chocolates in the next room, and I couldn't resist them. The chocolates were that I wanted to write fact instead of fiction. There were so many things that I knew I could investigate, so many things that I knew I could find out about. Suddenly the newspapers all came alive, and I realized that I was in terrible trouble as a fiction writer.

In that mood he opened the *New York Times* on Monday, November 16, 1959. There, all but hidden in the middle of page 39, was a one-column story headlined, "WEALTHY FARMER, 3 OF FAMILY SLAIN." The dateline was Holcomb, Kansas, November 15, and the story began: "A wealthy wheat farmer, his wife and their two young children were found shot to death today in their home. They had been killed by shotgun blasts at close range after being bound and gagged."[8]

Pausing to take breath and help the reader appreciate the significance of this moment not only in Capote's career, but in the history of modern nonfiction, Clarke began a new chapter of his biography with the following passage:

> In describing the genesis of a successful work, a writer often will say that he stumbled across his idea, giving the impression that it was purely a matter of luck, like finding a hundred-dollar bill on the sidewalk. The truth, as Henry James observed, is usually different: "His discoveries are, like those of the navigator, the chemist, the biologist, scarce more than alert recognitions. He comes upon the interesting thing as Columbus came upon the isle of San Salvador, because he had moved in the right direction for it."
>
> So it was that Truman, who had been moving in the right direction for several years, came across his San Salvador, his interesting thing, in that brief account of cruel death in far-off Kansas: he had been looking for it, or something very much like it. For no apparent reason, four people had been slain: Herbert Clutter; his wife, Bonnie; and two of their four

children, Nancy, sixteen, and Kenyon, fifteen. As he read and reread those spartan paragraphs, Truman realized that a crime of such horrifying dimensions was a subject that was indeed beyond him, a truth he could not change. Even the location, a part of the country as alien to him as the steppes of Russia, had a perverse appeal. "Everything would seem freshly minted," he later explained, reconstructing his thinking at that time. "The people, their accents and attitude, the landscape, its contours, the weather. All this, it seemed to me, could only sharpen my eye and quicken my ear." Finally he said to himself, "Well, why not this crime? The Clutter case. Why not pack up and go to Kansas and see what happens?"[9]

Thus the genesis of *In Cold Blood:* related not by a literary scholar or a historian, but by a biographer who knew Capote well, who was completely candid in describing the offensive as well as the genial aspects of his character; who was determined to approach every possible archival repository in the search for manuscripts and letters; and who was willing to interview more than 250 witnesses and sources in order to portray Capote and explore the origins of his work.

Finding the Line

You wish to be a biographer? *Find the line.* It is the line not of least resistance, but of the most resistance: the one you draw in order to link the salient features of your subject's life-work, from genesis to fulfillment—or backward, if you so choose.

Sketch it first, as a painter might, beginning with a charcoal outline—the way Seurat prepared for his *Grande Jatte.* Write up the episodes you feel best convey the story, whether in events or themes. See where your narrative leads, how it begins to look. End your day's work in the middle of a sentence or thought, so that you can remind yourself, the next day, that you're opening windows onto a life, not closing them. Ask yourself, constantly: What is the thread running through this life-story?

Cut, cut, and keep cutting away the unnecessary, the superficial, the hyperbole. "One of the things that drives me is curiosity," Stephen Ambrose once explained, "and I never can know what really happened until I sit down and have to write it up." He fell into the habit of showing it to his wife, Moira. Moira "listens and then she jumps on me. She's always accusing me of triumphalism and makes me cut back on that. I like to fly the flag high, and Moira wants me to be a little more critical than that."[10]

Ambrose didn't always comply—but he tried.

Listen to Moira as the voice of your potential readers, to see whether your curiosity corresponds with theirs. But once you know what you're doing, be proud of it, like Matisse, or Truman Capote. Taking Harper Lee, his childhood friend, with him, Capote set off for the Midwest, pausing overnight to be feted by members of Kansas State University's English Department. "But if he had realized then what the future held," his biographer wrote, "he never would have stopped." And he quoted Capote's own words: "I would have driven straight on. Like a bat out of hell."[11]

ELEVEN

The Twilight Years

The old begin to complain of the conduct of the young
when they themselves are no longer able to set a bad
example.

—LA ROCHEFOUCAULD, *Maxims*, no. 93

*C*hronicling the midlife achievements of your subject is demanding enough in terms of research, understanding, insight, evaluation, storytelling. But what of the
later years, when that "bubble reputation" has been
achieved and you must chronicle the inevitable decline of
your subject?

Though there are exceptions, the later years of most
life-stories have tended traditionally to be glossed over in

biography. Individuals who have excelled in their profession through middle years become more cantankerous or, like Evelyn Waugh, isolated and unhappy. They are tested by illness, as well as by bereavement, which presages their own death. Yet in today's developed nations, where, thanks to better nutrition and health care, we live on average so much longer than previous generations, the result has been a deepening biographical interest in the later stages of life.

In the "evening of life," as Bernard Montgomery called it, he was a model for me because I actually knew him during his later years—from the 1950s, when I was still a schoolboy in short pants, until his death in 1976. He was a striking figure, with piercing blue-gray eyes and an iron will—very much the field marshal. He asked constant questions, like a prosecutor. He went through a long period where he would not speak to his own son David, who had dared to get divorced—indeed, his unwillingness to show parental affection and his brittle, boastful ego made him a lonely old man, living by himself in a converted watermill in Hampshire, southwest of London. Yet it was that very mask that drew me to him when I was a youngster, since I knew there had to be more to his personality than that— and I was right.

The years exacted their toll, and Montgomery eventually took to his bed, for good. With his spare, angular face and parchment-like skin, he was, by the end of my third volume, no longer the same man who had served and sparred with Ike, and who had led two million American, British, Canadian, and Free French soldiers ashore in the liberation of France in 1944.

> Monty's memory, always so sharp and exact for names, faces and dates, began to fade after a bout of illness in 1972, and he tired quickly in conversation. The gardens, once so immaculately kept and weeded, began to fall into disorder without his watchful supervising eye. The caravans in which he had lived and commanded from Alamein to Lüneburg lay locked in the barns. By the Spring of 1973 his once unshakeably clear, schoolboy handwriting had deteriorated into barely legible hieroglyphics. When signing a copy of one of his books for the Chinese ambassador he could no longer recall the proper spelling of Alamein, his proud title. He had seemed determined to live to one hundred, not to surrender to death; now he appeared not to care, and was like a small boy, alone in the school sanatorium, looked after by his faithful housekeeper Miss Cox.
>
> Those who had known Monty in his prime were

disappointed at this seeming abdication of will. His whole career had been a triumph of the will to fight and to succeed. Field Marshal Sir Gerald Templer, the "Tiger of Malaya," penned in a note among his papers: "He takes not the slightest interest in anything, does not read though he can do so without using glasses, and will not see anybody. We were told to be there at 3.30 P.M., which we were punctually, and that we should go at 3.50 P.M. Actually he asked us to go as he felt tired at precisely 3.45 P.M. A terrible end of the life of a once great man."[1]

Was the story so terrible, though? If the act of biography is whittling down the human being to human size from the mass of accumulated myth and surviving information (and misinformation), then the telling of a great individual's final years is a vital part of the biographer's responsibility. It is the opportunity to counterbalance the years of achievement and, on behalf of the reader, bring the subject to earth, where he or she will eventually lie. The aim is not to denigrate, but to remind ourselves that we are all, in the end, only human.

Sometimes, of course, the later years of a biographee actually provide a whole *new* life—as is the case with some women who outlive their husbands, such as Alma Mahler, Frieda Lawrence, Katharine Graham, Pamela Harriman, Jacqueline Kennedy, and a host of others. The reader is curious to know: What was it like to be the closest companion to a genius or star or dominant personality—and then be on one's own, the central figure at last, free to choose new partners, new companions, new outlets for one's passions?

From dependent muses, consorts, mothers, housewives, and domestic companions, widows can become major personalities in their own right—often with tremendous power, fortunes, or status. This can happen, too, for widowers— as it did for Leonard Woolf, John Bayley (Iris Murdoch's doting husband), and numerous other men. The biographical moral is that, if conflict be the stuff of drama and suspenseful fiction, then reversal of fortune or situation can, for biographers, offer an equally compelling narrative element.

Late-Life Creativity—and Its Opposite

Later years can certainly prove as fecund as early years, or more so—especially in cases of artists who by temperament seek ever-new modes of creative expression. Paul Gauguin, Pablo Picasso, Henri Matisse, George Orwell,

Thomas Mann, Igor Stravinsky, Arthur Miller, John Updike, Philip Roth—in many such cases the later work turns out to be the artist's finest, and the chronicle of that late-life creativity is fascinating to investigate.

I remember, when I was writing my dual biography of the brothers Mann, how moving I found their later years of exile from Germany, after Hitler became chancellor—in fact, how their years in Switzerland, France, and America were already prefigured in the biblical story of Joseph, which Thomas Mann in middle age had begun weaving into a tetralogy, one of his finest fictional achievements. In old age, exactly as the Joseph story had presaged, Thomas Mann, the younger brother, became the provider for his older sibling; he arranged for Heinrich to be given a life-saving visa to America in 1941 and supported him financially when Heinrich's contract with MGM Studios ran out. Thomas wrote his late masterpiece, *Doctor Faustus,* at the age of seventy-two. Heinrich dedicated one of his own later works "an meinem grossem Bruder" ("to my big/ great brother")—acknowledging that his little brother had, in his later years, become his big and justly celebrated brother.

Neither Heinrich nor Thomas was very active sexually in later life (though Heinrich—who became famous for his novel *Professor Unrat,* which was filmed as *The Blue An-*

gel, did cohabit with, and later married in exile, a Berlin bargirl, in an amazing example of life imitating art). In most lives the romantic and sexual element will be less pronounced in the evening of life than earlier—but by no means should you assume that this is always the case! Consider the life of Charlie Chaplin, or Bertrand Russell. Ronald Clark's portrait of Russell remains one of the most engaging of modern biographies, though published more than thirty years ago. A mathematician, philosopher, peace activist, Nobel Prize winner, educator, aristocrat, writer, and lover, Russell was one of the most extraordinary individuals of the twentieth century—wonderfully captured in Clark's 639-page opus. Most of all, Clark brilliantly conveyed the contradictions and incessant fireworks of Russell's long life, which lasted nearly a century.

Outraged by the nuclear brinkmanship of the Cuban Missile Crisis, Russell, from his home in North Wales, issued a series of *pronunciamentos* which he was convinced had an influence on the Soviets. Believing that he was the most articulate spokesman on behalf of peace and of young people, he became their guru, especially on the matter of nuclear disarmament and America's war in Vietnam. "This was one reason," Clark explained in a choice phrase, "and a strong one, for carrying on with a policy of lordly intervention in international affairs.

There were others. Russell was approaching his ninety-first birthday; he knew he had little time left and he intended to make the most of it. Moreover, he had one great advantage: he could afford to fail. Just as Einstein, his reputation firmly base on Relativity, could mortgage the second half of his life on a desperate search for a viable Unified Field Theory, so could Russell, already among the greatest philosophers of the century, afford to spend his last few years hammering on the world's chancellery doors with the demand that men should behave rationally.[2]

Furthermore, given Russell's writings on marriage and morals, Clark could unabashedly narrate, in tandem with the philosopher's achievements, his amazing love-life. This proved as comical as his work for world peace was serious, since Russell pursued sex with an almost endless sequence of married and unmarried mistresses and casual lovers.

Using letters and diaries, Clark painted an unforgettable portrait of a man who united romantic passion with an ice-cold intellect. Russell's lover Ottoline Morrell likened him to a "psychological surgeon." Using the many hundred of letters of their frank correspondence, Russell's later memoirs, and Ottoline's diary, Clark was able to recount not only their much-deliberated adultery—including their decision to tell their spouses before consummation of their relationship—but Russell's simultaneous, love-inspired writing of his classic book *The Problems of Philosophy*. "To my shame," Ottoline later confessed, "however much I was thrilled with the beauty and transcendence of his thoughts, I could hardly bear the lack of physical attraction, the lack of charm and gentleness and sympathy, that are so essential to me, and yet so rare."[3] Nevertheless, they remained close friends for the rest of their lives. Meanwhile, Russell's passion was transferred to a succession of other women, as he continued to pour out philosophical, political, and literary reflections right up until his own death.

Of course, there are lives that are cut short and have no later years: lives such as those of Albert Camus, Marilyn Monroe, Sylvia Plath, JFK, Robert Kennedy, Anne Sexton. The very abbreviation or amputation of their life-line provides a kind of suspense to the storytelling, since we know it can and must end abruptly—a fact that, as in tragedy, we can do nothing about. For the main part, though, biography encompasses all seven of Shakespeare's ages; and in the chronicling of the later years you, as biographer, will have the chance of a lifetime, so to speak: the opportunity to exercise judgment, understanding, and compassion.

Reversal of Fortune

Let's look at some examples of late-life storytelling that illustrate actual reversals of fortune in the later part of an individual's life. Richard Ellmann's biography of Oscar Wilde, published in 1988, is a classic account.

Ellmann, son of a Jewish immigrant from Kiev, managed in his own later years (he was sixty-nine when he died, just before publication of *Oscar Wilde*) to exceed his superb biography of James Joyce. In that account of Joyce's life, he told the story not of the proverbial wandering Jew but of a wandering Irishman, and did so with indefatigable wit and literary insight. In *Oscar Wilde,* however, Ellmann concentrated on Wilde's years of celebrity in London, reserving the last quarter of his text for the tale of Wilde's disastrous court case, disgrace, imprisonment, and exile: one of history's most striking turnabouts in literary and personal fortune.

All trials, Wilde had once written, are for one's life. In his case, his lawsuit against the homophobic Marquess of Queensbury became the deliberate sacrifice of his own career and literary genius in a doomed gesture to please his treacherous lover, "Bosie" (Alfred Douglas), at the height of his success as a playwright. (Three of Wilde's plays were running simultaneously in London when the libel suit was heard.) The result was ruin. Wilde suffered arrest, trial, conviction, and incarceration with hard labor. These did not, however, cure his predatory interest in attractive young men. A Paris journalist who saw him kissing a marine accused him of having "retourné à son vomissement" ("returned to his own vomit"). He had—but lacked the money to enjoy these last sinful pleasures, and was reduced to begging. Meeting the opera singer Nellie Melba on the street in Paris, he stunned her with the words, "Madame Melba, you don't know who I am? I'm Oscar Wilde, and I'm going to do a terrible thing. I'm going to ask you for money." "She took all she had in her purse," Ellmann chronicled, "and gave it to him; he muttered his thanks and went." Another London actress, on a visit to Paris, saw him "looking into the window of a pastry shop, biting his fingers."[4]

Could this have been the same man who gave the world plays like *The Importance of Being Earnest, An Ideal Husband,* and *Lady Windermere's Fan?* Never for a moment does Ellmann's honesty allow him to cover up Wilde's behavior, but never for a moment do we feel less than sorrow at his fall from grace. "Wilde was as infamous as he had been in the early nineties. In America a set of photographs in a scarlet cover entitled *The Sins of Oscar Wilde* was hawked about American colleges. Young men were being warned of the peril he represented."[5] When an American college freshman named Armstrong wrote to his family saying that he'd met Wilde by the banks of the Seine and had treated the penniless celebrity to dinner, he was "ordered home by the next boat." When the Marquess of Queensbury died in 1900, Bosie inherited a fortune which he was free to spend on whomsoever and whatever he wished. He refused, however, to give a penny to Wilde—"I can't afford to spend anything except on myself"—and accused Wilde of wheedling "like an old whore."[6]

"I can write, but have lost the joy of writing," Wilde lamented in exile, quite understandably. Eventually, the reader longs—as Wilde did—for release from such purgatory: marveling at Wilde's genius, lamenting his failings, sad at his penury, infuriated by the surrender of his once creative spirit, repelled by the hypocrisy and self-righteousness of his abusers, moved by the sheer immutability of his chosen fate. "I wrote when I did not know life," he told Anna de Bremont, a friend of his mother's. "Now that I know the meaning of life, I have no more to write."[7]

Churchill's Resignation

Wilde surrendered his greatness; Churchill wouldn't. He achieved greatness in his later years in a multitude of ways—as writer (winner of the Nobel Prize for Literature), as generalissimo, and as statesman. But relinquishing the prime ministership of Great Britain was the hardest thing of all for him.

For his official biographer, Martin Gilbert, the vainglorious aspect of Churchill's personality was tough to accept. Gilbert was loath to criticize his hero but had to recount how, after suffering a stroke and becoming less and less able to conduct affairs as prime minister (the last surviving member of Parliament to have been elected in the reign of Queen Victoria), Churchill was pressed to retire not only by the opposition, but by his own cabinet.

Few prime ministers retire save by *force majeure*—indeed, Neville Chamberlain, aged seventy-one, had resigned only after Hitler invaded France and the Low Countries in May 1940, and the majority of members of Parliament turned against Chamberlain—Leo Amery having thundered famously across the aisle, "In the name of God, go!" Fearing such a fate, Churchill ultimately made a private agreement with his foreign secretary, Anthony Eden, to hand over the prime ministership on April 5, 1955.

Yet a message from Sir Roger Makins, the British ambassador to the United States, gave Churchill a new reason to hang on. President Eisenhower, it appeared, wished to come to Paris in May to "lay plans for a meeting with the Soviets in a sustained effort to reduce tensions and the risk of war." This news caused Churchill to renege on his promise—and drove his loyal foreign secretary to exasperation. Gilbert described the subsequent confrontation, before members of the assembled Cabinet at No. 10 Downing Street, with commendable *sang froid:*

> The Cabinet now discussed the possibility that the Paris meeting would be held in May as proposed by Eisenhower, to be followed by a Four-Power meeting in June. Churchill then suggested that perhaps the June meeting, at which the Russians would be present, could be held in London. Was it the mention of June that suddenly made Eden see red? To the mystification of his colleagues, who knew nothing of the April 5 hand-over date, he then asked, slowly and deliberately, "Does that mean, Prime Minister, that the arrangements you have made with me are at an end?"
>
> Churchill was angered that Eden should raise the resignation issue in this way. He began to reply somewhat indistinctly about "the national interest" and "this has been my ambition," whereupon Eden broke in with the words, "I have been Foreign Minister for ten years. Am I not to be trusted?"
>
> "It seems certain facts are not known to all of

us," interrupted Lord Salisbury, who knew nothing of the April 5 date, and who now insisted that the Cabinet be told what was going on between Churchill and Eden. But Churchill refused. "I cannot assent to such a discussion," he said. "I know my duty and will perform it. If any member of the Cabinet dissents, his way is open."[8]

All of Churchill's visionary hope, egoism, obstinacy, and toughness is there still, at age eighty—captured by a dedicated researcher, historian, and, above all, biographer who brought the great statesman into human scale.

The First Académicienne

To tell the stories of an individual's later years is thus to open a window onto waning life that permits you, as narrator, to bring your biographical task to a moving conclusion.

How wide the window on old age can be opened, of course, depends on the accessibility of the sources that will make your portrait of the later years credible rather than speculative.

Josyane Savigneau at first felt somewhat thwarted, when embarking on her life of the great French novelist Marguerite Yourcenar (1903–1987), since Yourcenar's diaries had been sealed until 2037. Nevertheless, Savigneau had interviewed Yourcenar (author of *The Memoirs of Hadrian*) in her later years, and was able to piece together a moving interim account of Yourcenar's "Boston marriage" to an American woman, Grace Frick.

Yourcenar and Frick lived together for many years in Maine, where Yourcenar fashioned a quality of classical French prose that would win her the first-ever seat held by a woman in the venerable French Academy. Accepting the honor at an induction ceremony in Paris, in the evening of her life, Yourcenar came face to face with male chauvinism at its most exclusive: a men's club (limited to forty members, elected for life), penetrated by a woman's woman:

> The Académie was probably for Yourcenar the first site of confrontation with men. For the first, perhaps the only, time in her life, she felt their—irrational—reprobation. It was a reprobation founded uniquely on her belonging to the other sex. Their hostility toward her was, and remains, greater still than the hostility borne women who fight for women's rights. Yourcenar didn't even *clash* with men socially. She ignored them. And this they could never tolerate.[9]

Yourcenar appeared only a single time at the academy—namely, on the occasion of her induction. She was dressed in a specially designed outfit by Yves Saint-Laurent: a long velvet cloak with a large white silk shawl. Describing the occasion, Savigneau noted the members' "fearsome abhorrence for women," quoting this phrase from the diary of the writer and broadcaster Mathieu Galey.[10] With the president of France officiating, the scene, peopled with academicians wearing their distinctive costumes (black frock coats heavily embroidered in leaf-green, worn with swords and cocked hats), was more akin to Queen Victoria's jubilee than an academic reception, as Galey described it:

> A consecration, to the sound of a drum. A Franciscan tertiary, followed by a high priest (the Reverend Father Carré), or an old empress being judged in the High Court by all these strange magistrates with green tails. With their insectlike appearance, one also got the impression of some mysterious confrairy; it was as if a large termite, inseminated by her insects, which were buzzing excitedly around her, were going to lay some eggs, beneath the gaze of the presidential couple, impassively perched on their Louis XV chairs.[11]

Savigneau's account of the Battle of the Academy is, in it-self, a jewel of human observation—but it is trumped, in turn, by her account of Yourcenar's even more extraordi-nary late-life love affair, after Grace Frick's prolonged and painful death. The academicians had, according to tradi-tion, given Yourcenar a word to define for the ninth edition of their official dictionary, which had reached the letter M. A rumor went around that they were going to give her the slang word for "lesbian." In fact, tasked with giving her the word "madwoman," they balked—giving her instead the adverb "madly." As Yourcenar had fallen "madly" in love with a young gay man named Jerry Wilson (he be-came her life's companion, accompanying her on her trav-els around the world as the most famous French woman of letters), this was, she believed, magical serendipity. Though many found the *Académicienne* arrogant, opinionated, and inflexible, Savigneau beautifully conveys how her mental armor protected her from a patriarchal French world full of conceit and intellectual snobbery, and allowed her to en-joy her years with Jerry Wilson, before his early death from AIDS.

The Riefenstahl Case

Finally, let's look briefly at an example of how, in the con-text of a reversal of fortune later in life, truth may become available to, or legally usable by, the biographer only when the subject dies and can no longer sue for libel. Such was the case of the greatest woman filmmaker of the twentieth century, Leni Riefenstahl.

Riefenstahl's films *Triumph of the Will* and *Olympia* set new standards for documentary filmmaking—and Nazi propaganda. Denied the financing to make films in Europe after World War II, owing to her refusal to admit culpability or remorse for her part in the Nazi nightmare, she decided eventually to film black African tribesmen in the Sudan.

In his 2007 biography, *Leni*, Steven Bach recounted how this happened. Riefenstahl saw, in 1951, a photograph of a "majestic African athlete, naked but for a single earring, riding on the shoulders of his defeated rival after a tribal wrestling match." Filming African athletes would be her way of demonstrating she was not guilty of racial prejudice. Contacting the British photographer George Rodger, she offered him a thousand dollars for an introduction to the tribe.

Rodger, unfortunately for Riefenstahl, had been the first photographer allowed by Montgomery into the Bergen-Belsen concentration camp upon its liberation six years before. "Dear Madam," he wrote back, "knowing your background and mine, I don't really have anything to say to you at all."[12] This didn't stop Riefenstahl, however. Eleven years later she managed to travel to the Sudan by attaching herself to a Nansen Society anthropological expedition.

As Bach told the story, Riefenstahl was interested neither in science nor in education. Just as she'd shamelessly gotten gypsies from Teresienstadt to play in her unfinished wartime feature film *Tiefland*—gypsies who were then exterminated by the Nazis—so now she exploited the Nuba to the point where the Nansen team cast her off. But for Riefenstahl, the chance to photograph—and hopefully film—the naked Nuba was too important to pass up, and she stayed on for eight months, returning six times in the ensuing fifteen years, determined to reestablish her name as the greatest woman photographer-filmmaker of her time.

Like Gitta Sereny's inquisitorial biography *Albert Speer: His Battle with Truth* (1995), Bach's *Leni* lays bare, side by side with Riefenstahl's dogged, perfectionist pursuit of visually captured beauty, the truth behind Riefenstahl's endless late-life prevarications, lies, and lawsuits aimed at preventing the facts from emerging. She was, he wrote, the "inexhaustible curator of her own legend"[13]—largely because, as one of the most manipulative individuals of her era, she insisted on total control not only of everything she did, but of everything that might be said or printed about her. She instigated lawsuit after lawsuit, in a never-ending campaign of self-justification and whitewashing. With her death, however, that control came to an end: the baton finally passed to biographers like Bach, who was able to recount her later years in a way that would do justice to her painstaking artistry, yet also to the truth. Suffering broken ribs and a back injury when her Russian helicopter was shot down in the Sudan, she lived to see the opening of her last film, *Underwater Impressions;* be sued for Holocaust denial by surviving *Tiefland* gypsies; and witness the beginning of the third millennium.

Long on example, short on advice? These passages illustrate, I hope, how modern biographers can, with rigor and yet delicacy, chart the later years of an individual in ways that are informative and moving, and that speak, indirectly, to our own lives—the fundamental purpose of serious biography.

Riefenstahl passed away at her house in Pöcking, Bavaria, near the Starnberger See, on September 8, 2003, at the age of a hundred and one. She had led an extraordinary life, by any standards. "Leni died," Bach concluded, "as she had lived: unrepentant, self-enamored, armor-clad"[14]—an epitaph which brings us to the dropping of life's curtain in biography: the last act.

TWELVE

Ending Your Story

Tell me, my soul, can this be death?

—ALEXANDER POPE,
"The Dying Christian to His Soul"

The end of life is death, which most of us fear. The death, or deathbed scene, in biography is thus more pregnant, in its way, than that of birth, for it is laden with our own morbid but understandable fascination. We want to know how our subject met his or her end, since death will be our end too.

Poets make sentiments noble, but do not always meet their maker nobly. Rimbaud, for example, endured an agonizing death in Marseille, where his leg had been amputated because of a cancerous tumor. A wooden leg was ordered, but after it was unpacked—the box having been first mistaken for a coffin—he exclaimed: "I shall never wear it. It's all over, I can feel that I'm dying."[1]

Rimbaud, at thirty-seven, was already legendary for his scandalous affair with his fellow poet Paul Verlaine, and for his subversive, hallucinatory poems. For ten years after his breakup with Verlaine he had sought, in exile, to reform, working as a trader across North Africa. As Rimbaud's English biographer, Graham Robb, told the story a century later, the reformation was cut short by sickness, necessitating a return to France. Though Rimbaud dreamed of going back to Africa, his cancer spread following surgery in Marseille. His right arm became paralyzed; his body shrank. Morphine now produced the same hallucinatory images that had once colored his verse. Writing to their mother, his sister Isabelle—who had arrived to care for him—invented a deathbed scene. Last rites had been refused by the hospital chaplain, concerned lest the patient, heaven forbid, "choke on the body of Christ." Undaunted, Isabelle was determined to ensure her brother's posterity on earth, if not in the afterlife. "Where biography is concerned, I allow only one theme," she stated candidly, "and that's my own."[2]

As Robb's biography comes to its sad close, the author quotes the poet's last, haunting, mad words. It is a letter Rimbaud dictated, addressed to a certain "Monsieur le Directeur." Whatever tale his sister might have invented for their mother, these actual last words are heart-rending to read today. The dying poet first listed a consignment of ivory to be shipped, then added a personal request: he wanted to sail on a different vessel. He was, he admitted to the directeur, "crippled and unhappy—any dog in the street could tell you that"—and wished to know the cost of a passage to Suez. "I am completely paralysed, and so I wish to embark in good time."[3]

At ten o'clock the next morning, the author of "Le Bateau Ivre" boarded the phantom boat for a final time, and passed away. By his exhaustive research, use of surviving documents, love of Rimbaud's poetry, and immersion in French cultural history, Robb was able to bring his tale to a final, moving conclusion—a scene no fiction writer could ever narrate with such authority.

Not Drowning but Waving

The death of the poet Stevie Smith, as recorded by her biographer Frances Spalding, was the opposite of hallucinatory. Known for her astringent, brave, elliptical lines of verse, Smith's end was sad and yet utterly in character. The author quotes one of Stevie's friends, Helen Fowler:

The room was full of flowers; outside the window was the hospital garden, wintry still, sodden grass to the hedge and hardly discernible hills under a cloudy sky, inside was the hum of the hospital, voices, footsteps, trolleys wheeled about, dishes clattered. James [MacGibbon] stroked her cheek, I patted her hand. Suddenly she was restless, fidgety and then was racked with paroxysms of shaking, twisting, shuddering, joking, twitching. We held her in our arms, feeling the light, small body racked and shaken. It was like holding a flailing child in an excess of grief or tantrum, but worse, much worse, for the passion that shook her body was from outside her will. Our eyes met once or twice over her; I know that we were both hoping she would die then at this moment. Incredibly, it seemed, of course she didn't. A nurse brought a feeding cup of tea or orange juice and she had a few sips and lay back on the pillows. We re-arranged her scarf, held her hands again; talked again to her. There was so much to say and no way to say it.[4]

Periods of lucidity were interspersed between approaching death throes—"days when her speech was relatively free of confusion and blocks," Spalding narrated. "One of these occurred at Torbay Hospital before her biopsy, when Molly Everett brought in 'Come Death,' which she had typed at Stevie's request. Stevie sat up cross-legged on her bed and to the astonishment of her visitors and others in the ward performed it there and then without a mistake"—ending with her appeal to "sweet Death" as the "only god / who comes as a servant when he is called," and urging that the servant "not be slow."[5]

How is it possible for readers, as they become acquainted with this extraordinary woman through her life, to be unmoved by her death? The account makes a mockery of literary purists who feel that knowledge of the life, as opposed to the art, diminishes a poet's verse.

> She read it again to Father Sebastian Wolfe when he visited, astonishing him with her fearless, welcoming attitude to death, an attitude he had rarely encountered even in those whose faith was strong. Inez Holden, in her obituary of Stevie, also recollected that on her visit to the hospital Stevie, though unable to sustain coherent conversation, indicated that she was not daunted by her approaching death. When showing "Come Death" to James MacGibbon, Stevie encircled the word "death," MacGibbon un-

derstanding from this that she wished him to obtain for her the means by which to end her life. He did not do so, but he showed the poem with the encircled word to Dr Wigram and thereafter Stevie was more and more heavily sedated. Even before this, she seemed to Sister Hornabrook to be peaceful in herself, perhaps at last finally disenchanted, for as she had written, "only / In heaven's permission / Are creatures quiet / In their condition." On 7 March [1971] she died.[6]

And there Frances Spalding leaves Smith and us, in a place that does not really exist in fiction. Although a great novel can make us weep over the demise of an invented character, we know he or she is fictional—whereas biography gives us immutable *reality*. Spalding's book tells us how a great poet met, indeed welcomed, her end—and thus by implication shows how we, too, might meet ours.

Oscar Wilde, James Joyce, Richard Wright . . . : How can we not be fascinated by the waning hours and last words of those for whom words have been their life-line? And nonverbal artists—painters such as Whistler, an American who died in London, or Gauguin, a Frenchman who died in the Marquesas: How can we not be moved by the fact that their departures were so unacknowledged in their own day, yet their colors and canvases are so vividly and famously alive today?

Suffering from recurrent pneumonia and heart disease, Whistler continued working to the last, his biographer Stanley Weintraub recorded. One small canvas, *The Daughter of Eve,* was a portrait of Dorothy Seton, Whistler's favorite Irish model, famed for her coppery red hair. He completed it in an hour and three quarters—as if knowing the time left to him was brief.[7] On July 17, 1903, the American master of color in portraiture passed away, before the doctor could reach his bedside.

"At the time of Whistler's death no public gallery in England held one of his pictures," Weintraub noted—adding that this was due not simply to the artistic blindness of his British contemporaries, but to the man himself, who had dared to sue the critic John Ruskin for libel (although Whistler won the case, the costs bankrupted him), and whose self-invented persona "grated against the smugness of late Victorian England."[8]

Weintraub's biography helped to restore Whistler's place in the artistic pantheon of the late twentieth century. Biographies of Paul Gauguin, including the one by David Sweetman, did the same for their subject a century after his death.

Gauguin's farewell to life was even more painful than

that of the bankrupted Whistler. Living in a small house in the Marquesas, suffering from syphilis, and facing imprisonment, Gauguin persuaded an American, Ben Varney, "to return his syringe so that he could once again inject himself with morphine," wrote Sweetman. Surrounded by photos and images of his wife, Mette, and his children in Denmark, as well as by his paintings stacked against his studio wall, the master post-Impressionist was at death's door.

> The portraits had all gone—Teha'amana and Pau'ura—why had he never painted Vaeoho? Most of his pictures had been despatched almost as soon as they were finished so that he had never had a chance to see them together, no opportunity to make a final judgement, and by then he had little idea what had become of them. It was strange that Mette was still there, among the children; her presence, even in black and white, must have been a harsh reminder of all his broken promises. She remains the most enigmatic of all the characters in his long and tortuous story. Mette with her love of mannish clothes, yet with her love of little luxuries. Mette who had fallen in love with him because he was unlike anything she had known, and who yet re-

mained inflexible in her determination to lead her life in her own way. Now she hung there among the pornography and the last remaining paintings, in strange but not entirely inappropriate company— the mannish Mette Gad, with the *mahu* and the half-naked bathers. Perhaps Gauguin really had gone to the remotest ends of the earth not so much to escape Western civilization as to flee from those strong women who had shaped him: Flora Tristan, the grandmother he had never known but whose life set the pattern for his own, Aline his mother, with her firm sharp hand, and Mette, so like them in many ways. . . .

Early on the morning of 8 May, at the urging of Tioka, Pastor Vernier called round and found Gauguin on the bed as usual, though by then unsure whether it was day or night. His servants had wandered off and he was worried—he had had two fainting fits and was now in pain "all over." The pastor tried to cheer him up; they talked briefly about books, about Flaubert's *Salammbô*, another beautiful woman, dominated by her emotions, and doomed to act out male fantasies of seduction, power and death. But Vernier could only stay briefly before going to teach at the little mission school. He left him lying on his back, looking calm and rested. . . .

Sometime mid-morning he woke in pain, turned to the morphine bottle and realized that he had taken it all. He swung one leg off the bed and tried to get up but the effort was too much. He fell back and did not move again.[9]

Gauguin was no more. The news was borne to Pastor Venier's Protestant mission with the shout: "Come, come, the White is dead!" This did not stop the Catholic bishop from stealing the body and interring it in the Catholic mission cemetery, "to win points over Vernier and the Protestants by showing the natives that the Catholic Church always triumphs in the end."[10]

Sweetman's biography maintained a fine balance between empathy and sympathy, respect and critical judgment—as demonstrated in his account of Gauguin's death. A. N. Wilson's life of Leo Tolstoy, too, shows how a good biographer can illuminate the death of his subject by focusing on the other members of the cast; for often the response of others to the death is more revealing than the individual's own last words. The story of Tolstoy's flight by train from his wife, Sofya, is certainly one such example.

Sofya had not known "of her husband's whereabouts until a newspaperman telegraphed her, asking for an interview," Wilson related. The journalist "assumed she knew that her husband was dying of pneumonia in the station master's house at Astopovo."

> The children tried to dissuade her from going, but it was hard to see how they could or—as several of them were to say afterwards—why they should. Tolstoy in his weakened and terrified state might assert that Chertkov, whom he had known for twenty-seven years (nearly ten of which had been spent by Chertkov in English exile), had devoted his "entire life" to the [Christian] cause. But Sofya Andreyevna, who had copied and recopied all his great literary masterpieces, protected him against editors and predators, managed his household and farms and money, been his lover and his slave, and borne him thirteen children, could also have been said to have some claim on Tolstoy's gratitude and affection. The fact that it had all ended in hatred and bitterness was— Ilya, among the children, argued—all the more reason why the two tragic old people should be reconciled at the end.[11]

The story of Tolstoy's last hours, with Sofya arriving by special train, and reporters and cameramen assembling from around the world, is told by Wilson with quiet pathos.

Religion—state religion—played its inevitable role. Since Tolstoy, as a Christian radical, had been excommunicated, there was pressure on all sides to effect not only a marital reconciliation, but a reconciliation with the church. As the great master of the Russian novel was slipping away from life, Chertkov left the room and Sofya was permitted to join her dying spouse:

> The tiny room was crowded with people, as the pathetic figure of Sofya was allowed to squeeze through. She fell to her knees by the bed. Weeping, she whispered, "Forgive me, forgive me!" One of the doctors was afraid she would wake the old man. What would it have mattered if she had? But she was led from the room, and stood in the freezing porch for two hours, from half-past three until half-past five on the morning of November 7. Then the door opened, and her son Sergy was standing there. He led her back into the room. "I have never loved anyone but you," she said to the figure in the bed.

But by now he was fast ebbing away. After only a few more breaths he was gone. Sofya stood up, and leaned on the body with her head on its chest. There was no movement, no breath, no heartbeat.[12]

Denied an Orthodox church funeral, Tolstoy's body was buried two days later on his estate at Yasnaya Polyana, in a wooded place where his brother Nikolay had buried "the green stick on which was written the secret of how peace could come to the earth, and evil could be banished."[13]

It is a deeply evocative image. In the end, Wilson writes, "Tolstoy had come no nearer to discovering this secret than anyone else, but the return to the place of the green stick had an obvious appropriateness. Whatever muddled instincts had made him run out into the night less than a fortnight before, he had, at least in part, been running back towards his childhood, towards his sister, the last link with the Ant Brotherhood."[14]

Wilson's plain, almost understated style seems to me perfectly suited to narrating the life of one of the greatest novelists in all literature. It sets up no discordant harmonies between the biographer's work and Tolstoy's own incomparable writings, and allows the biographer to be dispassionate in chronicling the battles among members of the subject's family.

The Official Record

The disposal of the body—like the distribution of assets in a will—can cast a revealing light on the characters you describe in your book, and on the passage of the subject from life into afterlife (his or her posthumous reputation). You'd do well to research, reflect upon, and record the treatment of the remains carefully, whether putting the account at the end of your biography or—as is perfectly appropriate in storytelling—at the very beginning, in your prologue, so as to arouse the reader's curiosity about the individual who has passed away.

The level of detail should be, as always, commensurate with your agenda. In a work addressed to a wide audience, the postmortem will best be brief, if not redundant. If, by contrast, you are the official or authorized biographer, you must accept that your book will be not only a biography but a reference work, used by historians and students for its evidentiary, factual detail.

A good example of this is R. F. Foster's two-volume life of W. B. Yeats, which is tough reading for a general audience, but a mine of valuable research for the specialist. It nears its end with an account of the Irish poet's death and interment in southern France in 1939—but then treats us to the tale of an extraordinary mixup over "WBY's" body, which was wanted in Sligo, in his homeland, where Yeats was considered the nation's greatest poet. Because of the outbreak of World War II the remains could not be delivered—and once the war ended, they were no longer in the grave!

The reason for this was simple. A ten-year temporary lease had been taken on the grave, but in June 1947 it turned out that there had been complications with this arrangement.

> Edith Shackleton Heald came back to Roquebrune for the first time since she had stood by the graveside in the freezing cold on 30 January 1939—and could not find it. To her horror, the Curé told her that the temporary "concession" had run out after five years and the remains had been removed to the ossuary.
>
> Unsubstantiated accusations of carelessness were privately levelled: George [Yeats's widow] took the matter up with the French government, and the transference of her late husband's remains became an official affair. However, given the lack of documentation at Roquebrune and the increasingly inconsistent accounts from the local clergy, it was hard to find out precisely what had happened.

The likelihood is that George correctly took a ten-year concession, but that the church authorities had mistakenly situated the grave in the part of the cemetery owned by the municipality rather than by private families, where leases usually ran out after five years. Certainly the body had been exhumed, without anyone informing the family. Exactly the same thing had happened to the adjacent grave, where an Englishman called Alfred Hollis had been buried a few days after WBY, also with a ten-year "concession" which was not honoured. In any case, it proved necessary in March 1948 for French officials to identify the remains [duly found in the ossuary], which was done to the satisfaction of both local authorities and representatives from Paris. The identified remains were placed in a new coffin, with the old plate affixed. Though great care had been taken to preserve discretion, rumours of confusion reached the newspapers, and some murmurs would haunt the re-interment; later, perhaps inevitably, messages on the subject even came through at a séance attended by Robinson. The legend of a mystery burial, or even an empty coffin, sustains a kind of mythic life, as with King Arthur, or—more appositely—Charles Stewart Parnell.[15]

Such detailed attention to fact, truth, and myth makes Foster's biography exhaustive and exhausting for the general reader—but as a record of Yeats's life and death, patiently researched and recounted, it is incomparable: a work that will not only delight aficionados of Yeats but fuel other biographical portraits of the poet for decades to come.

Final Words

The end of a biography, then, is not in itself the end of a life-story, which goes on in people's memories, and in further biographies.

The death scene, perhaps followed by the funeral, will often be the most suitable finale—but not always. An overlap into posterity may also complete your agenda more emphatically, allowing you greater scope to state or restate your aims in writing the book.

Yet this can prove a license to bad poetry, rather than good. Let me give an example: that of John Fuegi's ending to his book *Brecht and Company*, a brilliant biography of the greatest German dramatist of the mid-twentieth century.

Fuegi had spent a lifetime editing and researching Brecht's work—only to find that significant portions of it had been written by Brecht's mistresses Margarete Steffin, Elisabeth Hauptmann, and Ruth Berlau, as well as by Martin Pohl, none of whom had received adequate acknowledgment from Brecht. Fuegi's biography came toward its end with an extraordinary account of Brecht's death and funeral in East Berlin in 1956 (having a fear of being interred alive, he had ordered that a stiletto be stabbed through his heart, which was done by one of the attending doctors, thereafter known as Mack the Knife). But Fuegi then added a final chapter: he described the subsequent lives of Brecht's friends and companions, and issued an impassioned plea for those forgotten coauthors to be publicly recognized. "It is, in my view, unconscionable (though it happens all the time) to stage [without correct attribution] *The Threepenny Opera* or *Happy End,* to name but two works for which Elisabeth Hauptmann is mainly responsible. If private property is an outmoded concept, as Brecht argued when accused of stealing in the 1920s, then why do we keep 'Brecht' as his and his heirs' private allotment garden?" This led Fuegi to a denunciation that was sincere but wholly unnecessary, since his point about Brecht's creative theft had been well made in the biography itself:

> Should people in future years still be asking the question, Where were the women dramatists of world rank in the first half of the twentieth century, point them under the mask of the brutal male "lover" Shui Ta, at the hidden face of the woman

who loves him despite his brutality, Shen Te in *The Good Woman of Setzuan*. Or, having heard the boasting of murderer, rapist, racist Mack the Knife, we can urge people to listen to words sung "in a different voice," the voices of Hauptman's Polly and Jenny as they dream of a tomorrow when women are recognized in their own right, no longer brutalized and silenced by Mackie and his kind.

Having taken off the stage masks that Steffin and Hauptmann and Berlau and Pohl all donned for reasons they knew best, we can look with new wonder at what they achieved despite living in one of the most brutal periods of human history. If they, in a deeply prejudiced world, could achieve so much, what might now be done?[16]

Such well-intended appeals for coauthor acknowledgment were, of course, turned down by the Brecht estate. Certainly they expressed the deeply felt views of a biographer who was striving to tell the truth as he saw it. But is it worth imposing a "political" agenda on the finale of a great biography, especially if the author has already made those points in his narrative?

Though I respect the purpose, it a dangerous tactic, especially in the immediate aftermath of a life, when the subject's legacy is unclear. Posterity and cultural interests are fickle, and an impassioned appeal in one era can seem silly in the next. Beware!

Peter Guralnick's otherwise excellent two-volume biography of Elvis Presley (1999) likewise suffers from a weak conclusion. "Long before he was laid in the grave," Guralnick wrote, "the legend of Elvis' success, the one trademark it was impossible for even the Colonel to register, had been retailed over and over again, but now it was overwhelmed in a flood of reminiscences that at first strove to deny the 'frail humanity' that bound him to the rest of the human race, then rushed to condemn him for it." (Guralnick is referring to Presley's dependence on drugs and alcohol.) "The cacophony of voices that have joined together to create a chorus of informed opinion, uninformed speculation, hagiography, symbolism, and blame, can be difficult at times to drown out," the biographer noted—but then permitted himself a personal tribute that, in a new millennium, sounds childishly sincere but defensive and off-key in a life of a singer who couldn't read music but had perfect pitch:

> It is the one voice that counts. It is the voice that the world first heard on those bright yellow 78s, whose original insignia, a crowing rooster surrounded by

boldly stylized sunbeams and a border of musical notes, sought to proclaim a new day. It is impossible to silence that voice; you cannot miss it when you listen to "That's All Right" or "Mystery Train" or "Blue Moon of Kentucky" or any of the songs with which Elvis continued to convey his sense of unlimited possibilities almost to the end of his life. It is that sense of aspiration as much as any historical signposts or goals that continues to communicate directly with a public that recognized in Elvis a kindred spirit from the first. That is what we have to remember. In the face of facts, for all that we have come to know, it is necessary to listen unprejudiced and unencumbered if we are to hear Elvis' message: the proclamation of emotions long suppressed, the embrace of a vulnerability culturally denied, the unabashed striving for freedom. Elvis Presley may have lost his way, but even in his darkest moments, he still retained some of the same innocent transparency that first defined the difference in the music and the man. More than most, he had an awareness of his limitations; his very faith was tested by his recognition of how far he had fallen from what he had set out to achieve—but for all of his doubt, for all of his disappointment, for all of the self-loathing that he

> frequently felt, and all of the disillusionment and
> fear, he continued to believe in a democratic ideal
> of redemptive transformation, he continued to seek
> out a connection with a public that embraced him
> not for what he was but for what he sought to be.[17]

"Redemptive transformation"? As a member of that very
public for half a century, I was not alone in finding such an
ending entirely unnecessary—especially as it was followed
by a final quotation from Presley himself, about "behav-
ing well" with strangers! "We were always considerate of
other people's feelings," Guralnick quotes his hero. As the
last words of one of the greatest rock-and-roll singers of
all time, they strike the feeblest of notes, musically and
biographically.

Better to keep a tight rein on authorial emotion, in order to allow the reader to make his or her own judgment;
this is the inevitable moral. If you have done your job
properly, you will have sewn into your story all that needs
to be said—save perhaps a mention of the survivors of
your tale.

Want an example of a perfectly modulated ending? Try
this: the postscript to Michael Holroyd's biography of the
English roué and portrait painter Augustus John, who died
in 1961. By the end of the decade, John's quasi-widow,

Dodo, his long-time, long-suffering companion and the Mona Lisa of his oeuvre, was aging; at the same time, Fryern Court, John's house near the South Coast, was decaying:

> Dry rot burrowed through the house; the large studio stood deserted, like an empty warehouse; brambles and nettles made the path to the old studio impenetrable. Vandals had broken in and covered the vast triptych of Sainte Sara with graffiti and explosions of paint. Under Dodo's orders, Romilly [John's son by a first marriage] laboured heroically in the garden among the wilderness of giant weeds. Yet even in disarray, a magic, like some sultry atmosphere, clung to the place. Kittens still nested in the matted stems of the clematis; the magnolias and yellow azaleas flowered with the same colours John had painted; the hammock still swung between the apple and the Judas tree; the faded brick, the long windows leading to cool dark rooms, the crazy paving inaccurately sprayed with weed-killer, the roses, the huge yew tree and, outgrowing everything, the mountainous rubbish dump: all were part of this magic.

On 19 December 1968 Dodo was eighty-seven. She had been getting visibly weaker and, to her consternation, able to do less. On the evening of 23 July 1969, Romilly found her fallen on the dining-room floor. He and Kathie [his wife] got her to bed, and she slept. Next morning when they went in she lay in the same position. She had died in her sleep.[18]

That, to me, is a beautifully symbolic ending to the life of a grand bohemian whose behavior had outraged polite society—but whose other son, Caspar, became an admiral in the Royal Navy!

Listening to the Lions

Richard Ellmann's life of James Joyce likewise ends with an account of the last years of Joyce's beloved wife, Nora. "Nora Joyce lived on in Zurich," Ellmann wrote, "often complaining, 'Things are very dull now. There was always something doing when he was about.' Someone asked her if she was Molly Bloom, and she replied, 'I'm not—she was much fatter.'" The "turbulence of her husband, and his keen pleasure in sounds, were her dominant recollections of him. She took visitors to the cemetery, which adjoins the zoological garden that he had compared to the one in the Phoenix Park, and said, 'My husband is buried there. He was awfully fond of the lions—I like to think of him lying there and listening to them roar.'"

Nora died in April 1951, of uremic poisoning. "She had not renounced Catholicism as thoroughly as her husband, and in her last years she occasionally went to church and prayer. When she was dying at the convent hospital she allowed a priest to be brought, and received the last rites. At her funeral a priest delivered, after the Swiss custom, a funeral speech at the grave, and described her as 'eine grosse Sünderin' ('a great sinner'). Few epithets could have been less apt," Ellmann commented. "She was buried in the same cemetery as Joyce but not next to him, for the space was already filled. The casualness of their lodgings in life was kept after death."

Listing the fates of their children, of Joyce's brother (who died on Bloomsday 1955), and of his sisters, Ellmann concluded:

> The surface of the life Joyce lived seemed always erratic and provisional. But its central meaning was directed as consciously as his work. The ingenuity with which he wrote his books was the same with which he forced the world to read them; the smiling affection he extended to Bloom and his

other principal characters was the same that he gave the members of his family; his disregard for bourgeois thrift and convention was the splendid extravagance which enabled him in literature to make an intractable wilderness into a new state. In whatever he did, his two profound interests—his family and his writings—kept their place. These passions never dwindled. The intensity of the first gave his work its sympathy and humanity; the intensity of the second raised his life to dignity and high dedication.[19]

Like the opening bars of your biography, the final cadences should be cut back until they express no more than is germane and necessary. In the above examples, we see a scrupulous author at work—one who preserves his sense of balance, humor, and exactitude, with a mix of distance and empathy that seems just right, but who does not himself step onto the stage.

If you wish, however, you are at liberty to take a walk-on role. Hermione Lee ended her biography of the novelist Edith Wharton with a personal visit to the house near Paris where Wharton died, the Pavillon Colombe, subsequently purchased by the Duc and Duchesse de Tallyrand. She then walked to the grave itself:

The cemetery is mixed: the guardian at the gate, who spoke no English, told me there were Protestants and Catholics and even "some Israelites" buried there. He looked Wharton up for me in his filing cabinet of old index cards, her entry hand-written in the same copperplate italic handwriting as the card written, ten years before hers, for Walter Berry [Wharton's closest friend]. Mme Wharton's details—married, divorced, "perpetuelle" resident in the graveyard, depth of body 1 m 50 cm—are given on the card, as well as her location. She is up the hill in a plain, rather ugly grave, with its carved motto, "O CRUX AVE SPES UNICA" ["O cross, hail to our only hope"], her two names, Edith Wharton and Edith Newbold Jones, her dates (in French) and no other detail. Another grave has been fitted in between hers and Walter Berry's. A cotoneaster had been planted in the earth frame around the stone, but the tomb was covered with weeds, old bottles and a very ancient pot of dead flowers. Clearly no one had been there for a long time. It struck me as an unvisited and lonely tomb, of a person who died without close relatives nearby to look after it, the casualty of a disputed will. There is no "Society for the Preservation of the Grave of Edith Wharton," as there undoubtedly would have been if she had been buried, like [her former husband] Teddy Wharton, in Lenox [Massachusetts]. It said something to me, in parting, about Edith Wharton's relationship to France: part "perpetuelle" inhabitant, part stranger in exile. She herself was a dedicated visitor and keeper-up of the graves of her loved ones and, as she said of herself, a very housekeeperish person. So this neglect seemed sad. In the rain, I weeded Edith, and planted a single white silk azalea, bought from the flower-shop at the cemetery gate. She would probably have been scornful about the artificial flower, but would, I felt, have been glad to have her grave tidied up.[20]

This sad, elegiac conclusion also ends our own journey through the various stages of composition in undertaking a biography—leading us to biography's sister genre: the biography of oneself.

III

Variations on a Theme

THIRTEEN

Autobiography and Memoirs

"It's a poor sort of memory that only works backwards,"
the Queen remarked.

—LEWIS CARROLL, *Through the Looking-Glass*

Among the many mansions of life-writing is the biography of oneself. Although we are, in this primer, mainly concerned with biography, biographers use autobiography as one of the most valuable ingredients or sources for a life-study. Looking at the genre of autobiography will, I hope, help you understand its purpose and praxis. And who knows? You may decide that you wish to write about yourself, rather than about somebody else.

To confuse us mightily, the words "autobiography" and

"*an* autobiography" mean two very different things. So first off, let's be clear.

As a generic term, "autobiography" encompasses everything written by an individual: from a book of memoirs to diaries, blogs, letters, and journals.

"An autobiography" refers, however, to a print biography of oneself, composed according to a formula developed over the past two hundred years. And to confuse us still further, an autobiography is markedly different from a person's memoirs.

Eyewitness to History

Let's start with memoirs, since these really began the business of self-depiction. From the ancient Greeks onward, memoirs—or *mémoires,* since the word was first coined, centuries later, in France—have been straightforward accounts by individuals, describing their life-experiences during particular eras of history. The accent is on their times, and on the way in which the memoirists did (or did not) influence them.

One of the first writers in this genre was the Greek general Xenophon, who had already written a superb biography of Cyrus the Younger but had his own personal story to tell. In 401 B.C. he had marched with Cyrus in the grand campaign to seize the throne of Persia, and had then helped to lead the famous Retreat of the Ten Thousand when Cyrus failed and was killed. Xenophon's memoirs, *Anabasis* or *The Persian Expedition,* written about thirty years later (circa 370 B.C.) and in the third person, became a classic in their own day. They still have the ring of lived experience in the face of death and the breakdown of an army's morale:

> Some people brought charges against Xenophon, alleging that they had been beaten by him and making the basis of their accusations that he had behaved in an overbearing manner. Xenophon asked the man who had spoken first to say where the incident had taken place. "It happened," he said, "in the place where we were dying of cold and where there was all that snow."
>
> "Well," said Xenophon, "when the weather was like you say it was, when our food was giving out and we had not even a smell of wine, when a lot of us were sinking under all our hardships and the enemy were following us up behind, if I really acted in an overbearing way, then I admit that I must have a more overbearing character than the donkey has; and they say that donkeys are so overbearing that they never get tired. . . .

But you all ought to hear what actually happened. It is worth listening to. A man was being left behind, because he could no longer go on marching. All I knew of the man was that he was one of us. I compelled you to carry him so that his life might be saved. . . . And did I not then come up to you again with the rearguard and find you digging a hole in order to bury the man? I stood by you, did I not, and commended you for it? Then, when we were standing by, the man drew in his leg and the people shouted that he was alive; but you said, 'He can be as much alive as he likes, I am not going to carry him.' It was at this point that I struck you, and you are quite right about that. It was because I had the impression that you looked as though you knew that the man was alive."

"What about it?" the man replied. "He died all the same, did he not, after I had shown him to you?"

"No doubt we shall all die," said Xenophon. "Is that any reason why we should all be buried alive?"

Then they all shouted the man down, saying that Xenophon had not beaten him half enough.[1]

Xenophon's memoirs are still one of the first prose works used in language classes in ancient Greek; they are famous for their simple, direct, clear style. So, too, are Julius Caesar's memoirs, *De Bello Gallico* (*The Gallic War*), written in Latin. From that literary foundation, memoirs by celebrated people became a distinctive narrative genre: personal reminiscences telling us of real people, places, and events as the authors remembered them.

"I am the son of a peasant; my father, my grandfather, my great-grandfather were all mere peasants," wrote Martin Luther in a version of his memoirs edited by the great French historian Jules Michelet in 1835 and translated into English the following year.

> My father went to Mansfeldt, and became a miner there. It was there I was born. That I was afterwards to become bachelor of arts, doctor of divinity, and what not, was assuredly not written in the stars, at least, not to ordinary readers. How I astonished everybody when I turned monk! And again, when I exchanged the brown cap for another. These things greatly vexed my father—nay made him quite ill for a time. After that I got pulling the pope about by the hair of his head; I married a runaway nun; I had children by her. Who saw these things in the stars? Who would have told anyone beforehand they were to happen?[2]

Such memoirs were straightforward to write, provided the author followed certain narrative conventions—as Robert Graves clearly recognized. Like a rich fruitcake, they had to be filled with interesting characters, confrontations, experiences, and events, in order to keep general readers entertained. And informed: until the advent of modern journalism, with its paid foreign correspondents and professional reportage, memoirs offered readers vital clues to what had really happened in the recent past, filtered (and often embellished) through the eyes of the writer. Consider this passage in which Thomas Jefferson recalls his days as American representative to the court of King Louis XVI, and describes his memories of the French Revolution and Marie Antoinette:

> The king was still at Marly. Nobody was permitted to approach him but friends. He was assailed by falsehoods in all shapes. He was made to believe that the Commons were about to absolve the army from their oath of fidelity to him, and to raise their pay. The court party were now all rage and desperation. . . . I was quite alarmed at this state of things. . . .
>
> The king was now become a passive machine in the hands of the National Assembly, and had he

been left to himself, he would have willingly acqui-
esced in whatever they should devise as best for
the nation. A wise constitution would have been
formed, hereditary in his line, himself placed at its
head, with powers so large as to enable him to do all
the good of his station, and so limited as to restrain
him from its abuse. This he would have faithfully ad-
ministered, and more than this I do not believe he
ever wished. But he had a queen of absolute sway
over his weak mind, and timid virtue; and of a character the reverse of his in all points. This angel,
as gaudily painted in the rhapsodies of the Rhetor
Burke, with some smartness of fancy, but no sound
sense, was proud, disdainful of restraint, indignant
at all obstacles to her will, eager in the pursuit of
pleasure, and firm enough to hold to her desires, or
perish in their wreck. Her inordinate gambling and
dissipations, with those of the Count d'Artois and
others of her clique, had been a sensible item in the
exhaustion of the treasury, which called into action
the reforming hand of the nation; and her opposition to it, her inflexible perverseness, and dauntless
spirit, led herself to the Guillotine, & drew the king
on with her, and plunged the world into crimes &

> calamities which will forever stain the pages of mod-
> ern history. I have ever believed that had there been
> no queen, there would have been no revolution.[3]

Was Jefferson fair to Marie-Antoinette? At all events he was *there,* in Paris and Versailles, at the time. The memoirs of warriors, diplomats, travelers, and adventurers were unashamedly subjective—an antidote as well as a complement to the history written by historians.

As memoirs became more popular, their authors (and publishers) sought to exploit growing public curiosity in an age of increasing literacy. One of the best-selling books of reminiscences of the early nineteenth century was the *Memoirs of Harriette Wilson,* which began with an opening sentence as memorable, in its challenging way, as Jane Austen's had been a dozen years earlier. "I shall not say why and how I became, at the age of fifteen, the mistress of the Earl of Craven."

Wilson continued with equal high-handedness: "Whether it was love, or the severity of my father, the depravity of my heart, or the winning arts of the noble Lord, which induced me to leave my paternal roof and place myself under his protection, does not now signify: or if it does, I am not in the humour to gratify curiosity in this matter."[4] Thereupon Miss Wilson, née Dubochet, proceeded to tell a story of paid strumpetry that so terrified the gentry of her time that large sums of money were handed over to her by people who desperately wanted to be *omitted* from her memoirs. (The average was two hundred pounds.) Many aristocrats were said to have paid up—though not the Duke of Wellington, who famously scrawled "Publish, and be damned" in red ink when returning her blackmail letter.

Wellington's refusal to pay spurred Harriette to write a vengeful account of the duke's return from Spain. It was, she wrote, "such a pity that [the Duke of] Argyle got to my house first. . . . My tender swain Wellington stood in the gutter at two in the morning, pouring forth his amorous wishes in the pouring rain, in strains replete with heart-rending grief." She also wrote that Wellington was a bore both in bed and out, and that, when wearing his "broad red ribbon," he looked "very much like a rat catcher."[5]

Though spiteful, Harriette's memoirs were certainly witty, and had the ring of truth about them. In his diary, Sir Walter Scott noted that "she has some good retailing of conversations, in which the style of the speaker, so far as is known to me, is exactly imitated."[6] Most important was the fact that, in terms of cultural history, her memoirs fanned a popular interest in reminiscences as *gossip* rather than history. Harriette's chief rival as arch-courtesan of

England, Julia Johnstone, immediately published her coun-ter-memoirs, *The True Confessions of Julia Johnstone, Written by Herself, in Contradiction to the Fables of Harriette Wilson*. Jealous and mean-spirited, they bombed.

In other words, the wheels of popular memoirs were oiled by irony, spice, and humor—crucial ingredients that made the books enjoyable as well as informative. Mark Twain, in his memoirs, attributed his "way" with facts to his dear mother:

> Any person who is familiar with me knows how to strike my average, and therefore knows how to get at the jewel of any fact of mine and dig it out of its blue-clay matrix. My mother knew that art. When I was seven or eight, or ten, or twelve years old—along there—a neighbor said to her,
>
> "Do you believe anything that that boy says?"
>
> My mother said, "He is the well-spring of truth, but you can't bring up the whole well with one bucket"—and she added, "I know his average, there-fore he never deceives me. I discount him thirty per cent. for embroidery, and what is left is priceless truth, without a flaw in it anywhere."[7]

As every popular memoirist knew, the best gossip re-lated to celebrities. Gertrude Stein, an expatriate in Paris, collected modernist paintings in the early years of the twentieth century. By the 1930s she was able to translate them into a literary goldmine, setting them out in the form of a personalized art gallery on paper—not only using Xenophon's third person, but appropriating the invented voice of her American companion, Alice B. Toklas:

> I went to see Mrs. Stein who had in the meantime returned to Paris, and there at her house I met Gertrude Stein. I was impressed by the coral brooch she wore and by her voice. I may say that only three times in my life have I met a genius and each time a bell within me rang and I was not mistaken, and I may say in each case it was before there was any recognition of the quality of genius in them. The three geniuses of whom I wish to speak are Gertrude Stein, Pablo Picasso and Alfred Whitehead. . . .
>
> At that time there was [on the walls of Stein's atelier] a great deal of Matisse, Picasso, Renoir, Cézanne but there were also a great many other things. There were two Gauguins, there were Manguins, there was a big nude by Valloton that felt like only it was not like the Odalisque of Manet, there was a Toulouse-Lautrec. Once about this time Picasso looking at this and greatly daring said, but all the same I do paint better than he did. Toulouse-

Lautrec had been the most important of his early influences. I later bought a little tiny picture by Picasso of that epoch. There was a portrait of Gertrude Stein by Valloton that might have been a David but was not, there was a Maurice Denis, a little Daumier, many Cézanne water colours, there was in short everything, there was even a little Delacroix and a moderate sized Greco. There were enormous Picassos of the Harlequin period, there were two rows of Matisses, there was a big portrait of a woman by Cézanne and some little Cézannes, all these pictures had a history and I will soon tell them.[8]

Name dropping, in other words, guarantees the memoirist immortality-by-association, an aspect the arch-comedian Spike Milligan later immortalized in his memoirs, entitled *Hitler: My Part in His Downfall.*

Despite their inevitably boastful, self-advertising character, memoirs still have historical, evidentiary value—and are straightforward to narrate. In fact, if you don't have time to pen your memoirs yourself, or feel you lack the writing skills necessary for extended narrative, you may employ the services of a ghostwriter as coauthor—a practice which readers will find perfectly understandable. It is the eyewitness account they want, rather than a literary masterpiece.

Memoirs may be manipulated and selective, especially in an individual's old age, but they remain, after all, a record of the author's personal window onto a particular era. Amusing, informative, possibly deceitful, often self-deceiving, memoirs are extended self-portraits that, whether pompous or humble, reflect the time in which they are composed—even when they do not shed much light on their author's own character.

If you wish to write your memoirs, then, *enjoy* the telling! Marshal the same elements of composition that we've rehearsed in previous chapters, and you will hopefully satisfy the reader's curiosity. You'll also make a small but lasting contribution to the way future historians will look at us.

What, though, of that other kind of autobiography we call *"an* autobiography"—a work not of straight memoirs or reminiscences, but of intimate, revealing, public self-exploration?

Autobiography as Confession

Saint Augustine is the patron saint of autobiography as confession. "In the meantime, during my sixteenth year, the narrow means of my family obliged me to leave school and live idly at home with my parents," Augustine wrote in his *Confessions* (397 A.D.). "The brambles of lust grew high above my head and there was no one to root them out, certainly not my father."

Augustine's biography of himself took the form of an extended apologia to God. He was not above telling God about his first erection:

> One day at the public baths he [Augustine's father] saw the active signs of fresh virility coming to life in me and this was enough to make him relish the thought of having grandchildren. He was happy to tell my mother about it, for his happiness was due to the intoxication which causes the world to forget you, its Creator, and to love the things you have created instead of loving you, because the world is drunk with the invisible wine of its own perverted, earthbound will. But in my mother's heart you had already begun to build your temple and laid the foundations of your holy dwelling, while my father was still a catechumen and a new one at that. So, in her piety, she became alarmed and apprehensive, and although I had not yet been baptized, she began to dread that I might follow in the crooked path of

those who do not keep their eyes on you but turn their backs instead.

How presumptuous it was of me to say that you were silent, my God, when I drifted farther and farther away from you! Can it be true that you said nothing to me at that time? Surely the words which rang in my ears, spoken by your faithful servant, my mother, could have come from none but you? Yet none of them sank into my heart to make me do as you said. I well remember what her wishes were and how she most earnestly warned me not to commit fornication and above all not to seduce any man's wife. It all seemed womanish advice to me and I should have blushed to accept it. Yet the words were yours, though I did not know it. I thought that you were silent and that she was speaking, but all the while you were speaking to me through her, and when I disregarded her, your handmaid, I was disregarding you, though I was both her son and your servant. But I did this unawares and continued headlong on my way. I was so blinded to the truth that among my companions I was ashamed to be less dissolute than they were. For I heard them bragging of their depravity, and the greater the sin the more they gloried in it, so that I took pleasure in the same vices not only for the enjoyment of what I did, but also for the applause I won.[9]

For centuries, Christian followers modeled themselves on Saint Augustine's relentlessly honest self-examination and his redeeming shame. Margery Kempe's confessions, for example, attested to a similar power of confession, and the need to expose the temptations of Satan. Dictating them to a monk (who recounted her confession in the third person) a thousand years after Augustine, Margery was completely candid in telling about the forbidden fruit that had lured her:

In the second year of her temptations it so happened that a man whom she liked said to her on St Margaret's Eve before evensong that, for anything, he would sleep with her and enjoy the lust of his body, and she should not withstand him, for if he might not have his desire that time, he said, he would have it another time instead—she should not choose. And he did it to test what she would do, but she imagined that he meant it in earnest and said very little in reply. So they parted then and both went to hear evensong, for her church was dedicated to St Margaret. This woman was so troubled with the man's words that she could not listen to evensong, not say her paternoster, nor think any other good thought, but was more troubled than she ever was before. . . .

She lay beside her husband, and to have intercourse with him was so abominable to her that she could not bear it, and yet it was permissible and at a rightful time if she had wished it. But all the time she was tormented to sin with the other man because he had spoken to her. At last—through the importunings of temptation, and a lack of discretion—she was overcome and consented in her mind, and went to the man to know if he would then consent to have her. And he said he would not for all the wealth in this world; he would rather be chopped up as small as meat for the pot.[10]

Margery's confessions are considered the earliest surviving autobiography in English by a woman—though they were considered too scandalous to be printed in her own time, indeed for centuries afterward. (They were finally published in 1933.) In the meantime, the book that inaugurated modern autobiographies, as distinct from a person's memoirs, was Rousseau's *Confessions,* written in the late

1760s—confessions that were also considered too scandalous for publication, despite having been written by a man.

Rousseau's patron, Madame d'Epinay, was so shocked when Rousseau read from his manuscript that she sought a police ban. Yet in the 1770s and 1780s, in a world being turned upside down by revolutionary movements, it was inevitable that Rousseau's autobiography would eventually see the light of day—particularly in parts of Europe where the clergy were abhorred.

Rousseau's self-portrait was deliberately and proudly a *secular* document. It grappled with sexual sin, but its objective was absolute truth-telling about the self, for the self. It was intended to win favor not with God but with the *reader,* as validation of the author's self. "If there is one circumstance in my life which well describes my character, it is that which I am about to relate," Rousseau wrote, eschewing any "false feeling of delicacy" which would prevent him from fulfilling the truth-telling "purpose of my book":

> Whoever you may be, who desire to know the inmost heart of a man, have the courage to read the next two or three pages; you will become thoroughly acquainted with Jean-Jacques Rousseau.
>
> I entered the room of a courtesan as if it had

been the sanctuary of love and beauty; in her person I thought I beheld its divinity. I should never have believed that, without respect and esteem, I could have experienced the emotions with which she inspired me. No sooner had I recognized, in the preliminary familiarities, the value of her charms and caresses than, for fear of losing the fruit of them in advance, I was anxious to make haste and pluck it. Suddenly, in place of the flames which consumed me, I felt a deathly chill run through my veins; my legs trembled under me; and feeling ready to faint, I sat down and cried.

Who would guess the reason of my tears, and the thoughts that passed through my head at that moment?[11]

Ruthless psychological self-examination now characterized the genre. Such an approach no longer consisted of self-satisfied memoirs written in old age. It was a rigorous, bracing, self-analytical *investigation:* a forensic journey into the past, in a determination to locate and share, openly, the absolute truth about oneself, so that by confronting it with humility, honesty, courage, and humanity, one might free oneself of the endless filters and extirpations of religion.

From 1782, then, although a work *of* autobiography remained the correct way of describing, generally, any text written from the vantage point of the author's own life, *"an* autobiography" became a new, mostly secular genre in its own right. Consider, for example, the autobiography written by the runaway slave Frederick Douglass sixty-three years later, in 1845:

> Just at this point of my progress, Mr. Auld found out what was going on, and at once forbade Mrs. Auld to instruct me further, telling her, among other things, that it was unlawful, as well as unsafe, to teach a slave to read. To use his own words, further, he said, "If you give a nigger an inch, he will take an ell. A nigger should know nothing but to obey his master—to do as he is told to do. Learning would *spoil* the best nigger in the world. Now," said he, "if you teach that nigger (speaking of myself) how to read, there would be no keeping him. It would forever unfit him to be a slave. He would at once become unmanageable, and of no value to his master. As to himself, it could do him no good, but a great deal of harm. It would make him discontented and unhappy." These words sank deep into my heart, stirred up sentiments within that lay slumbering, and called into existence an entirely new train of

thought. It was a new and special revelation, explaining dark and mysterious things, with which my youthful understanding had struggled, but struggled in vain. I now understood what had been to me a most perplexing difficulty—to wit, the white man's power to enslave the black man. It was a grand achievement, and I prized it highly. From that moment, I understood the pathway from slavery to freedom. . . .

Though conscious of the difficulty of learning without a teacher, I set out with high hope, and a fixed purpose, at whatever cost of trouble, to learn how to read. The very decided manner with which he spoke, and strove to impress his wife with the evil consequences of giving me instruction, served to convince me that he was deeply sensible of the truths he was uttering. It gave me the best assurance that I might rely with the utmost confidence on the results which, he said, would flow from teaching me to read. What he most dreaded, that I most desired. What he most loved, that I most hated. That which to him was a great evil, to be carefully shunned, was to me a great good, to be diligently sought; and the argument which he so warmly urged, against my learning to read, only served to inspire me with a desire and determination to learn. In learning to read, I owe almost as much to the bitter opposition of my master, as to the kindly aid of my mistress. I acknowledge the benefit of both.[12]

Anxious not to be caught and returned to his former owner, Douglass sailed, on the advice of friends, to Scotland, while his protectors sought to release him from his legal bondage as a slave in the American South. Moreover, to differentiate between true faith and religion used as a means to enslave others, Douglass added a profoundly felt coda, or appendix:

What I have said respecting and against religion, I mean strictly to apply to the *slaveholding religion* of this land, and with no possible reference to Christianity proper; for, between the Christianity of this land, and the Christianity of Christ, I recognize the widest possible difference—so wide, that to receive the one as good, pure, and holy, is of necessity to reject the other as bad, corrupt, and wicked. To be the friend of the one, is of necessity to be the enemy of the other. I love the pure, peaceable, and impartial Christianity of Christ: I therefore hate the corrupt, slaveholding, women-whipping, cradle-plundering,

partial and hypocritical Christianity of this land. Indeed, I can see no reason, but the most deceitful
one, for calling the religion of this land Christianity.
I look upon it as the climax of all misnomers, the
boldest of all frauds, and the grossest of all libels.[13]

Passionate, demanding, denunciatory, self-analytical: "autobiographies" now differed from people's "memoirs," as
their authors challenged themselves and the world to be
honest about their own lives, and those around them—
even their own families.

A century after Douglass, the diary of a Jewish victim
of the Holocaust was published as *The Autobiography of
Anne Frank*. Comprising Anne's mock-letters to a fictional
friend ("Kitty"), written in hiding in the secret back-rooms
of her father's spice warehouse on the Prinsengracht in
German-occupied Amsterdam during World War II, the
book does not have the usual form of an autobiography.
Yet Anne Frank's constant questioning of herself and others goes to the heart of what had, since Rousseau, been
deemed *an* autobiography. Here are her last recorded
words, at the age of sixteen:

One of the many questions that have often bothered
me is why women have been, and still are, thought

to be so inferior to men. It's easy to say it's unfair, but that's not enough for me; I'd really like to know the reason for this injustice!

Men presumably dominated women from the very beginning because of their greater strength; it's men who earn a living, beget children and do as they please. . . . Until recently, women silently went along with this, which was stupid, since the longer it's kept up, the more deeply entrenched it becomes. Fortunately, education, work and progress have opened women's eyes. In many countries they've been granted equal rights; many people, mainly women, but also men, now realize how wrong it was to tolerate this state of affairs for so long. Modern women want the right to be completely independent! . . .

As I've told you many times, I'm split in two. One side contains my exuberant cheerfulness, my flippancy, my joy in life and, above all, my ability to appreciate the lighter side of things. By that I mean not finding anything wrong with flirtations, a kiss, an embrace, a saucy joke. This side of me is usually lying in wait to ambush the other one, which is much purer, deeper, finer. . . . So the nice Anne is never seen in company. She's never made a single appearance, though she almost always takes the stage when I'm alone. I know exactly how I'd like to be, how I am . . . on the inside. But unfortunately I'm only like that with myself. And perhaps that's why— no, I'm sure that's the reason why—I think of myself as happy on the inside and other people think I'm happy on the outside. I'm guided by the pure Anne within, but on the outside I'm nothing but a frolicsome little goat tugging at its tether.[14]

An autobiography, then, is the relentless record and attempted examination of one's own life: a quest for mental freedom through truthfulness. To write a true autobiography, in the Rousseauian sense, you will not be able to use a ghostwriter. The work, the passion as well as the self-exposure, must be done by you alone—and for this you will need great courage and storytelling skills. To qualify for the designation "autobiographer," you must publicly *question* life—your own. It is not, repeat *not*, simple. Indeed, it is probably the most challenging, bar *none*, of all biographical undertakings. For this reason I urge you to think twice before embarking on such a venture.

There are, however, alternatives—as we shall see in the next chapter.

FOURTEEN

Memoir

The mischievous consequences of vice and folly, of irregular desires and predominant passions, are best discovered
by those relations which are levelled with the general sur-
face of life, which tells not how any man became great,
but how he was made happy; not how he lost the favour of
his prince, but how he became discontented with himself.
Those relations are therefore commonly of most value in
which the writer tells his own story.

—SAMUEL JOHNSON,
The Idler, 84 (November 24, 1759)

*I*n 1929, short of money, and with his domestic life
in chaos owing to a failing *ménage à quatre,* Robert Graves
suffered yet another blow. His American mistress, Laura

Riding, threw herself out of a fourth-floor window in Hammersmith, London, after bidding good-bye to the other members of the menagerie (Graves's wife, Nancy, and Laura's other lover, Geoffrey Phibbs). Graves followed her from a window on the floor below.

Laura Reichenthal (her real name) almost died from her fall, and required months of hospitalization and back surgery; Graves, miraculously, was only bruised. Beset by guilt at having in part caused Riding's suicide attempt, he decided to pull himself together, get divorced, and take her abroad, if she survived. Thereafter he would, he was determined, devote his life to Laura—his White Goddess, or muse.

To earn the money for this adventure, Graves dictated to a stenographer in six weeks not only the course of his brief life (he was still only thirty-four) but one of the most evocative personal narratives of World War I, as seen from the trenches rather than from the chancellories of Europe or châteaux of the generals. Composed in a relentless, staccato, machine-gun style, his memoirs never flagged, or showed pain. The Grim Reaper reaped in Flanders' fields— Graves recounting the experience as if in shell shock, a decade later. (In 1917 he had, in fact, accompanied Siegfried Sassoon to hospital for shell shock at Craiglockhart, in Scotland, where the great World War I poet, Wilfred

Owen, was under the care of the psychiatrist Dr. William Rivers.) Into this heady war-brew Graves threw everything, heedless of the effect until the work was finished, when he realized it was—like Xenophon's *Persian Expedition*— unique.

Was *Good-bye to All That* a young veteran's precocious memoirs—or a true autobiography?

Good-bye to All That certainly painted a human life (Graves's own) with uncompromising realism and apparent honesty—so much so that his mother, ashamed, cut him out of her will. What the "autobiography" did *not* do, however, was tell the true story of the breakdown of his marriage, and the events leading up to the dictation of the book: a story that was far too private—and scandalous in 1929—to reveal. Graves had poured his energy, hurt, shame, guilt, and rage into a work that was part autobiography, part blistering memoirs: a sort of manifesto exposing the callous inhumanity of war and the behavior of the people around him—from the boy he loved (platonically) at boarding school, before the war, to the officers and men he served with in the Royal Welch Fusiliers. Stunned readers in 1929 could only puzzle, however, over the strange "Dedicatory Epilogue," in which Graves publicly addressed his American mistress, without naming her. The book had been written, he publicly declared, not from the point of view of a person looking back across his life in order to look forward to more of the same, but from the opposite perspective. He was, he asserted, writing "against myself." Laura, by contrast, was someone "living invisibly, against kind, as dead, beyond event"—and he apologized abjectly to her for not including her in the tome.[1]

Graves's parents were shocked by the savage tone of the work; but, knowing the scandalous domestic circumstances, they were relieved that at least Robert hadn't, in the manner of Saint Augustine or Jean-Jacques Rousseau, hung out the dirtiest of his linen to sully the family honor. His "Dedicatory Epilogue," with its byzantine circumlocutions in opposition to the brilliantly clear narrative of the book itself, was an act of filial mercy. At the end of the epilogue's obscure narrative, recording how he'd traveled to Ireland and then Huntingdonshire and sipped wine with the writer David Garnett (in fact, he had gone to try to persuade Geoffrey Phibbs to return to Riding's bed, or be killed) Graves had ended with the (for him) sacred date: April 27, 1929, which signified, in his *Lebenslauf*, "a fourth-storey window and a stone area and you were dying. . . . After which, anecdotes fail."[2]

What this mumbo-jumbo really meant was beyond the capacity of most readers at the time to divine—and was in any case removed from later editions of the book, once

Graves's quasi-marriage to Laura Riding fell apart, in America. Laura married the writer Schyler Jackson in 1941; Graves returned to England, where he ultimately became professor of poetry at Oxford. The actual meaning of the title *Good-bye to All That* was not revealed until his nephew Richard Perceval Graves wrote his biography at the end of the century, long after the poet's death.[3]

The moral is that a true autobiography—rather than a person's merely truthful memoirs—is the hardest thing of all to do in the biographical arena. So long as you're recounting your life course in terms of the people and places you've known, as well as depicting your times, you're simply doing your job as a writer of your memoirs. It's when the spotlight falls on you, the author, and your actual self, that the trouble starts. How can you genuinely lay out your whole life—the truth about your whole life—to public view, voyeuristic interest, and possible condemnation? Rousseau had done it—but Rousseau was a genius, and in any case his *Confessions* were published only after his death.

Since Rousseau, there have been very few great autobiographies. Nevertheless, in the shadow of the classical form of memoirs—books recording, for example, the lives of retired celebrities, from princes to politicians, actresses to artists—there had always been an off-limits area, even a current of subversion: a barely controlled authorial desire to tell not just the stories the public supposedly wanted, or was allowed to hear, as glorified name-dropping, but the *true* stories of one's life—especially where they concerned unconventional, unmentionable, sometimes illegal matters, from sexual preference to drug use.

By the second half of the twentieth century, then, with the approaching end of censorship and with battles raging over civil rights, gay rights, decolonization, and feminism, a need arose for a new genre that would go beyond conventional reminiscences and people's memoirs. World War II—which affected civilians as well as soldiers—had opened the floodgates to reminiscences of war in all theaters and in all dimensions: the air war, submarine warfare, war on the high seas, war on land, war on the home front, including Blitzkrieg and Blitz, POW camps and concentration camps. Class distinctions had been erased by Nazis and Communists as a feature of their ideologies, but in the Western democratic nations, too, there had been a sea change in the structure of social, racial, and gender relations—raising profound and unsettling questions of identity and self amid the deluge of people's reminiscences. The result was the gradual development of a hybrid form that would combine elements both of people's memoirs and of autobiography: the "memoir"—singular.

The New Genre

Let's look at some examples of this hybrid form—beginning with Brendan Behan's famous memoir, *Borstal Boy*, published in 1959.

Behan's account of the three years he spent in a prison for young offenders, following his arrest in Liverpool in 1939 for possession of explosives in an IRA bombing campaign, typified the genre that was beginning to emerge: not an autobiography of a whole life, but the record of a discrete part of it, told as a challenge both to oneself, in terms of truth-telling, and to the world, in terms of a larger political or quasi-political agenda. The personal was, in this way, licensed to become political.

Friday, in the evening, the landlady shouted up the stairs:

"Oh, God, oh Jesus, oh Sacred Heart. Boy, there's two gentlemen to see you."

I knew by the screeches of her that these gentlemen were not calling to enquire after my health, or to know if I'd had a good trip. I grabbed my suitcase, containing Pot. Chlor, Sulph Ac, gelignite, detonators, electrical and ignition, and the rest of my

Sinn Fein conjuror's outfit, and carried it to the window. Then the gentlemen arrived.

A young one, with a blonde, Herrenvolk head and a BBC accent shouted, "I say, greb him, the bestud."

When I was safely grabbed, the blonde one gave me several punches in the face, though not very damaging ones. An older man, in heavy Lancashire speech, told him to leave me alone, and to stop making an —— of himself. . . . There were now two or three others in the room, and this old man was the sergeant and in charge of the raid.[4]

In 1942, soon after his release, Behan was again arrested, for the attempted murder of two English detectives; he was granted amnesty in 1945. Thereafter the former terrorist turned to a different stage, becoming one of the foremost playwrights of his generation. But he was unable to overcome his addiction to alcohol. Never one to ask for sympathy, he characterized himself as a "drunk with a writing problem." He died at forty-one. His last words, spoken to the Catholic nun wiping his brow, were: "Ah, bless you, Sister, may your sons all be bishops."[5]

Humor, struggle, survival, passion, vivid recall: the new

genre offered a platform for brief, touching narratives of real life and real people—novellas in contrast to novels— but also, at its most exalted level, a chance to do even more: to change the world at least a little, by exposing injustice or suffering, or the real truth about institutions or people or pursuits, through the very act of self-exposure. No footnotes or sources were required, for this was personal witness: lived, experienced, artfully narrated.

It was not only in the political and cultural realm of protest that the new genre of short, novella-like memoir scored. In science, too, the focus on telling the raw truth about a specific moment or period in one's life held especial promise. The memoirist was newly licensed to peel away layers of taboo and politeness in the cause of political, social, cultural, and scientific honesty.

James Watson's discovery, with Francis Crick, of the double helical structure of DNA, in 1953, had led the way to deciphering the genetic code. Written over several years in the 1960s, Watson's memoir, *The Double Helix,* was turned down by the press at Watson's own university for being, unfortunately, *too* truthful.

Watson's nickname in the biochemical scientific community was "Honest Jim," since the young researcher never stood on ceremony. "I have never seen Francis Crick in a modest mood," he famously opened his story. "Perhaps in other company he is that way, but I have never had reason so to judge him."

Crick was certainly a character. "On two occasions the corridor outside his office was flooded with water pouring out of a laboratory in which Crick was working. Francis, with his interest in theory, had neglected to fasten securely the rubber tubing around his suction pump," Watson related.

> At the time of my arrival, Francis's theories spread far beyond the confines of protein crystallography. Anything important would attract him, and he frequently visited other labs to see which new experiments had been done. . . . The quick manner in which he seized their facts and tried to reduce them to coherent patterns frequently made his friends' stomachs sink with the apprehension that, all too often in the near future, he would succeed, and expose to the world the fuzziness of minds hidden from direct view by the considerate, well-spoken manners of the Cambridge colleges.

If Watson failed to kowtow to convention in describing his fellow scientists, he was even more candid about himself. "My doodling of the [molecule] bases on paper at first got

nowhere . . . and I fell asleep hoping that an undergradu-
ate party the next afternoon at Downing [College] would
be full of pretty girls. But my expectations," he recalled
frankly, "were dashed as soon as I arrived to spot a group
of healthy hockey players and several pallid debutantes."

Not until the middle of the next week, however, did
a non-trivial idea emerge. It came while I was drawing the used rings of adenine on paper. Suddenly I
realized the potentially profound implications of a
DNA structure in which the adenine residue formed
hydrogen bonds similar to those found in crystals of
pure adenine. If DNA was like this, each adenine
residue would form two hydrogen bonds to an adenine residue related to it by a 180-degree rotation.
. . . Despite the messy backbone, my pulse began
to race. If this was DNA, I should create a bomb-
shell [at age twenty-four] by announcing its discovery. The existence of two intertwined chains with
identical base sequences could not be a chance matter. Instead it would strongly suggest that one chain
in each molecule had at some earlier stage served as
the template for the synthesis of the other chain.
Under this scheme, gene replication starts with the
separation of its two identical chains. . . . For over

two hours I happily lay awake with pairs of adenine residues whirling in front of my closed eyes. Only for a brief moment did the fear shoot through me that an idea this good could be wrong.[6]

The race to reveal the secret of human replication was moving toward its climax.

Sir Peter Medawar, a Nobel Prize winner, welcomed Watson's account after it was published in New York, pointing out that Watson had, for posterity, recorded his personal witness to the "greatest achievement of science in the twentieth century."

> A good many people will read *The Double Helix* for the insight they hope it will bring them into the nature of the creative process in science. It may indeed become a standard case history of the so-called "hypothetic-deductive" method at work. Hypothesis and inference, feedback and modified hypothesis, the rapid alternation of imaginative critical episodes of thought—here it can all be seen in motion, and every scientist will recognize the same intellectual structure in the research he does himself. . . . No layman who reads this book with any kind of understanding will ever again think of the scientist as a

man who cranks a machine of discovery. No beginner in science will henceforth believe that discovery is bound to come his way if only he practices a certain Method, goes through a certain well-defined performance of hand and mind.[7]

Another Nobel Prize winner, André Lwoff, defended Watson's controversial candor. The memoir was embarrassingly personal for a scientist, yes—but Watson's "taste for scandal, although revealing, is certainly not the main characteristic of this dedicated scientist," Lwoff declared. "His most profound motivation was, and still is, his fascination with life and its secrets."[8]

The book became a worldwide sensation—changing forever, as Medawar had predicted, the way people saw the process of scientific discovery.

Contested and argued over, the hybrid combination of ruthless autobiographical self-depiction and reminiscences was being born as "a memoir," and swiftly took root in the burgeoning Western world of the 1960s, where privacy was being discarded like old clothes. The year after Watson's memoir appeared, another memoir was published that was destined to become equally classic: Maya Angelou's *I Know Why The Caged Bird Sings*.

"Even if Mother hadn't been such a pretty woman,

light-skinned with straight hair, he was lucky to get her, and he knew it," Angelou wrote of her mother's boyfriend, Mr. Freeman. "She was educated, from a well-known family. After all, wasn't she born in St. Louis?"

> She laughed all the time and made jokes. He was grateful. I think he must have been many years older than she, but if not, he still had the sluggish inferiority of old men married to younger women. He watched her every move and when she left the room, his eyes allowed her reluctantly to go. . . .
>
> Because of the need for stability, children easily become creatures of habit. After the third time in Mother's bed, I thought there was nothing strange about sleeping there. . . .
>
> Mother usually brought milk when she came in, but that morning as Baily [Angelou's brother] and I straightened the living room her bedroom door had been open, and we knew that she hadn't come home the night before.
>
> He gave me money and I rushed to the store and back to the house. After putting the milk in the icebox, I turned and had just reached the front door when I heard, "Ritie, come here." I didn't think about the holding time [when she had been forced

to hold Freemen's penis, in bed] until I got close to him. His pants were open and his "thing" was standing out of his britches by itself.

"No, sir, Mr. Freeman." I started to back away. I didn't want to touch that mushy-hard thing again, and I didn't need him to hold me anymore. He grabbed my arm and pulled me between his legs. His face was still and looked kind, but he didn't smile or blink his eyes. Nothing. He did nothing, except reach his left hand around to turn on the radio without even looking at it. Over the noise of the music and static, he said, "Now, this ain't gonna hurt you much. You liked it before, didn't you?"[9]

Angelou's rape at the age of eight—and the subsequent murder of Mr. Freeman by her uncles—was only one of many childhood afflictions she recounted. Pregnant by sixteen, she became a singer, dancer, brothel madam, cook, drug user, prostitute, and finally one of the foremost black writers and poets of her generation. Her reputation, like Watson's, was established by her extraordinarily candid memoir.

Scientific discovery in the face of obstinate older colleagues, success despite childhood sexual abuse—soon, oppressions of every kind were being retailed. When these were combined with stories of the author's survival, they offered beacons of hope for others.

Political oppression was one such theme. "Several days later [after ending a hunger strike] a warder came to fetch me," wrote Anatoly Marchenko in his memoir of political protest in Soviet Russia, *My Testimony*, published in the West in 1969, the same year as Angelou's memoir. "He led me via a staircase and various corridors to the first floor and directed me through a door lined with black oilcloth. A little nameplate said: 'Prison Governor.'"

> In the office inside sat the prison governor at his desk, beneath a large portrait of Dzerzhinsky [founder of the Cheka, the Bolshevik secret police]; on the couch were two men familiar to me from the investigation of my case, the legal inspector of prisons and the head of the investigation department. The fourth man was a stranger. One glance at him and I shuddered, so unnatural and repulsive was his appearance: a tiny little eggshaped body, minuscule legs that barely reached to the floor, and the thinnest scraggy little neck crowned by an enormous flattened globe: his head. The slits of his eyes, the barely discernible little nose and the thin smiling

mouth were sunk in a sea of taut, yellow, gleaming, dough. How could that neck hold such a load?

They told me that this was the Deputy Public Prosecutor of the Turkmen Republic, and invited me to sit down. The conversation was conducted in an informal and familiar tone. They asked me how I felt and whether I had ended my hunger strike. Thanking them for their touching delicacy and interest I informed them that it was ended and asked in turn: "Can you tell me, please, when and where I will be sent?"

"You are going to a Komsomol site. You'll be a Komsomol worker," answered the monster, absolutely wreathed in smiles as he enjoyed his little joke.[10]

Marchenko—who died in a Soviet prison in 1986, almost twenty years later, as the result of yet another hunger strike for the release of political prisoners—exemplified personal political courage in the face of tyranny. Indeed, intellectual, psychological, political, and sheer human *courage* were perhaps the guiding spirits of the new genre, which climaxed in America with a flood of memoirs in the 1990s, which the educator William Zinsser would later declare "the age of the memoir." Never, he wrote, "have personal narratives gushed so profusely from the American soil as in the closing decade of the twentieth century. Everyone has a story to tell, and everyone is telling it."[11] Zinsser welcomed the phenomenon—a flood that reached its highest point with the publication, in 1996, of *Angela's Ashes*, a memoir by an American immigrant that would stand for millions of such true stories.

Unlike Marchenko's memoir, Frank McCourt's book about the ravages of alcoholism in an Irish immigrant family is a survivor's tale, told with great love and compassion. "It's dark on Atlantic Avenue and all the bars around the Long Island Railroad Station are bright and noisy," McCourt wrote, recalling a scene from his early childhood.

> We go from bar to bar looking for Dad. Mam leaves us outside with the pram while she goes in or she sends me. There are crowds of noisy men and stale smells that remind me of Dad when he comes with the smell of the whiskey on him.
>
> The man behind the bar says, Yeah, sonny, whaddya want? You're not supposeta be in here, y'know.
>
> I'm looking for my father. Is my father here?
>
> Now sonny, how'd I know dat? Who's your fawdah? . . .

Mam tries all the bars around the station [Brooklyn] before she gives up. She leans against a wall and cries. Jesus, we still have to walk all the way to Classon Avenue and I have four starving children. She sends me back into the bar where Pete offered me the sip to see if the barman would fill the twins' bottles with water and maybe a little sugar in each. The men in the bar think it's very funny that the barman should be filling baby bottles but he's big and he tells them to shut their lip. He tells me babies should be drinking milk not water and when I tell him Mam doesn't have the money he empties the baby bottles and fills them with milk. He says, Tell ya mom they need that for the teeth an' bones. Ya drink water an' sugar an' all ya get is rickets. Tell ya Mam.[12]

Given the emotional power of its subject, and the depth of compassion applied to its reconstruction as memoir, *Angela's Ashes* rightly won the Pulitzer Prize, and was dramatized as a feature film.

Memoir offered authors the double challenge of a new narrative art form demanding absolute personal candor. Yet the growing popularity of the genre brought with it certain dangers—which you would do well to reflect upon if you're of a mind to write a memoir.

Faux-Memoir

Starved for new material to deconstruct, French poststructuralists and academic literary theorists flocked around the singular new memoir bandwagon beginning in the 1960s, eager to address the literary and linguistic issues of identity formation, self-image, self-invention, self-accusation, and self-exculpation it raised, as well as the obscure codes in which these matters were addressed. However myopic their interest (since none were interested in the second part of the hybrid: the history and social issues being chronicled), poststructuralists did at least spotlight the matters of truth-telling and audience gullibility. Thus, when James Frey published his supposedly truthful memoir *A Million Little Pieces* (2003), the world came crashing down around his ears.

Amid the seemingly endless opportunities for exhibitionist confession in tabloids, on television, and on the Internet, greed finally trumped truthfulness. Faux-memoir as personal exhibitionism had become all too inviting to would-be authors, artists, and critics. The new genre was at once academically pukka (being taught in thousands of new and aptly named "creative writing" classes, while the study of biography and its ethics languished with virtually no representation), yet also commercially popular and remunerative.

A Million Little Pieces described how Frey supposedly became, in his early twenties, a convict, an alcoholic, and a drug abuser. Unfortunately for him, he was soon found to have invented most of the saga.

The fate of Frey's purported memoir provides a fascinating warning to all would-be memoir writers. His book was selected in 2005 by the hugely influential TV host Oprah Winfrey, for her Book Club. Not only did it look set to sell millions of copies, but it would probably be made into a film.

Unfortunately for James Frey, the Internet provided the public with a new forum for web-based discussion of issues and people, without fear of libel suits. The website TheSmokingGun.com, after a six-week investigation, electronically published what neither Oprah Winfrey nor members of the print press were willing to countenance: that much of the detail behind Frey's self-lacerating and seemingly sincere *apologia pro vita mea* was fabricated. The revelation proved more sensational than Frey's memoir, racing across the Internet before Frey could think of a response or excuse.

Doubleday, Frey's publisher, was soon rumored to be offering refunds to anyone who had bought the book. This wasn't true; but Random House, Inc., did eventually compel the author to issue a statement, to be inserted in all editions of the book, saying that "people cope with adversity in many different ways, ways that are deeply personal." The mistake he'd made, Frey confessed, was creating a past self "in my mind, to help me cope." Unfortunately, this self was not actually "the person who went through the experience," he admitted. To make matters still worse, "I wanted the stories in the book to ebb and flow, to have dramatic arcs, to have the tension that all great stories require"—a literary urge which had carried him to excess.[13] He had, to his credit, first offered the book to his publisher as fiction, but had been told it wouldn't sell, whereas as a *memoir*, a species of autobiography, it would—and, for a while, it did.

A Million Little Lies became a joke. Lest the public be misled—and bring a lawsuit—the Brooklyn Public Library recatalogued the book not as memoir but as fiction—as Frey had originally intended it to be. That did not end Frey's ignominy, however, for he was eventually sued—this time for plagiarism!

If you are intending to write a memoir, then: be warned! In his book *Inventing the Truth,* William Zinsser observed

how a genre that had promised so much to so many became, in the wrong or unseasoned hands, a sort of tsu-
nami. For years, Zinsser had criss-crossed the country, quietly teaching the art of memoir; but in the late 1990s, he
suddenly found it "was getting a bad name." "Talk shows
on cable television spawned a national appetite for true
confession," he wrote. They "swept away all the old codes
of civility and taste. The result was an avalanche of memoirs that were little more than therapy, the authors bashing
their parents and siblings and exulting in lurid details of
their tussle with drink, drug addiction, anorexia, obesity,
co-dependency, depression, attempted suicide and other
talk-show syndromes."[14]

Zinsser recommended a return to more civilized values of modesty and self-control, even a relearning of the
meaning of shame. But in the modern world of instant
text-messaging and visual primacy, was he talking to the
wind?

Exhibitionism and self-revelation are, like today's craze
for tattoos, too much a part of youth culture to be halted
by admonition. Thus, my most urgent advice to the
would-be memoir writer is: ponder in advance the consequences of self-exposure, before you go too far—literally
and metaphorically!

FIFTEEN

Truth—and Its Consequences

April is the cruellest month, breeding
Lilacs out of the dead land, mixing
Memory and desire, stirring
Dull roots with spring rain.

—T. S. ELIOT, *The Waste Land*

*Y*ou have written a draft manuscript: a biography—perhaps even an autobiography, or your memoirs, or a memoir. Before you touch up the portrait and place it before the world, however, you must think again about the consequences of its publication.

Publishing a truthful biography is a very different matter from composing it. In any course on doing biography, Ian Hamilton's book about J. D. Salinger should be mandatory reading. It is the only book I know of that illustrates with absolute candor the perils of attempting to publish a biography if the subject is still alive and can take the author to court—which Salinger famously did.

Hamilton, who had written an authorized life of the poet Robert Lowell that was well received, had on the strength of this been commissioned to write a life of the reclusive author of *Catcher in the Rye*. His proposal set out his agenda as a sort of *Quest for Corvo:* an account of an investigation to find the true Salinger, through the novelist's early work and life-story. The research and the eventual manuscript, however, were a disaster.

As expected, Salinger did not authorize the work. Indeed, he made certain that no one of any note or intimacy (such as his ex-wife) would cooperate. What Salinger could not police, however, was access to his letters and papers that had found their way into archival collections, open to researchers and the public. Armed with these letters, Hamilton, in the mid-1980s, composed his half-life, ending it in 1965, when Salinger was forty-four. In this way, Hamilton hoped to show the world, and Salinger himself, that he was not invading Salinger's much-prized privacy—merely recording his early creative life. But it didn't work. Salinger sued to stop publication, using the law of copyright as a privacy-protective weapon.

Under existing U.S. laws governing "fair use," Hamilton and his publishers believed they had a right to "free speech," in a book that was respectful, scholarly, and educational. They did not expect that Salinger, a recluse, would submit to legal deposition on the matter.

Salinger was not only a hermit—he was a hoarder, and was adamant that he would not allow a single word he had ever written to be published without his express permission. In his eyes, fair use was unfair; it exposed him to public view, which he found repugnant. Disregarding the effect that a new ruling on fair use might have on scholarship in America (since critical work, without the right to quote, is impossible), Salinger insisted on taking his lawsuit to trial. Though the judge ruled in Hamilton's favor, two subsequent appeals judges ruled in favor of Salinger. The Supreme Court refused to hear the case—and the whole notion of fair-use quotation in biography in America was sundered.

Hamilton, who had received a large advance, was forced to repay his publisher. As a serious biographer, he was, effectively, ruined. Apart from a short life of Matthew Arnold, and his brilliant survey of Salinger-like cases, *Keepers of the Flame,* he never wrote another biography. He died in 2001.

Moral Issues

One of Hamilton's many insights in his painful record of biographical failure, recorded in his book *In Search of J. D. Salinger,* was his self-portrait as two people. The first was

Ian Hamilton the person, agonizing over the moral questions entailed in writing a book about a famous fellow writer who didn't wish to be written about. The second was Ian Hamilton the professional biographer, who simply wanted to "get on with the job."[1]

This dichotomy goes to the heart of biographical ethics—not only if you are writing about another individual, but equally so if you are writing about yourself. The problem, you see, is not only in researching and setting down the truth, but in making that truth public, where people can—and do—get, or feel, hurt.

Let's examine some examples of this business of hurt, for it may well affect decisions you will have to make regarding publication of your completed manuscript. James Watson's *Double Helix* is a good illustration.

Far from being an instant best-seller, *The Double Helix* was rejected in 1967 by the first publisher Watson submitted it to, Harvard University Press (he was on the Harvard faculty at the time). Francis Crick and Maurice Wilkins—who won the 1962 Nobel Prize along with Crick and Watson for their 1953 discovery—were not amused by Watson's potentially embarrassing depiction, especially the unsparing portraits of their colleagues. For a time, it was rumored that Crick would sue his former colleague if Watson went ahead with publication of the memoir. The president of Harvard, Dr. Nathan Pusey, overruled the university press's Board of Syndics when it wanted to accept the manuscript. Pusey—as Harvard's student paper, the *Crimson*, protested—preferred "bland tranquillity" to "diversity of viewpoint."[2]

In the end, Watson's memoir (which he'd begun writing in 1962) was brought out in New York in 1968 by a mainstream publisher—his former Harvard editor having resigned and taken the book to Atheneum. Extracts were also published in the *Atlantic Monthly*.

Overnight, Watson found himself being lauded for his vivid tale: the inside story of the quest for DNA's structure. The book sold a million copies. But Watson was nevertheless vilified for his uncharitable description of Dr. Rosalind Franklin, his London University colleague—whose work on crystallography, or X-ray diffraction, had first enabled Watson and Crick to discern the helical structure of DNA. Dr. Franklin died young, at thirty-seven, and thus missed by four years the Nobel Prize which the other members of the double-helix team garnered.[3] Watson's sexist, posthumous description of "Rosy" seemed therefore inexplicably cruel:

> By choice she did not emphasize her feminine qualities. Though her features were strong, she was not

unattractive and might have been quite stunning had she taken even a mild interest in clothes. This she did not. There was never lipstick to contrast with her straight black hair, while at the age of thirty-one her dresses showed all the imagination of English blue-stocking adolescents. So it was quite easy to imagine her the product of an unsatisfied mother who unduly stressed the desirability of professional careers that could save bright girls from marriages to full men.[4]

In fact, as Watson pointed out, Dr. Franklin came from a very "comfortable, erudite" Jewish family—but the posthumous damage of the portrayal was done. Watson was prevailed upon to publish an apology, in the form of an epilogue. He admitted that his "initial impressions of Dr. Franklin, both scientific and personal," were "often wrong"—adding a brief tribute to the physical chemist who had not only done so much groundbreaking work to identify the structure of the DNA molecule and to confirm Crick and Watson's theory, but had subsequently done innovative work on viruses. Yet if Watson was prepared to admit his initial impressions were wrong, André Lwoff asked in retrospect, "why not eliminate them" from the book he was publishing? "Death," Lwoff commented pithily, "is a high price to pay for rehabilitation."[5]

The ethics of writing and publishing a memoir are, in other words, as controversial as those entailed in producing a biography—sometimes more so. Death may end the danger of a libel suit, but it does not reduce the hurt which revelation can inflict on the living.

Dr. Johnson was acutely aware of the problem—that of genuine lifelikeness and its capacity to give offense. Most accounts of "particular persons are barren and useless," he wrote in 1750, because they are written too late. "If a life be delayed till interest and envy are at an end," he pointed out, "we may hope for impartiality, but expect little intelligence; for the incidents which give excellence to biography are of a volatile and evanescent kind, such as soon escape the memory." Such portraits end up losing "all resemblance to the original."[6]

A memoir, in other words, requires the very things likely to most upset the living: ruthless honesty and vividness of recall! Certainly the accuracy of Johnson's observation was manifested when James Watson's delayed sequel to his *Double Helix* was published three decades later, in 2001. *The Double Helix* had told a truly riveting story of scientific discovery, employing memoir—the hybrid of autobiography and memoirs—as his nonscientific instrument. The sequel, *Genes, Girls and Gamow: After the Double Helix,* turned out to be an old man's somewhat tedious, name-dropping memoirs. Far from employing the hybrid form Watson himself had helped to establish, his reminiscences were complacent and self-satisfied—a recitation of the past with no focal drama other than the increasingly hysterical search for a good woman who would end his nightmare of sexual marauding, and marry him.

Thus, publishing a biography or a memoir that is truly challenging demands courage, even foolhardiness. It will be a struggle between sensitivity and almost necessary in-sensitivity, a contest between your agenda and what the real world will tolerate. How you deal with those ethical issues is something only you (and your publisher) can de-cide—but decide you must.

Let me give one further example of what I mean. Three years after publication of *The Double Helix,* the poet A. Alvarez published an account of suicide, *The Savage God.* It began with a personal memoir: the story of Alvarez's re-lationship with his fellow poet, Sylvia Plath: a friendship that came to a sudden, tragic end when Plath took her own life in the winter of 1963.

Page by page, Alvarez—who had been the poetry edi-tor at the London *Observer*—recalled Plath's determination to become a great poet, the sad breakdown of her marriage to Ted Hughes, their separation, her extraordinary final poems, and her enigmatic death: enigmatic, since Alvarez—a suicide survivor himself—did not believe that Plath had really meant to take her own life. "Had everything worked out as it should—had the gas not drugged the man downstairs, preventing him from opening the front door to the *au pair* girl—there is no doubt she would have been saved. I think she wanted to be," he posited. "Why else leave her doctor's telephone number?"[7]

Hughes had asked Alvarez to attend the inquest.

> Earlier that morning I had gone with Ted to the undertaker in Mornington Crescent. The coffin was at the far end of a bare, draped room. She lay stiffly, a ludicrous ruff at her neck. Only her face showed. It was grey and slightly transparent, like wax. I had never before seen a dead person and I hardly recognized her; her features seemed too thin and sharp. The room smelled of apples, faint, sweet but somehow unclean, as though the apples were beginning to rot. I was glad to get out into the cold and noise of the dingy streets. It seemed impossible that she was dead.
>
> Even now I find it hard to believe. There was too

much life in her long, flat, strongly boned body, and her longish face with its fine brown eyes, shrewd and full of feeling. She was practical and candid, passionate and compassionate. I believe she was a genius. I sometimes catch myself thinking I'll run into her walking on Primrose Hill or the [Hampstead] Heath, and we'll pick up the conversation where we left off. But perhaps that is because her poems still speak so distinctly in her accents: quick, sardonic, unpredictable, effortlessly inventive, a bit angry, and always utterly her own.[8]

Sensitive, compassionate, elegiac, Alvarez's memoir, when serialized in the *Observer* eight years after Plath's suicide, was considered a beautiful tribute to the dead poet by most readers. Not by Ted Hughes, however. "It is humiliating to me and to her mother and brother to have her last days exhumed in this way, as you do in your memoir, for classroom discussion," he protested after the first extract was published.

You kept saying you would show me what you were writing about her—why didn't you? For you, it was something you wrote, no doubt against great inner resistance, for your readers, it's five interesting minutes, but for us it is permanent dynamite.

For you, she is a topic of intellectual discussion, a poetic, existential phenomenon. . . . But for F. and N. [Hughes's children by Plath: Frieda and Nicholas, then eleven and nine], she is the absolute centrepin—they have made her very important, the more so because of her obvious absence. Throughout the mess I've been making of replacing her these last years, their image of her—of what she did and was—is going to decide their lives. . . . Before your details, it was vague, it was a mystery. But now you have defined the whole thing, and handed it to the public. In a real way, you have robbed them of her death, of any natural way of dealing with her death. This will add up through every year they live. For you and everybody else, it is fading fast—you've solved the mystery of exactly what happened, and how. (You've given a version, anyway.) But for F. and N., it has not yet properly begun; the presiding fact of their future will only really dawn on them when somehow they meet your memoir. . . .

They had enough of the facts and the truths living in the mausoleum Sylvia left for them. What

> your memoir supplies is not just facts—(so few of
> the facts—so many fictions and mere speculations
> trying to be facts)—but poison. Poison is no less poi-
> son for being a fact.[9]

Accused of "sensationalism," and chagrined by Hughes's
personal invective, poor Alvarez could only withdraw the
second part of the *Observer*'s serialization—though he did
publish the memoir in his book, which had a smaller, perhaps more discerning readership. Two decades later, when
writing her seminal book on Plath, *The Silent Woman,* Janet
Malcolm took Hughes's side: the ever-tormented widower,
reviled by feminists who strove to chip his name off her
gravestone, in the little cemetery in Yorkshire where he
had buried her.

But how sincere were Hughes's protests?

Alvarez—who had done so much to promote Hughes's
poetry, as well as Plath's—was "terribly hurt" by Hughes's
letters accusing him of sensationalism. "I have not intruded
into your marriage or made public any intimate details
about it," he defended his motives and behavior. "They did
not seem to me to have anything to do with what I was
writing about, or to be anybody's business. So I kept them
out, although, obviously, I knew about it, and, equally obviously, Sylvia talked about it at times." Nor did he under-

stand Hughes's insistence on keeping his and Plath's children in the dark about their mother's suicide. "As for the children, God knows that is an appallingly difficult thing. But I would have thought it better for them eventually to see this [memoir], which is at least written with some kind of consideration and feeling for their mother, rather than a cloud of vague and malicious rumors. . . . I did not know you hadn't yet told them about it, but there is no way in which they won't eventually find out. I would have thought the pop distortions going around would be a great deal more harmful."[10]

Alvarez's response only incurred further wrath from Hughes, who terminated their friendship. The true "mess" of Hughes's life—especially his relationship with Assia Wevill, and *her* suicide in 1969 (she gassed herself and Shura, her little daughter by Hughes), as well as his compulsive womanizing and seduction of other men's wives—would not be published for another decade, following Hughes's death in 1998. Traumatized by the two suicides, Hughes had, biographers finally realized, played his bleak cards with amazing skill: effacing Assia Wevill's memory (and that of his daughter Shura) from the public record during his lifetime, exploiting the copyright to his first wife's literary works with extraordinary effectiveness (despite the fact that she had begun divorce proceedings against him, citing his adultery with Assia), "losing" Sylvia's priceless final diaries and draft novel (which portrayed him in a bad light), and becoming Poet Laureate of England.

A man of huge talent and powerful masculine charisma, Hughes had managed to gain the fame and wealth he coveted, two wives, and many lovers, with near-impunity. He even stunned those who defended his absolute right to privacy and silence in the matter of his dead wife: shortly before he died, he published a book entitled *Birthday Letters* (which excluded Assia and Shura)—his own intimate, and bestselling, account of his relationship with Plath.

Poison had turned, in Hughes's hands, into lucre.

The moral here is that the ethics of biography are complex and challenging. They take us back to the largely unchronicled history of life writing (and life depiction in other media, such as painting, film, radio, and television), for there is really nothing new in this.

The fact is, since biography first began, it has given rise to controversy, pitting private against public, honesty against hypocrisy, truth against consequences—the consequences of revealing the truth about real people. And these consequences don't lessen, even when you imagine you are telling your own story in a memoir. Indeed, they are often worse.

The novelist Elizabeth Hardwick, widow of the poet Robert Lowell, spoke for all those who sneer at, yet fear, biography and memoir. "Biography is a scrofulous cottage industry," she told the *Paris Review*'s Darryl Pinckney. "How seldom it is that one has ever heard of the person writing the biography. What are the models, what are the qualifications? And it is not only the full-scale computer printout that these things [biographies] are, but the books [memoirs] brought forth by lovers, friends from youth, cousins, whatever. I remember how horrified Dickens was when he met, in later life, the model for Dora in David Copperfield. Now Dora would hire a hack and write about Dickens."[11]

Snobbery and ignorance, sadly, will inevitably greet your work in some quarters; but they will be the least of your worries. Whether writing a biography or memoir, you will have to weigh the consequences as far as you can anticipate them: legal, social, psychological. It is not a subject that is ever, to my knowledge, discussed in manuals of writing, save in the vaguest or most superficial way. Yet in a world wedded to the rights of the individual, it marks the very fault-line of modern democracy.

How much truth-telling can a democracy permit without shooting itself in the foot? Has the mania for revelation and gossip become socially self-destructive? Whether at a

local, private level, or at a national, public level, the likely
consequences of publication must be taken into account—
and you may well have to accept compromises that offend
your notions of absolute truth, yet reflect the real world: a
world in which the truth can sometimes cause more damage and hurt than lies.

A Punitive Mistress

Telling the truth is a troubled arena in which almost no
fiction writer, and few historians, need fear to tread, but biographers *must!* Suetonius was dismissed from his job at
Rome's imperial headquarters; Sir Walter Raleigh was executed; Sir Edmund Gosse had to publish his truthful memoir of his father anonymously; and many a biographer—
myself included—has reeled from a lost lawsuit.

Take heed! Make sure you do not rush into print a work
that you will regret. Be careful with your facts, as well as
your assertions, in memoir and in biography. Memoir may
look easier than biography, because it has no need for formal research, or sources beyond the author's memory. But
as the saga of Frey's *Million Little Pieces* demonstrated, that
memory had better be truthful, or you will be found out—
and exposed in a manner that may be very painful.

Even if you do take especial care, you cannot, of course,
meet all eventualities—as Doris Kearns Goodwin and her

publishers, Simon and Schuster, found to their cost. Pressured first by competitive academics at Harvard to publish her biography of Lyndon Johnson before she was truly ready, then by major publishing contracts for further biographies, Goodwin—the most intelligent, compassionate, and sympathetic of biographers, who confessed on television that while writing of the Roosevelts' marriage "I almost felt like I wanted to push them together because I could feel the love between them"[12]—gave way to sloppy research, was discovered to have inadvertently plagiarized other author's works, found herself vilified across the Internet, and felt compelled to resign from the Pulitzer Prize Committee in 2002.[13] Even Stephen Ambrose, bestselling military writer and biographer of Presidents Eisenhower and Nixon, underwent a similar experience before his death, accused of the theft of other people's manuscripts and work. These were distressing codas to many years of well-intentioned and dedicated labor. They are also a reminder that biography today, though it offers great fulfillment, and even rewards on occasion, can still be a hard taskmaster, and—as Sir Walter Raleigh noted—a punitive mistress.

Let me dispel the gloom, however. Telling someone's story well may be the most life-affirming thing you'll ever do!

SIXTEEN

The Afterlife

By labour and intent study (which I take to be my portion
in this life) joined with the strong propensity of nature, I
might perhaps leave something so written to after-times,
as they should not willingly let it die.

—JOHN MILTON, *The Reason of Church Government*

*F*or the fitting out of the *Titanic,* a huge 300-page
"builder's specification book" was printed for the army of
joiners, painters, plumbers, tillers, carpet layers, and elec-
tricians who prepared the ship for its maiden voyage, beginning on April 10, 1912.

After taking on board more passengers off Cherbourg
and then Queenstown (the *Titanic* was too large to dock
at either port), the liner sailed across the Atlantic on its

maiden voyage, though it never reached its destination, New York City.

No builder's specification book, however detailed, will ensure the safe passage of your biography! Your work could end up foundering like the *Titanic,* or living as long as the *Queen Mary,* which won the Blue Ribbon and sailed successfully for over thirty years—despite Hitler's offer of a bounty and the Iron Cross to any U-boat captain who could sink her! All I can do, as a biographer who has had an assortment of successes, near-disasters, and failures over the past forty years, is offer a few final, practical hints on the "fitting out" of your text, and some last words of advice. For, just as fitters go aboard a liner in its last weeks of preparation to ensure all is shipshape for the eventual passengers, so will you have time, from the first draft up to the last proof galley, to effect changes, from major overhaul to minutiae. Use it!

Let's start with some of the major fittings.

The first is subdivision—and signage. Books, parts, chapters, subsections: these are the time-tested ways of *partitioning* the finished opus—not for the sake of fragmentation, but to help the reader pause for breath and enable the writer to start afresh on a new theme or period in the subject's life. Just as a playwright inserts act and scene divisions in order to change time, place, scenery, and actors on stage, so too are you given, by virtue of the convention of part and chapter divisions, a reader-friendly license to stop, jump, change the subject, reverse the sequence, or revisit the moment you are describing. As a picture is said to be worth a thousand words, so too may a chapter break.

If you don't believe me, look carefully at any major biography. See how the author ends a chapter, and begins another. See how subheads, interspersed throughout a long chapter, can make your detailed narrative more accommodating, by giving the reader a chance to pause, or you yourself a chance to alter the position of your authorial lens. In telling the story of Thomas and Heinrich Mann, where I needed to keep switching from one brother to the other, I found this simple mechanical device a godsend. As my own biographies have become ever longer, spread across more and more volumes, so the simple expedient of partitioning has become more and more necessary for maintaining clarity and readability.

The next "fitting out" task is editing: both self-editing and submitting your work to the edits of others—that is to say, your acquiring editor and your manuscript editor.

Self-editing can be a grueling task—but it's your last chance to check your text, in terms of both design and professionalism, before you hand the manuscript over to the publisher's editor. Somehow you have to summon the energy and the distance required for you to see it as others will see it.

Does it open well? Is the structure satisfactory? Do the chapter breaks work? Are the chapter titles interesting? Does it end appropriately?

At a more detailed level, you must check your quotations for accuracy. You must count the number of words quoted, to ensure that the excerpts fall within the bounds of fair use. Consult with your editor about this. If the excerpts are long, you will have to obtain written permission-to-quote from the original publisher or source. Footnotes or endnotes need to be double-checked, as well. You will have to compile a bibliography (if this is part of your contractual obligation), and write a section of acknowledgments. Be generous in giving credit—but not embarrassingly so, as Norman Sherry was in the final volume of his Graham Greene biography (in which he thanked his local Texas restaurateur for giving him a special table), lest you cause embarrassment for the people who've helped you. Then hand over the manuscript—and let the publication battle begin!

Each book is the cherished child of the creative and constructive energies of its author. Now this child is going away, as if to college—and will come back hopefully enriched, but in all probability different.

Your editor may have been kind and encouraging in the past, but now he or she must—both on your behalf and on behalf of the reader—be tough. At worst, your manuscript may be rejected, and you will be asked to begin again or to substantially rewrite your text. You will be obliged to keep to the word limit specified in your contract.

Even in the best-case scenario, the editor will suggest (with greater or lesser forcefulness) cuts and alterations; and though you will at first be horrified, you must consider them dispassionately. You are in the metaphorical and literal cutting room. Your editor would not be doing a proper job unless the raw manuscript were subjected to his or her experienced, critical eye. Edmund Morris recalled the process of conferring with the editor of his first *Theodore Roosevelt* volume: "I remember I had my huge manuscript of basic text, typescript, and he wanted the odd sentence out. And he had a little jar of Wite-Out. He'd be sitting there with my manuscript, slop, slop, with this obscuring fluid. And I remember him saying to me, 'Don't you just love Wite-Out?' I could see he was an editor in action here. They love to obliterate. I said, 'That's my words you're obliterating, fellow.'"[1]

Negotiation will ensue, as the merits and disadvantages of the suggested edits are batted back and forth. If the acquiring editor is also copyediting, every single page of your manuscript will be defaced. Deal with it. If the editor is handing the manuscript on to a copyeditor, don't be fooled by clean-looking pages. They'll be marked up all too soon!

Gradually, your manuscript is metamorphosing into a book—which is both a constructive and mechanical process, with a number of stages, following a set timetable. More people will become involved: a production department, a book designer, a marketing department, a publicity department. In morphing into a book, your biography will become, to all intents and purposes, a commodity, to be produced, bought, and sold.

Do your best for your book. Take seriously the suggested edits and comply as far as possible with the advice of your editors. After the book is typeset, read the proofs very carefully for errors, both of electronic conversion and of judgments made in the final text. If you are responsible for obtaining illustrations, invest the necessary time and trouble in obtaining them and in securing the legal copyright permission for their use. Again, ask your publisher for guidance. Agree with your editor and book designer on the appropriate length for the captions—and take care over their composition, since captions and illustrations may be the first thing a prospective buyer looks at. Ensure that the correct source is given in each case. Check that the index does what you wish (guiding readers to the important themes of the work, as well as names), and is accurate; if you prepare it yourself, ensure that someone else double-checks the entries. Help as far as you can with jacket copy, advertising copy, PR material, prospective media, people, institutions who will be interested in your subject.

I spell out these obligations for a reason: writing a biography or memoir entails more than research and writing. Beginning from the publisher's receipt of the manuscript, no serious book can be produced in less than a year. If the average time taken to write a biography is two to three years, then the production process comprises a quarter and possibly a third of the time required to complete a biography. Be prepared! But take comfort, too—for somewhere in the editing and production process, you will, I guarantee, experience a small epiphany: a moment when, after all the many months and years you have labored over your manuscript, you can finally see it in your mind's eye as *right,* a finished work of which you can be proud. It has finally come together, and does what you have wanted it and fashioned it to do.

However brief, this epiphany is important because it is likely to be the summit of your creative satisfaction: the spiritual reward for all your thought, application, perseverance, determination. After that, the ascent is over, and you must come back down to earth.

No longer yours, your book is more than simply a commodity. It is a sacrifice, which the gods of critical reception will pronounce upon before it is read by the public at large. Advance copies will have been sent to reviewers and the media, and it is to their critical responses that you must next submit—an experience which requires a tougher skin than you might imagine.

Some authors go into a deep depression—not necessarily because their books are poorly reviewed (or, worse still, ignored), but because they themselves are exhausted by the creative process and need to regain their equilibrium. James Reston, for example, had first intended to write a life of Jesse Helms, but had been beaten to the punch by another biographer. Texas governor John Connally, his next subject, gave him no cooperation—"Absolutely none at all, zero," Reston recalled. In fact, Connally "would put these blocks in my way" (John Connally had been shot alongside President Kennedy on November 22, 1963, but survived, only to undergo another disaster when he went bankrupt). Yet Reston persevered, determined to tell the archetypal story of a man who had "been so big and high in American powerful circles [and] had fallen so far, so fast," a trajectory that gave the saga a "Shakespearean or Grecian quality." Afterward, "I was very, very keen to get cracking on another book and be well into the research by the time this one was out," he recounted—but it was not so simple. "The publication process," he admitted, "has always paralyzed me." For months he was unable to work. "You can't do anything. Then when the book comes out, you wait for the reviews, and you wait for the television people to attack you. You see, the destiny and the fate of the book really is not in for six to eight months. So if you give yourself over to this kind of paralysis, it can be really quite a large block of time."[2]

Reston's reaction is a common one. Somehow, if possible, you need to guard against such apprehensions. Robert Caro, writing his four-volume life of Lyndon Johnson, learned to move on immediately to research the next volume—telling Brian Lamb, who interviewed him in 1990: "This book we're talking about, the one that was just published [*Means of Ascent*, covering Johnson's pre-Senate political career], is to me almost—it's behind me. That's the funny feeling. My mind is on the third volume. Johnson is in the Senate"—and so was Caro, mentally.[3]

Other biographers feel intense excitement as the days of ivory-tower research and writing give way to public attention, even applause. Each author responds differently—but whatever happens, you will need to accept, as a biographer, a level of critical comment that will be professionally disappointing. It's no good expecting reviewers to appreciate your construction, style, or narrative, since they invariably ignore such aspects of a work. The best you can hope for, as a biographer, is that reviewers will provide readers with a brief discussion of the life and personality of your subject, and thus spark public interest in your work—irrespective of your organizational and narrative skill. The worst will be reviewers who are interested only in revelations—including fresh tidbits that they can use to spice up their essays. If the publisher has mounted a publicity campaign to generate reader-interest, you may have control at least over what you yourself say about your work and the subject—but it will be tempered by the fact that interviewers will simply not have time, in a busy broadcasting life, to actually read your book, and are really concerned only with audience entertainment.

How can you avoid being disappointed, after investing so many years in the undertaking, so much research in laying the foundation of your story, so much thought in its composition, so much care in its production? As one writer recently remarked, a good review you forget in seven minutes; a bad one takes you seven years!

Leon Edel put the problem beautifully almost forty years

ago. Readers of biography tend to read "with delight" the story of a real life that interests them, without thinking too much about the construction of the narrative, if it is done well. But critics, who *should* be able to write with intelligence about the effort involved, were, in his experience, "wholly negligent in not informing" the public about what goes into a biography. "I know of no critics in modern times," Edel wrote, "who have chosen to deal with biography as one deals with poetry or the novel. The critics fall into the easy trap of writing pieces about the life that was lived, when their business is to discuss how the life was told."[4]

How the life was told is still, sadly, a closed book to reviewers and critics. Take courage, though! "Reception" and "promotion" are the price you must pay these days, in order to be a biographer. If you do not publish, you cannot be a biographer; so you have to go through with what often feels like a senseless charade.

My best advice—after many years of sweat, toil, and tears—is that you should brace yourself, in advance, for a test of your patience and humor. If there is a media trial, think of it as a brief interlude before your book is read by readers who *want* to read your work, not bash or trivialize it. It is for them, after all, that you wrote—and they will write to you, or email, if they are so minded. "I get lovely letters from people from all over," Stephen Ambrose remarked following the success of his *D-Day, June 6, 1944,* "and it just means the world to me. People say nice things to me about the books. They tell me about them, and that's the big, the principal payoff." Ambrose was aware that his own life was changing. "I don't like this taste of celebrityhood," he confessed. "I like being a writer, and I was pretty well known before this last month, but nobody knew my face. I wish it were back that way," he added—and he thought it still would be, as soon as the fiftieth anniversary of D-Day was past.[5]

But it never was the same again. Fame, fortune, and accusations of literary theft irrevocably changed his life. If you rub the magic lamp, therefore, be careful what you wish for!

In the meantime, be of good cheer. The search for truth is a noble endeavor, for all the pitfalls. As Dr. Johnson wrote, "that which is fully known cannot be falsified but with reluctance of understanding, and alarm of conscience"—conscience being "the sentinel of virtue."[6] Moreover, without biographers in our democratic world, where would we be?

As the Latin poet Horace wrote, in the century before

the birth of Jesus of Nazareth, "Many heroes lived before Agamemnon; but all are unknown and unwept, extinguished in everlasting night, because they have no spirited chronicler." Be proud that you can rectify this, as a biographer, in our own time.

NOTES

SELECTED BIBLIOGRAPHY

ACKNOWLEDGMENTS

INDEX

Notes

CHAPTER 1. THE TASK OF BIOGRAPHY

1. *The Rambler,* 60 (October 13, 1750).

2. James Boswell, *Boswell's Life of Johnson,* ed. George Birkbeck Hill (Oxford: Clarendon, 1950), 79.

3. *The Rambler,* 60 (October 13, 1750).

4. *The Idler,* 84 (November 24, 1759).

5. *The Rambler,* 60 (October 13, 1750).

6. Ibid.

7. *The Idler,* 84 (November 24, 1759).

8. *The Rambler,* 60 (October 13, 1750).

9. *The Rambler,* 68 (November 10, 1750).

10. Sir Walter Raleigh, *History of the World* (1614), Preface, paragraph 73.

11. Virginia Woolf, *Orlando: A Biography* (Harmondsworth: Penguin, 1963; orig. pub. 1928), 161.

12. Ibid., 172.

CHAPTER 2. WHAT IS YOUR AGENDA?

1. Robert Caro, interview with Brian Lamb, *Booknotes,* C-SPAN (April 29, 1990).

2. Bernard Crick, "On the Difficulties of Writing Biography in General and of Orwell's in Particular," quoted in Janet Malcolm, *The Silent Woman: Sylvia Plath and Ted Hughes* (New York: Knopf, 1994), 11.

3. Bernard Crick, *George Orwell: A Life* (Boston: Little, Brown, 1980).

4. Nicholas Von Hoffman, "Robert Caro's Holy Fire," *Vanity Fair* (April 1990).

5. Later, when the copyright on Woolf's books expired, neither Penguin nor Oxford World's Classics would even reprint it. See Julia Briggs, *Virginia Woolf: An Inner Life* (New York: Holt, 2005), 367.

6. Malcolm, *The Silent Woman*, 102.

7. David McCullough, in Brian Lamb, *Booknotes: America's Finest Authors on Reading, Writing, and the Power of Ideas* (New York: Times Books, 1997), 4.

8. Caro, interview with Lamb, *Booknotes*, C-SPAN.

9. Ibid.

10. Ibid.

11. Sigmund Freud, *Leonardo da Vinci and a Memory of His Childhood*, trans. Alan Tyson, ed. James Strachey (New York: Norton, 1961; orig. German ed. 1910).

CHAPTER 3. DEFINING YOUR AUDIENCE

1. David McCullough, in Brian Lamb, *Booknotes: America's Finest Authors on Reading, Writing, and the Power of Ideas* (New York: Times Books, 1997), 5.

2. Edmund Morris, speaking about his book *Dutch: A Memoir of Ronald Reagan*, on Brian Lamb's *Booknotes*, C-SPAN (December 5, 1999).

3. Ibid.

4. The play was called *But It Still Goes On*. See Richard Perceval Graves, *Robert Graves: The Years with Laura, 1926–40* (London: Weidenfeld and Nicolson, 1990), 101–102.

5. Michael Holroyd, *Lytton Strachey*, vol. 2: *The Years of Achievement, 1910–1932* (London: Heinemann, 1968), 234.

6. Ibid., 267 and 329.

CHAPTER 4. RESEARCHING YOUR SUBJECT

1. Tracy Chevalier, *Girl with a Pearl Earring* (New York: Dutton, 1999).

2. Martin Postle and William Vaughan, *The Artist's Model: From Etty to Spencer* (London: Merrell Holberton, 1999).

3. Thomas Carlyle, "On Sir Walter Scott," in *Memoirs of the Life of Sir Walter Scott, Baronet*, vols. 1–6, first published in *London and Westminster Review*, 12 (Edinburgh, 1837). Republished in the Harvard Classics, ed. Charles W. Eliot, vol. 25, part 5, as Thomas Carlyle, "Sir Walter Scott" (New York: Collier, 1909–1914).

4. James Watson, *The Double Helix* (New York: Athenaeum, 1968).

5. F. H. Hinsley et al., *British Intelligence in the Second World War: Its Influence on Strategy and Operations* (London: Her Majesty's Stationery Office, 1979, 1981, 1984, 1988, and 1990).

6. Plutarch, *Demosthenes*, trans. John Dryden, in Plutarch, *Lives of the Noble Grecians and Romans*, ch. 56, numerous editions including Internet.

7. Philip Ziegler, *Mountbatten* (New York: Knopf, 1985), 701.

8. See *The Holocaust*, Channel 4 (London), at channel4.com/history/microsites/H/holocaust/later2a.html.

9. Several distinguished historians afterward found this troubling, contending that close examination of *any* scholar's working notes and diaries would show the messy, often contradictory process involved before a historical verdict is reached. Like sausage making, it is not appealing when exposed to public view. Was it fair, then, to single out "poor" Irving, they asked? Deborah Lipstadt could scarcely believe her eyes when she read such sympathetic remarks by distinguished fellow practitioners of history. She wondered, in fact, whether journalists and the public had forgotten who was su-

ing whom and how serious the stakes were. See Deborah Lipstadt, *History on Trial: My Day in Court with David Irving* (London: Penguin, 2005). See also Richard Evans's *Telling Lies about Hitler: The Holocaust, History and the David Irving Trial* (London: Verso, 2002).

CHAPTER 5. THE SHAPE OF A LIFE

1. R. W. B. Lewis, *Edith Wharton: A Biography* (New York: Harper and Row, 1975).

2. Millicent Bell, *Edith Wharton and Henry James* (New York: George Braziller, 1965).

3. Hermione Lee, *Edith Wharton* (New York: Knopf, 2007).

4. Edward Hallett Carr, *What Is History?* (New York: Vintage, 1961), 33.

5. Lytton Strachey, *Eminent Victorians* (Harmondsworth: Penguin, 1986; orig. pub. 1918), 10.

6. Ibid.

7. Robert Penn Warren, *New and Selected Essays* (New York: Random House, 1989), 53.

8. Christopher Booker, *The Seven Basic Plots: Why We Tell Stories* (London: Continuum, 2004), 3.

9. Ibid., 701.

10. Strachey, *Eminent Victorians*, 104.

11. Ibid., 108.

12. A. J. A. Symons, *The Quest for Corvo* (Harmondsworth: Penguin, 1966; orig. pub. 1934).

13. Leon Edel, "The Figure under the Carpet," in Marc Pachter, ed., *Telling Lives: The Biographer's Art* (Washington, D.C.: New Republic Books, 1979), 18.

14. Ibid., 27.

15. Ibid.

16. Edel, "The Figure under the Carpet," 18.

17. Samuel Johnson, *The Rambler*, 60 (October 13, 1750).

18. Ibid.

19. Warren, *New and Selected Essays,* 56.

20. James Prior, *The Life of Oliver Goldsmith, M.B., from a Variety of Original Sources,* vol. 1 (London: John Murray, 1837), 396. Goldsmith included the anecdote in an introduction he wrote for an edition of Plutarch, and published anonymously.

21. Ibid.

22. A. S. Byatt, *On Histories and Stories: Selected Essays* (Cambridge, Mass.: Harvard University Press, 2001), 166.

CHAPTER 6. THE STARTING POINT

1. Herman J. Mankiewicz and Orson Welles, *The Citizen Kane Book: The Shooting Scrip* (Boston: Atlantic Monthly Press, 1971), 123.

2. David McCullough, *John Adams* (New York: Simon and Schuster, 2001), 17.

3. Edmund Morris, *The Rise of Theodore Roosevelt* (New York: Random House, 1979), 313–314.

4. Letter to Ruth Fry (August 28, 1940), in Virginia Woolf, *The Letters of Virginia Woolf,* ed. Nigel Nicolson and Joanne Trautmann, 6 vols. (New York: Harcourt, Brace, Jovanovich, 1975–1980), vol. 6, 423.

5. Letter to Clive Bell (August 12, 1940), ibid., 411.

6. Michael Holroyd, *Lytton Strachey, Volume 1: The Unknown Years* (London: Heinemann, 1967), 3.

7. Michael Holroyd, *Lytton Strachey: The New Biography* (New York: Farrar, Straus and Giroux, 1994), 3.

8. Hermione Lee, *Virginia Woolf* (London: Chatto and Windus, 1996), 3.

9. Edmund Morris, *Dutch* (New York: Random House, 1999), xi.

10. Nigel Hamilton, *JFK: Reckless Youth* (New York: Random House, 1992), xix.

11. Ron Chernow, *Alexander Hamilton* (New York: Penguin, 2004), 1.

12. Willard Sterne Randall, *Alexander Hamilton* (New York: Harper Collins, 2003), 1–2.

CHAPTER 7. BIRTHING YOUR SUBJECT

1. Doris Kearns Goodwin, in Brian Lamb, *Booknotes: America's Finest Authors on Reading, Writing, and the Power of Ideas* (New York: Times Books, 1997), 23.

2. Marc Pachter, ed., *Telling Lives: The Biographer's Art* (Washington, D.C.: New Republic Books, 1979), 102–103.

3. Virginia Woolf, *Orlando* (Harmondsworth: Penguin, 1963; orig. pub. 1928), 46.

4. A. O. Scott, "A French Songbird's Life, in Chronological Disorder," *New York Times* (June 8, 2007).

5. Humphrey Carpenter, *W. H. Auden: A Biography* (Boston: Houghton Mifflin, 1981), 1.

6. James Atlas, *Bellow: A Biography* (New York: Random House, 2000), 8–9.

7. Joanna Richardson, *Stendhal* (New York: Coward, McCann and Geoghehan, 1974), 15.

8. Judith Thurman, *Secrets of the Flesh: A Life of Colette* (New York: Knopf, 1999), 3.

9. Ibid., 6–7.

10. Ted Morgan, *Maugham* (New York: Simon and Schuster, 1980), 4.

11. Humphrey Burton, *Leonard Bernstein* (New York: Doubleday, 1994), 4–5.

12. Michael Ignatieff, *Isaiah Berlin: A Life* (New York: Henry Holt, 1998), 10.

CHAPTER 8. CHILDHOOD AND YOUTH

1. Peter Gay, *Freud: A Life for Our Time* (New York: Doubleday, 1988), 10–11.

2. Stanley Sadie, *Mozart: The Early Years, 1756–1781* (New York: Norton, 2006), 548.

3. Christopher Sawyer-Lauçanno, *E. E. Cummings* (Naperville, Ill.: Sourcebooks, 2004), 69.

4. Ibid.

5. Noël Riley Fitch, *Anaïs: The Erotic Life of Anaïs Nin* (Boston: Little, Brown, 1993), 4.

6. Ibid., 9.

7. Ibid., 4–5.

8. Nigel Hamilton, *JFK: Reckless Youth* (New York: Random House, 1992), 391.

9. Ibid., 796–797.

CHAPTER 9. LOVE STORIES

1. Janet Malcolm, *The Silent Woman* (New York: Knopf, 1994), 9.

2. Michael Beschloss, *The Boston Globe* (November 22, 1992).

3. Michiko Kakutani, "A Daunting Father, A Brother's Shadow," *New York Times* (November 27, 1992).

4. Michiko Kakutani, "Portrait of a President, Warts and . . . More Warts," *New York Times* (September 23, 2003).

5. John Cruickshank, "Toilet-Wall Biography," *Chicago Sun-Times* (September 28, 2003).

6. Suetonius, *The Twelve Caesars,* trans. Robert Graves, rev. Michael Grant (London: Allen Lane, 1979), 119.

7. Ibid., 123–124.

8. Samuel Johnson, *The Rambler,* 60 (October 13, 1750), 19.

9. Martin Stannard, *Evelyn Waugh: The Early Years, 1903–1939* (London: J. M. Dent, 1986), 180.

10. Ibid., 181.

11. Ibid., 182.

12. Ibid., 183.

13. Stannard, *Evelyn Waugh,* 181.

14. Deirdre Bair, *Simone de Beauvoir: A Biography* (London: Jonathan Cape, 1990), 333.

15. Ibid.

16. Ibid., 335–336.

17. Ibid., 336.

18. Ibid., 334.

19. Ibid., 333.

20. Ibid., 343.

21. Ibid., 353.

22. *The Rambler,* 68 (November 10, 1750).

CHAPTER 10. LIFE'S WORK

1. Plutarch, *The Age of Alexander: Nine Greek Lives,* trans. Ian Scott-Kilvert (London: Penguin, 1973), 252.

2. Kai Bird and Martin J. Sherwin, *American Prometheus: The Triumph and Tragedy of J. Robert Oppenheimer* (New York: Knopf, 2005), 541.

3. Ibid., 541–542.

4. Hilary Spurling, *Matisse the Master: A Life of Henri Matisse, the Conqueror of Colour, 1909–1954* (New York: Knopf, 2005), 138–140.

5. John E. Mack, *A Prince of Our Disorder: The Life of T. E. Lawrence* (Boston: Little, Brown, 1976), 240.

6. T. E. Lawrence, *Seven Pillars of Wisdom* (Garden City, N.Y.: Doubleday, Doran, 1936), 659.

7. Mack, *A Prince of Our Disorder,* 241–242.

8. Gerald Clarke, *Capote: A Biography* (London: Hamish Hamilton, 1988), 317.

9. Ibid., 318.

10. Stephen Ambrose (June 5, 1994), in Brian Lamb, *Booknotes: America's Finest Authors on Reading, Writing, and the Power of Ideas* (New York: Times Books, 1997), 55.

11. Clarke, *Capote,* 320.

CHAPTER 11. THE TWILIGHT YEARS

1. Nigel Hamilton, *Monty: Final Years of the Field Marshal* (New York: McGraw-Hill, 1986), 940.

2. Ronald W. Clark, *The Life of Bertrand Russell* (New York: Knopf, 1976), 602.

3. Ibid., 139.

4. Richard Ellmann, *Oscar Wilde* (New York: Knopf, 1988), 573.

5. Ibid., 575.

6. Ibid., 577–578.

7. Ibid., 578.

8. Martin Gilbert, *Churchill: A Life* (New York: Holt, 1991), 937–938.

9. Josyane Savigneau, *Marguerite Yourcenar: Inventing a Life* (Chicago: University of Chicago Press, 1993), 401.

10. Savigneau, *Marguerite Yourcenar,* 398–399.

11. Mathieu Galey, *Journal, 1974–1986* (Paris: Grasset, 1989), 161, quoted in Savigneau, *Marguerite Yourcenar,* 399.

12. Steven Bach, *Leni: The Life and Work of Leni Riefenstahl* (New York: Knopf, 2007), 261.

13. Ibid., 278.

14. Ibid., 299.

CHAPTER 12. ENDING YOUR STORY

1. Graham Robb, *Rimbaud* (New York: Norton, 2000), 436.

2. Ibid., 439.

3. Ibid., 440.

4. Frances Spalding, *Stevie Smith: A Biography* (New York: Norton, 1988), 301.

5. Ibid.

6. Ibid., 301–302.

7. Stanley Weintraub, *Whistler: A Biography* (New York: Weybright and Talley, 1974), 462.

8. Ibid., 465.

9. David Sweetman, *Paul Gauguin: A Life* (New York: Simon and Schuster, 1995), 533–534.

10. Ibid., 535.

11. A. N. Wilson, *Tolstoy* (New York: Norton, 1988), 513.

12. Ibid., 515–516.

13. Ibid., 517.

14. Ibid.

15. R. F. Foster, *W. B. Yeats: A Life*, vol. 2: *The Arch-Poet, 1915–1939* (Oxford: Oxford University Press, 2003), 657–658.

16. John Fuegi, *Brecht and Company* (New York: Grove, 1994), 620–621.

17. Peter Guralnick, *Careless Love: The Unmaking of Elvis Presley* (Boston: Little, Brown, 1999), 660–661.

18. Michael Holroyd, *Augustus John: A Biography*, rev. ed. (Harmondsworth: Penguin, 1976; orig. pub. 1974), 722–723.

19. Richard Ellmann, *James Joyce*, rev. ed. (New York: Oxford University Press, 1982; orig. pub. 1959), 743–744.

20. Hermione Lee, *Edith Wharton* (New York: Knopf, 2007), 761–762.

CHAPTER 13. AUTOBIOGRAPHY AND MEMOIRS

1. Xenophon, *The Persian Expedition*, trans. Rex Warner (Harmondsworth: Penguin, 1949; rpt. 1972), 256–257.

2. Jules Michelet, trans. and ed., *Mémoires de Luther, écrits par lui-même* (Paris, 1835). The *Mémoires* were quickly translated into English for American Protestants as *The Life of Martin Luther, Gathered from His Own Writings* (1846).

3. Thomas Jefferson, *Memoir* (1821), in volume 1 of *Memoir, Correspondence, and Miscellanies from the Papers of Thomas Jefferson*, ed. Thomas Jefferson Randolph (1829).

4. Harriette Wilson, *The Memoirs of Harriette Wilson* (London: Douglas, 1825).

5. Ibid.

6. Sir Walter Scott, quoted in Lesley Blanch, ed., *The Game of Hearts: Harriette Wilson's Memoirs, Interspersed with Excerpts from the Confessions of Julia Johnstone, Her Rival* (New York: Simon and Schuster, 1955), 37.

7. Mark Twain, *Mark Twain's Own Autobiography* (Madison: University of Wisconsin Press, 1990), 143.

8. Gertrude Stein, *The Autobiography of Alice B. Toklas* (New York: Vintage, 1961; orig. pub. 1933), 5, 10–11.

9. Saint Augustine, *Confessions,* trans. R. S. Pine-Coffin (Harmondsworth: Penguin, 1961), 45–46.

10. *The Book of Margery Kempe* (1433), trans. B. A. Windeatte (Harmondsworth: Penguin, 1985), 49–50.

11. Jean-Jacques Rousseau, *The Confessions* (Ware, Hertfordshire: Wordsworth, 1996), 309.

12. Frederick Douglass, *Narrative of the Life of Frederick Douglass, an American Slave, Written by Himself* (Boston: Anti-Slavery Office, 1845), ch. 6; Frederick Douglass, *Autobiographies* (New York: Library of America, 1994), 37–38.

13. Douglass, *Autobiographies,* 97.

14. Anne Frank, *Diary of a Young Girl* (1942–1944), trans. Susan Massotty (Harmondsworth: Penguin, 1997), 333–334, entry for August 1, 1944.

CHAPTER 14. MEMOIR

1. Robert Graves, *Good-bye to All That* (London: Jonathan Cape, 1929), epilogue.

2. Ibid.

3. Robert Perceval Graves, *Robert Graves: The Years with Laura Riding, 1926–1940* (London: Weidenfeld and Nicolson, 1990).

4. Brendan Behan, *Borstal Boy* (New York: Knopf, 1959), 3.

5. Lance Morrow, "A Dying Art: The Classy Exit Line," *Time* (January 16, 1984).

6. James D. Watson, *The Double Helix: A Personal Account of the Discovery of DNA,* ed. Gunther S. Stent, Norton Critical Edition (New York: Norton, 1980), 106–108.

7. Ibid., 225.

8. Ibid., 233.

9. Maya Angelou, *I Know Why the Caged Bird Sings* (New York: Random House, 1969), 67–68, 75–76.

10. Anatoly Marchenko, *My Testimony,* trans. Michael Scammell, in

Ross Mackenzie and Todd Culbertson, eds., *Eyewitness: Writings from the Ordeal of Communism* (New York: Freedom House, 1992; orig. pub. 1969), 264, 266.

11. William Zinsser, ed., *Inventing the Truth: The Art and Craft of Memoir* (Boston: Mariner Books, 1998), 3.

12. Frank McCourt, *Angela's Ashes* (New York: Scribner, 1996), 26–27.

13. Edward Wyatt, "Fray Says Falsehoods Improved His Tale," *New York Times* (February 2, 2006). Frey's note, dated January 2006, was printed on page v of subsequent editions of James Frey, *A Million Little Pieces* (New York: Anchor, 2006; orig. pub. 2003).

14. Ibid. See also Nick Taylor, "Truth and Memoir: A Conversation with William Zinsser," *Author's Guild Bulletin* (Spring 2006), 7–9, 42–43.

CHAPTER 15. TRUTH—AND ITS CONSEQUENCES

1. Ian Hamilton, *In Search of J. D. Salinger* (New York: Random House, 1988), 9. See also Rachel Donadio, "Bio Engineering," *New York Times Book Review* (November 4, 2007).

2. *Harvard Crimson* (February 14, 1968).

3. Later, Watson would wonder "how the prize would have been divided if Rosalind Franklin had not died so tragically young. Then, as today, the Nobel's rules preclude dividing any given prize among more than three individuals." James D. Watson, *Genes, Girls and Gamow* (Oxford: Oxford University Press, 2001), 250.

4. James Watson, *The Double Helix: A Personal Account of the Discovery of DNA,* ed. Gunther S. Stent, Norton Critical Edition (New York: Norton, 1980), 14.

5. André Lwoff, "Truth, What Is Truth (About How the Structure of DNA Was Discovered)," in Watson, *The Double Helix,* 225.

6. Samuel Johnson, *The Rambler,* 60 (October 13, 1750).

7. A. Alvarez, *The Savage God: A Study of Suicide* (Harmondsworth: Penguin, 1974; orig. pub. 1971), 53.

8. Ibid., 56.

9. Hughes to Alvarez, September/October 1986, in British Library, quoted in Janet Malcolm, *The Silent Woman: Sylvia Plath and Ted Hughes* (New York: Knopf, 1994), 124.

10. Ibid., 130, 126.

11. Elizabeth Hardwick, in George Plimpton, ed., *The Writer's Chapbook* (New York: Viking, 1989), 240.

12. Doris Kearns Goodwin, in Brian Lamb, *Booknotes: America's Finest Authors on Reading, Writing, and the Power of Ideas* (New York: Times Books, 1997), 25.

13. Four years later Goodwin reasserted her biographical credentials in a brilliant biography, *Team of Rivals: The Political Genius of Abraham Lincoln* (New York: Simon and Schuster, 2006).

CHAPTER 16. THE AFTERLIFE

1. Edmund Morris on the writing of *Dutch*, in Brian Lamb, *Booknotes: America's Finest Authors on Reading, Writing, and the Power of Ideas* (New York: Times Books, 1997), 20.

2. James Reston Jr., on the writing of *The Lone Star: The Life of John Connally*, in Lamb, *Booknotes*, 15–17.

3. Robert Caro, interviewed by Brian Lamb, *Booknotes*, C-SPAN (April 19, 1990).

4. Leon Edel, "The Figure under the Carpet, in Marc Pachter, ed., *Telling Lives: The Biographer's Art* (Washington, D.C.: New Republic Books, 1979), 19.

5. Stephen Ambrose, in Lamb, *Booknotes*, 55–56, referring to Ambrose, *D-Day, June 6, 1944: The Climactic Battle of World War II* (New York: Simon and Schuster, 1994).

6. Samuel Johnson, *The Idler*, 84 (November 24, 1759).

Selected Bibliography

Altick, Richard D. *Lives and Letters: A History of Literary Biography in England and America.* New York: Knopf, 1966.

Backscheider, Paula R. *Reflections on Biography.* Oxford: Oxford University Press, 1999.

Barnes, Julian. *Flaubert's Parrot.* London: Cape, 1984.

Barrington, Judith. *Writing the Memoir: From Truth to Art.* Portland, Ore.: Eight Mountain Press, 2002.

Batchelor, John, ed. *The Art of Literary Biography.* Oxford: Clarendon, 1995.

Bell, Susan Groag, and Marilyn Yalom, eds. *Revealing Lives: Autobiography, Biography, and Gender.* Albany: State University of New York Press, 1990.

Boswell, James. *Boswell's Life of Johnson,* ed. G. H. Hill. Oxford: Oxford University Press, 1934.

Bowen, Catherine Drinker. *Biography: The Craft and the Calling.* Boston: Little, Brown, 1969.

Bradford, Gamaliel. *Biography and the Human Heart.* Boston: Houghton Mifflin, 1932.

Burt, Daniel S. *The Biography Book: A Reader's Guide to Nonfiction, Fictional, and Film Biographies of More than 500 of the Most Fascinating Individuals of All Time.* Westport, Conn.: Oryx Press, 2001.

Caughie, John, ed. *Theories of Authorship: A Reader.* London: Routledge, 1981.

Cheney, Theodore A. Rees. *Fiction Techniques for Crafting Great Nonfiction.* Berkeley: Ten Speed Press, 2001.

Clifford, James L., ed. *Biography as an Art: Selected Criticism, 1560–1960.* New York: Oxford University Press, 1962.

Cockshut, A. O. J. *The Art of Autobiography in Nineteenth- and Twentieth-Century England.* New Haven: Yale University Press, 1984.

Couser, G. Thomas. *American Autobiography: The Prophetic Mode.* Amherst: University of Massachusetts Press, 1979.

Davenport, William H., and Ben Siegel, eds. *Biography Past and Present: Selections and Critical Essays.* New York: Scribner's, 1965.

Denzin, Norman K. *Interpretive Biography.* Thousand Oaks, Calif.: Sage, 1989.

Eakin, Paul J. *Fictions in Autobiography: Studies in the Art of Self-Invention.* Princeton: Princeton University Press, 1985.

———— *Touching the World: Reference in Autobiography.* Princeton: Princeton University Press, 1992.

———— *How Our Lives Become Stories: Making Selves.* Ithaca, N.Y.: Cornell University Press, 1999.

Eakin, Paul J., ed. *American Autobiography: Retrospect and Prospect.* Madison: University of Wisconsin Press, 1991.

———— *The Ethics of Life Writing.* Ithaca, N.Y.: Cornell University Press, 2004.

Edel, Leon. *Writing Lives: Principia Biographia.* New York: Norton, 1987.

Elms, Alan C. *Uncovering Lives: The Uneasy Alliance of Biography and Psychology.* New York: Oxford University Press, 1994.

Epstein, William H., ed. *Contesting the Subject: Essays in the Postmodern Theory and Practice of Biography and Biographical Criticism.* West Lafayette, Ind.: Purdue University Press, 1991.

Folkenfolk, Robert, ed. *The Culture of Autobiography: Constructions of Self-Representation.* Stanford, Calif.: Stanford University Press, 1993.

Forche, Carolyn, and Philip Gerard, eds. *Writing Creative Nonfiction: In-*

struction and Insights from the Teachers of the Associated Writing Programs. Cincinnati, Ohio: Story Press, 2001.

Freud, Sigmund. *Leonardo da Vinci and a Memory of His Childhood* (1910). Trans. Alan Tyson, ed. James Strachey. New York: Norton, 1961.

Gibbons, Randall, comp. *In Their Own Words.* New York: Random House, 1995.

Gilmore, Leigh. *Autobiographics: A Feminist Theory of Women's Self-Representation.* Ithaca, N.Y.: Cornell University Press, 1994.

Goodwin, James. *Autobiography: The Self Made Text.* New York: Twayne, 1993.

Hamilton, Ian. *Keepers of the Flame: Literary Estates and the Rise of Biography.* London: Hutchinson, 1992.

Hamilton, Nigel. *In Search of J. D. Salinger.* New York: Random House, 1988.

——— *Biography: A Brief History.* Cambridge, Mass.: Harvard University Press, 2007.

Holmes, Richard. *Footsteps: Adventures of a Romantic Biographer.* New York: Viking, 1985.

——— *Sidetracks: Explorations of a Romantic Biographer.* London: HarperCollins, 2000.

Homberger, Eric, and John Charmley, eds. *The Troubled Face of Biography.* New York: St. Martin's, 1988.

Iles, Theresa, ed. *All Sides of the Subject: Women and Biography.* New York: Teachers College Press, 1922.

Jolly, Margaretta, ed. *Encyclopedia of Life Writing: Autobiographical and Biographical Forms.* London: Fitzroy Dearborn, 2001.

Kendall, Paul Murray. *The Art of Biography.* London: Allen and Unwin, 1965.

Lehman, Daniel W. *Matters of Fact: Reading Nonfiction over the Edge.* Columbus: Ohio State University Press, 1997.

Lejeune, Philippe. *Le Pacte Autobiographique.* Paris: Seuil, 1975.

——— *On Autobiography.* Minneapolis: University of Minnesota Press, 1989.

Malcolm, Janet. *The Silent Woman*. New York: Knopf, 1994.

Maurois, André. *Aspects of Biography*. New York: Appleton, 1929.

Merrill, Dana K. *American Biography: Its Theory and Practice*. Portland, Maine: Bowker, 1957.

Meyers, Jeffrey, ed. *The Craft of Literary Biography*. London: Macmillan, 1985.

Miller, Robert, ed. *Biographical Research Methods*. 4 vols. London: Sage, 2005.

Moraitis, George, and George H. Pollock, eds. *Psychoanalytic Studies of Biography*. Madison, Conn.: International Universities Press, 1987.

Nadel, Ira Bruce. *Biography: Fiction, Fact and Form*. New York: St. Martin's, 1984.

Nicolson, Harold. *The Development of English Biography*. London: Hogarth, 1927.

Novarr, David. *The Lines of Life: Theories of Biography, 1880–1970*. West Lafayette, Ind.: Purdue University Press, 1986.

Oates, Stephen B., ed. *Biography as High Adventure: Life-Writers Speak on Their Art*. Amherst: University of Massachusetts Press, 1986.

Olney, James. *Metaphors of Self: The Meaning of Autobiography*. Princeton: Princeton University Press, 1972.

——— *Memory and Narrative: The Weave of Life-Writing*. Chicago: University of Chicago Press, 1998.

Olney, James, ed. *Autobiography: Essays Theoretical and Critical*. Princeton: Princeton University Press, 1980.

——— *Studies in Autobiography*. New York: Oxford University Press, 1998.

Parke, Catherine N. *Writing Lives*. New York: Twayne, 1996.

Plutarch. *The Lives of the Noble Grecians and Romans*. Trans. John Dryden, rev. Arthur Clough. New York: Modern Library, 1979.

Prose, Francine. *Reading Like a Writer: A Guide for People Who Love Books and for Those Who Want to Write Them*. New York: Harper Perennial, 2007.

Rainer, Christine. *Your Life as Story: Discovering the "New Autobiography" and Writing Memoir as Literature*. New York: Putnam, 1997.

Reid, B. L. *Necessary Lives: Biographical Reflections.* Columbia: University of Missouri Press, 1990.

Rhiel, Mary, and David Suchoff, eds. *The Seductions of Biography.* New York: Routledge, 1996.

Roberts, Brian. *Biographical Research.* Buckingham: Open University Press, 2002.

Rollyson, Carl E. *Biography: An Annotated Bibliography.* Pasadena: Salem Press, 1992.

—— *A Higher Form of Capitalism?: Adventures in the Art and Politics of Biography.* Chicago: Ivan R. Dee, 2005.

Secrest, Meryle. *Shoot the Widow.* New York: Knopf, 2007.

Seldon, Anthony, and Joanna Pappworth. *By Word of Mouth: "Elite" Oral History.* London: Methuen, 1983.

Smith, Sidonie, and Julia Watson, eds. *De/Colonizing the Subject: The Politics of Gender in Women's Autobiography.* Minneapolis: University of Minnesota Press, 1992.

—— *Getting a Life: Everyday Uses of Autobiography.* Minneapolis: University of Minnesota Press, 1996.

—— *Women, Autobiography, Theory: A Reader.* Madison: University of Wisconsin Press, 1998.

—— *Reading Autobiography: A Guide for Interpreting Life Narratives.* Minneapolis: University of Minnesota Press, 2001.

—— *Interfaces: Women, Autobiography, Image, Performance.* Ann Arbor: University of Michigan Press, 2002.

Stauffer, Donald A. *English Biography before 1700.* Cambridge, Mass.: Harvard University Press, 1930.

Strachey, Lytton. *Eminent Victorians* (1918). Harmondsworth: Penguin, 1986.

Suetonius. *The Twelve Caesars.* Trans. Robert Graves. Harmondsworth: Penguin, 1957. Revised by Michael Grant, 1979.

Thompson, Paul. *The Voice of the Past: Oral History.* Oxford: Oxford University Press, 1988.

Wheeler, David, ed. *Domestick Privacies: Samuel Johnson and the Art of Biography.* Lexington: University Press of Kentucky, 1987.

Whittemore, Reed. *Pure Lives: The Early Biographers.* Baltimore: Johns Hopkins University Press, 1988.

———— *Whole Lives: Shapers of Modern Biography.* Baltimore: Johns Hopkins University Press, 1989.

Young-Bruehl, Elisabeth. *Subject to Biography: Psychoanalysis, Feminism, and Writing Women's Lives.* Cambridge, Mass.: Harvard University Press, 1988.

Zinsser, William. *Inventing the Truth: The Art and Craft of Memoir.* Boston: Houghton Mifflin, 1987, 1995, 1998.

———— *Writing about Your Life: A Journey into the Past.* New York: Marlowe, 2005.

Acknowledgments

Like its predecessor volume, this book owes a great debt to others, whose names I have recorded at the end of *Biography: A Brief History*. Their inspiration, assistance, and goodwill have guided my passion for biography across the years of my life: family, friends, teachers, colleagues, fellow biographers, editors, readers, and students. Once again, I take this opportunity to thank them from the bottom of my heart.

In compiling this sequel I have, however, been encouraged and helped by a number of people whose contributions have directly marked the end-product, and whom I would like to thank in print. My editor at Harvard University Press, Joyce Seltzer, not only urged me to carry out my notion of a biographical primer, but when the first draft failed to meet her expectations, persuaded me to start over. The professor thus became the student once again. Painfully, after a number of iterations—each one subjected to her incisive criticism and suggested revisions—I was able to produce a hopefully more readable, more useful work. To her, along with my second grandchild, I have dedicated the resultant book.

I'd like, also, to thank the staff of Harvard University Press, in Cambridge, Mass., and in London, who did such an admirable job in preparing, designing, producing, and promoting *Biography: A Brief History,* and who have undertaken its sequel with such enthusiasm, most especially Maria Ascher, my manuscript editor.

My colleagues—faculty, fellows, staff—at the McCormack Graduate School of Policy Studies, under the leadership of Dean Steve Crosby, have also provided not only unstinting assistance but the goodhearted cheer that is just as vital, and appreciated.

The opportunity to teach biography to students over recent years, and to assist biographers and would-be biographers in addressing the many challenges of life writing, have helped me as much as I have been able, I hope, to help them—for which I am most grateful.

Dr. Craig Howes, director of the Biographical Research Center at the University of Hawaii at Manoa, invited me to address his colleagues and students in January 2006; I remain awed by the research and teaching, and the international interdisciplinary journal *Biography,* produced by the center, and I am immensely grateful for Dr. Howes's personal encouragement and advice.

Finally my beloved wife and companion, Dr. Raynel Shepard, read successive chapters with a teacher's uncompromising and constructive eye, while my friend of four and a half decades, Robin Whitby, helped me to prepare the final manuscript. Their collective contributions have saved me from untold errors of fact and judgment; for all residual mistakes and omissions I must, however, crave the reader's indulgence. I hope that, in however small a way, *How To Do Biography* will provide a practical, worthwhile primer.

Index